JERSEY'S GREAT WAR
An island and its people 1914-18

JERSEY'S GREAT WAR
An island and its people 1914-18

By Ian Ronayne

First published Jersey 2014
By the Jersey Heritage Trust
Jersey Museum, The Weighbridge,
St Helier, Jersey, JE2 3NG

ISBN 978-0-9562079-8-2

Text © Ian Ronayne 2014

Illustrations © individuals and organisations credited

All rights reserved. No part of this publication may be reproduced, stored in a retrieval system, or transmitted in any form or by any means, electronic, mechanical, photocopying, recording, or otherwise, without the prior permission of the copyright owner.

To the people of Jersey for their courage, commitment, sacrifice and independence between 1914 and 1918

CONTENTS

Foreword	xii
Introduction	xiii
Chapter 1: Peace, Progress and Prosperity An island and its people on the brink of war	1
Chapter 2: Call Out the Guards Jersey's defences, defenders and the mobilisation of the Militia on the eve of war	13
Chapter 3: Pour la Patrie Jersey's French community responds as France prepares for war	26
Chapter 4: An Entrenched Camp Preparing to defend Jersey as the enemy approached in 1914	45
Chapter 5: Your Island Needs You Kitchener's recruitment campaign and the response of Jersey's volunteers	62
Chapter 6: New Rules and Regulations Jersey's people and politicians adjust to wartime conditions	78
Chapter 7: The Enemy Among Us The treatment and fate of Jersey's 'Alien' community	94
Chapter 8: A Camp by the Sea German prisoners of war in Jersey	112

Chapter 9: England Expects National Registration and adopting compulsory military service in Jersey	135
Chapter 10: King or Countryside Dealing with the conflicting needs of military service and agricultural production	154
Chapter 11: A Woman's Work Wartime options and opportunities for the Island's women	174
Chapter 12: Money, Food and Men The challenges and demands faced by Jersey in a fourth year of war	190
Chapter 13: Tommies and Poilus Jerseymen in the service of Britain and France	213
Chapter 14: The Storm and the Calm Spanish Flu, the Armistice and the first challenges of peace	231
Chapter 15: One Hundred Years Since Assessing Jersey's Great War	247
Endnotes	259
Sources and Bibliography	263
Index	266

JERSEY'S GREAT WAR

ILLUSTRATIONS

Pre-war Jersey: an Island family enjoys a day out at Grève de Lecq in 1909	Page 37
Pre-war Jersey: the popularity of the Jersey Royal had led to a community of more than six thousand French nationals in the Island, many of whom worked in the agricultural industry	Page 37
Pre-war Jersey: marching soldiers were a familiar sight in the Island, such as these men of the East Surrey Regiment arriving in 1905 to take over British Army garrison duties	Page 38
Sir William Venables Vernon, Jersey's Bailiff since 1899 and civilian leader between 1914 and 1918	Page 39
The Militia mobilises on 30 July 1914: men of the Town Battalion armed and ready to take up guard duties in St Helier	Page 40
French reservists departing from St Helier harbour to rejoin their regiments at the start of August 1914	Page 40
French soldiers returning to the Island on leave were a familiar sight between 1914 and 1918	Page 41
'Our noble army of standbacks': some of those who had previously managed to avoid Militia service but who were called up in September 1914 to increase the number of men available to guard Jersey	Page 41
'Kitchener volunteers' arriving in St Helier for training in Jersey with the South Staffordshire Regiment	Page 42
South Staffordshire Regiment volunteers engage in bayonet practice on Peoples' Park, St Helier	Page 43
Officers of the South Staffordshire Regiment outside of St Helier's Grand Hotel, which was requisitioned in 1914 to house 750 soldiers	Page 43

Members of the Victoria College Officer Training Corps (OTC) played a part in the Island's defence by taking over a section of coastal defences every one night in five	Page 44
Major General Sir Alexander Rochfort, KCB, CMG, who was the Island's Lieutenant Governor and its military commander-in-chief from 1910 to October 1916	Page 127
Major General Alexander Wilson, KCB, who became Jersey's Lieutenant Governor in October 1916	Page 128
The Dean of Jersey, the Very Reverend Samuel Falle (seated in the centre) with members of the Jersey Contingent prior to their departure from the Island	Page 129
Cheery members of the Jersey Contingent on their departure from Jersey in March 1915	Page 129
One of the military ambulances purchased from funds raised in Jersey and sent to the front	Page 130
'Militant Suffragettes' Miss Lall Forsyth and Miss Agnes Buckton in Jersey before the war trying to raise local support for the campaign to win greater rights for women	Page 130
Preparing 'comfort' parcels to send to the troops was a popular and well supported civilian activity	Page 131
Fund raising campaigns were a way for Jersey's civilians to show their support for the war effort	Page 131
The Jersey Branch of the British Red Cross Society established a number of Voluntary Aid Detachments (VADs) soon after the outbreak of war with their members serving as nurses both in the Island and overseas	Page 132

JERSEY'S GREAT WAR

The 'enemy' in the Island – German prisoners of war march to attend the funeral of one of their own at St Peter's Parish Church watched by curious Islanders	Page 133
The Prisoner of War camp at Les Blanches Banques was home to nearly two thousand German soldiers and sailors at one point	Page 133
A shortage of men led to openings for women in the Island, including its first female 'posties'	Page 134
Volunteer now or face conscription: the Bailiff appeals to Militiamen in October 1915 to join the British Army or attest a willingness to do so under Britain's 'Derby Scheme'	Page 205
More men: the first Jersey conscripts leave the Island to join the British Army in March 1917	Page 205
More food: Jersey Royals on their way to Britain having been purchased by the Army Forage Corps	Page 206
Pour Le Patrie: the Island's French Consul, *Monsieur* Auguste Jouve, in a ceremony to decorate a wounded member of Jersey's French community	Page 206
Corporal John Veler who won a Military Medal on 1 July 1916 while serving with a Trench Mortar Battery and who would be killed later in the war, six months after his brother Peter	Page 207
George Le Gresley, who served with the Royal Engineers in Macedonia where he won a Military Medal in September 1918 for a display of courage that inspired all around him	Page 208
Nineteen-year-old Bienaime Tirel of the *41e régiment d'infanterie coloniale* won a *médaille militaire* and the *croix de guerre* in April 1917 on the *Chemin Des Dames* where he was severely wounded	Page 209

John Pinel, the Constable of St Helier, who was honoured   Page 210
for his efforts during the Spanish Flu epidemic in October
and November 1918

Crowds gather outside the offices of the *Evening Post*   Page 210
newspaper in St Helier's Charles Street for news at the end
of the war

Members of the Island's newly formed trades union take part   Page 211
in a victory march

The temporary cenotaph erected by the Constable of St Helier Page 212
John Pinel in the Parade that stood until replaced by the
permanent monument in 1923, which remains to the present
time

FOREWORD

I am delighted to have been asked to write a foreword for this important work by Ian Ronayne. As the author points out, while much has been written about the Occupation of the Island during the Second World War, there is little published material about the effect of the First World War on the people of Jersey.

In some ways this is not wholly surprising. In the first place, there are still many survivors of the Occupation who are able to tell their stories; and secondly, occupation by enemy forces had a dramatic effect on every single Islander whereas the effects of the First World War were more uneven.

Nevertheless, as the author shows, the Island was greatly affected in many different ways by the First World War and it is very important that the sacrifices made by so many are not forgotten. The official Roll of Honour prepared after the War contains the names of 862 men from Jersey who died whilst serving in the British armed forces and a further 264 who died whilst fighting in the French armed forces. The author suggests that the truer total is probably closer to 1600. It is difficult to overestimate the effect of such loss on so many families in a small community. The author also reminds us of the contribution made by the Jersey Company and of the losses which it suffered. In addition, there is an interesting analysis of the effect of the War in the wider context of social changes to society.

This is an important and readable book which contains a wealth of detail about a period which has not previously received much attention from Island historians. I commend the author for his research and would encourage all those with an interest in the Island's history to read it.

Sir Michael Birt
Bailiff

INTRODUCTION

When Britain declared war on Germany on 4 August 1914, by constitutional association the small British Channel Island of Jersey also entered the conflict. And when, after Allied victory, the guns finally fell silent on 11 November 1918, the war ended for Jersey as well. One hundred years on, these facts and dates are categorical; far less well known is what happened to the Island and its people during the four years, three months and seven days of conflict that took place in between.

It was not meant to be that way. At the end of First World War, the Island's government, the States of Jersey, created an account of the dramatic events that had affected the Island between August 1914 and November 1918. Yet it turned out to be, in the words of those who wrote it, just *a brief outline*. There was clearly an intention to go back and finish the job however. Even the writer of the 'brief outline' noted the *necessity of publishing a more complete account when time and opportunity permit.*[*] It never happened – until now. This book seeks to provide that complete account of Jersey's Great War.

It seems useful at this point to consider why it has taken one hundred years for a detailed account of Jersey during the First World War to actually appear. There is no shortage of general literature dealing with the conflict after all, although much of it has admittedly only appeared in recent years. The First World War has also been a subject for local school curriculums, consistently taught or discussed year after year at both secondary and primary levels. Furthermore, there is the annual Poppy Appeal and acts of remembrance that take place on and around 11 November to ensure that we never forget the sacrifices made on the battlefields of the First World War. It is curious, therefore, in the midst of all this frequent and collective focus that such an important period in the Island's history has been overlooked for so long.

To understand why this is the situation, we must firstly look towards those tragic 1914 - 1918 battlefields and the experiences of the soldiers who lived, fought and died on them. The trenches of the Western Front in France and Belgium have come to dominate the history of the First World War. We are drawn with incredulous and pitying fascination towards harrowing accounts of mud, blood and rats that were reportedly the size of cats. Depictions of brave soldiers advancing helplessly in the face of machine gun fire, choking on poison gas and caught in belts of barbed wire all make a compelling impression. So too do stories of chateau-bound generals callously ordering futile attacks against enemy positions with little understanding of the conditions that their

---

[*] Quoted text is taken from the Jersey Roll of Honour and Roll of Service created in 1919

men were fighting in. Set against such emotive 'Lions led by Donkeys' history, what chance had the story of one small island at war? Especially in view of the fact the enemy remained (mostly) at a considerable distance from Jersey during the First World War, in stark contrast to the one that followed. And we must look to the Second World War and the Island's occupation between 1940 and 1945 for a second reason as to why Jersey's earlier twentieth century history has been neglected.

Inconceivable though it must have seemed at the time, barely twenty years after the Treaty of Versailles had concluded 'the war to end all wars' the world was plunged back into a global conflict once more. In many respects, the Second World War was very different from the one that had preceded it. Technological advances and political reverses resulted in that conflict reaching out further than the First World War to enter civilian communities and lives more directly and forcibly, particularly in Western Europe. This is certainly true for Jersey and its people. There was to be no 'miracle of the Marne' in the summer of 1940, no stalemate in the trenches and no keeping the enemy a considerable distance from the Island. The new Western Front had crumbled before the German onslaught in just six weeks, leaving Jersey under German occupation for nearly five years. The collective experience of abandonment, isolation, deportations and threatened starvation seems to have helped cast a shroud over the admittedly less overtly dramatic events that had occurred between 1914 and 1918. After the joy of liberation, who can blame a community for neglecting its earlier history in favour of a more recent one, especially if it aroused the interest of the outside world as well?

In contrast to the Second World War, Jersey's experience between 1914 and 1918 has less clearly delineated points to explain it. After a very turbulent start, the First World War progressively rather than suddenly affected the lives of Islanders. And its impact was uneven; the conflict may have dramatically touched one family while another one could have been continuing its life almost as normal at times. Yet the First World War gradually came to affect most Islanders, whether they were soldiers or civilians. And it certainly affected Island life at all levels, opening tense divisions between community groups, challenging long-established relationships, imposing unwelcome restrictions and forcing Jersey at times to question what exactly its priorities were. In view of this, perhaps those in power after 1918 thought that it was best to look forward to the future rather than back into the past. If this was the case, it may suggest a third reason for neglecting Jersey's Great War. History could wait for another time, and, for whatever the actual reasons, it did just that.

Returning to the present, for an author this neglect presents both positive and negative challenges. Positively, it means that there is a relatively blank canvas on which to create an account with no preconceptions to challenge or myths to debunk. Negatively, it means that the sources from which to construct the story are limited and not necessarily created with a view to posterity. Sadly, given that one hundred years have now passed since that time, we can no longer call upon those who lived through the First World War to tell us what happened. This means that our understanding must be based on analysis, interpretation and a certain amount of conjecture. But then, that is always the lot of an historian and writer; it is just incumbent upon them to do the best possible job with the materials that are available.

This seems a good point to make an apology for any erroneous assumptions, misplaced interpretation or imprudent conjecture that the reader finds in this book. They are solely the author's responsibility. It also seems a good point to make an appeal for this to be a start rather than the conclusion of research into Jersey's Great War. For such a wide-ranging and multi-faceted story, this book can only provide a general history; others need to delve deeper and question further.

When it comes to this book, the starting point were two obvious and fundamental questions that required answering: firstly, how did the First World War impact on Jersey and its people? Secondly, how did Jersey and its people respond to the impact of the First World War?

Actually, we already have one very apparent answer to both questions. The Island's numerous war memorials with their hundreds of names are a sobering testament to the impact of the First World War on the lives of the Jerseymen who left to fight between 1914 and 1918, and the families that they left behind. The number of names inscribed on those memorials is a never-to-be-forgotten reminder of the sacrifice made by Jersey and its people. Recent years have witnessed a steadily growing and very welcome interest in the soldiers who both died in the First World War and those who survived it. Whether through individual stories arising from research undertaken by descendants and military history enthusiasts, or collective accounts, including one by this author in 2009[†], there is growing understanding and appreciation of the Jerseymen who served in the armed forces of Britain and France during the conflict.

Yet the experiences of the men who left to fight are only part of Jersey's Great War story, albeit a very important one. What has been absent until now is the story of the community that they left behind. In rushing to understand Tommies and trenches, we have overlooked the history of an island at war, how that war affected its people, its industries and its government and how they in turn responded to the challenges that it brought. The purpose of this book is to tell that story and, one hundred years after it began, to ensure that Jersey's

[†] Ours: The Jersey Pals in the First World War

Great War is no longer a neglected history.

Telling that story required the actions, advice and support of a number of people, and I must conclude by offering my thanks to them. To Jersey Heritage Trust, and particularly its Director, Jon Carter, and Community Learning Director, Doug Ford, for having the foresight to commission and publish this book and so help rectify a long-standing oversight. Special thanks to the present Bailiff of Jersey, Sir Michael Birt, for graciously agreeing to write a foreword. Thanks also to the keepers of records, including the Société Jersiaise, the Jersey Library, the National Archive, and, most importantly, the Jersey Archive for showing great support in first conserving and then willingly opening up the many files that relate to the period 1914 to 1918.

Finally but not least to my associates and good friends Barrie Bertram and Ned Malet De Carteret for their unstinting assistance in researching, editing and proofreading this book. Kindness given and gratefully accepted.

Ian Ronayne
Jersey, August 2014

1 PEACE, PROGRESS AND PROSPERITY

An island and its people on the brink of war

It had become tradition for Islanders to gather in St Helier's Royal Square on 31 December as midnight approached. The last New Year's Eve of peace was no exception.

The band of the Jersey Musical Union was present that evening, with good-humoured revellers dancing in groups to its lively tunes. All were keeping an eye on the clock sitting high up on the steeple of the nearby Town Church, with the excitement rising as twelve o'clock approached. In the final minutes of the old year, the doors of a gentlemen's club overlooking the square had swung open, and its well-dressed members emerged from the warmth onto their balcony to join the festivities. Among them was a photographer, who stepped forward to take a picture of the crowd below when the church bells chimed at midnight. As the strains of Auld Lange Syne faded into the cold night air, everyone turned to look-up at the balcony. With a flash, the sea of shining faces was captured for posterity; it was a last portrait of a people whose world was about to change forever.

Those gathered in the Royal Square on 31 December 1913 had no comprehension what the new year would bring of course; if they had a wish that evening, it would have surely been for more of the same. They were living on an island that was enjoying a time of peace, progress and prosperity after all. 'I question whether Jersey has ever had a more prosperous twelve months than 1913,' one commentator wrote at the time. 'The crops, the weather and the visitors all combined to fill the coffers of all sections of the community…in this sense we in Jersey may well hope that 1914 will be up to the level of 1913.'[1] There was no obvious reason to assume otherwise. The Island lay secure in its small part of the world, protected by the power and influence of the largest empire the world had ever seen. Confidence in the future was high, driven by the industrious and entrepreneurial spirit of the Islanders. Economic success in recent years had led to rising living standards and growing expectations of more to come. Not for everyone admittedly. Poverty was still found in the poorer streets of town and among the more deprived parts of the countryside. Yet most people had a little extra money to spend, and they were living in a world where there was more time and emphasis placed on spending it in pursuit of leisure. And all were benefiting from a programme of investment in public infrastructure that had come to fruition in the years leading up to 1914 with the opening of new schools, hospitals, churches, parks and grand municipal buildings.

The people in the photograph that evening were also living in a time of extraordinary advances. There must have seemed to be little that engineering and science could not conspire to achieve and at a pace that was increasing all the time. In the previous half century, Islanders had seen steamships, trains, telegrams and even aeroplanes arrive, along with the more mundane but equally revolutionary utilities of gas, electricity, telephones, water and sewerage. These were remarkable developments and although admittedly limited mostly to town and other urban areas at the time, their installation held the promise that one day everyone would benefit. There was a technical revolution in local transport occurring also. While the advent of steam train services in the 1870s had been groundbreaking, their reach in 1914 remained limited to linking St Helier with the small ports of Gorey in the east and St Aubin in the west, with an onward stretch from the latter to the Island's south-west corner. By the start of the twentieth century the first motor cars had appeared however. Motor buses that quickly established an ascendancy over train services when it came to public transport soon followed them. By 1914, buses had begun regularly running from town out into the country parishes and back. Pitchers of Cheapside in St Helier was one company offering such a service, carrying people between town and St Ouen four days a week, for a fare of one shilling and threepence return. The sight and sound of these early vehicles on the roads must have caused an enormous stir at a time when the horse and cart was still the dominant mode of transport for most people.

The presence of horses and carts, steam trains and shillings and pence serves as a reminder that many aspects of life for those who gathered in the Royal Square that night remained very different from the present time. While economic success, progress and technology may have greatly transformed Jersey and the wider world, some things were taking longer to change. Traditional Victorian beliefs and values still dominated society, strongly influencing the attitudes and behaviour of its people. These centred on the family and firmly established the expected roles for men, women and children. 'The bedrock for progress and existence is in the home,' lectured one local newspaper in 1914. 'Here the women should reign in a supremacy unchallenged even by man. Let us but abdicate this throne, and we shall have the "Ruin of Empires".'[2] As a result of such strongly entrenched views, real gender equality remained only a distant vision - or threat depending on one's viewpoint. There was a drive to change this, led by the Suffragette movement in Britain that had been forcefully championing the cause of equality in the years leading up to 1914. But they had yet to gain any significant concessions from the British Government when it came to women's rights, while in Jersey there were plenty of people with little time for such ideas. In 1914, the law permitted only men to vote in the Island's elections and permitted only men to stand for a seat in its government. By convention too, many professions and key roles in society were only open to men while women had to make do with lesser jobs and lower positions.

Education was another aspect of society different from the present time, with a clear disparity in what was available to the children of wealthy parents and those of everyone else. Although there had been great progress in standards and access between 1870 and 1914, schooling still ended at fourteen-years-old for all but a select few. Further education beyond that age was restricted to the small number of children whose families had the means to pay for it. This division was a factor helping to maintain a stratified society in 1914, with the gulf between those at the top and the bottom far more pronounced than can be presently found. In Britain, there was a growing support for change as socialism, the labour movement and trades unionism gained momentum among the working classes. While such ideas existed in Jersey, there remained a clear divide between employers and employees with the rights of latter distinctly lacking. As a result, those Islanders who had stood up on the balcony overlooking the Royal Square that New Year's Eve of 1913 would have had very different prospects from the majority of those that they saw below.

One other very marked difference from the present was that Jersey sat on the edge of a deeply divided and belligerent Europe at the start of 1914. War and the threat of war was nothing new to the Island of course. For centuries, it had been firmly in the front line of almost continuous conflict between England and France, suffering periodic raids and invasions and living under the constant threat of attack at other times. By 1914, however, this experience was now a fading memory for Islanders. The abdication of Napoleon Bonaparte one hundred years earlier had brought to an end more than three decades of almost continual warfare during which time Jersey had been strongly held as an important outpost against its hostile French neighbour. And although the flames of conflict had briefly flickered again after Napoleon escaped from Elba in 1815 and seized power once more, the Battle of Waterloo ensured his end and that one of the most intense periods of military activity in Jersey's history was over. It had been a period when Britain poured considerable resources into defending the Island, building forts, barracks, towers and cannon batteries to ensure that it remained secure from enemy hands. It all represented a very clear statement on Jersey's then strategic value to Britain, and of the determination to hold on to its oldest overseas possession.

Britain's hold on Jersey against a hostile French mainland dated back to a time six hundred years before the Napoleonic Wars. In 1204, King John of England lost control of Normandy to Philip II of France, thus ending a territorial union that had started in 1066 with William the Conqueror's victory at the Battle of Hastings. King John and his successors did not give up the prospect of regaining their lost lands in France, and were determined to retain Jersey and the other Channel Islands as a possession on the south side of the Channel. Fortified and garrisoned, Jersey had become a bastion for the English, and a thorn in the side of France. The loyalty of Islanders – or at least the loyalty of Jersey's prominent families of the time – was assured through the granting of certain rights and privileges when it came to self-government, trade and taxes. Over the centuries, these became enshrined in royal charters confirming the Island's relationship with, and independence from, England (and later Britain). In principle, they allowed England to retain overall responsibility for defence and foreign affairs, while Islanders were allowed to get on with managing their own civil matters.

In the years that followed 1204, two roles emerged to take responsibility for these important aspects of the Island's governance. The first was that of Governor. Originally called the Warden of the Isles when the responsibilities encompassed both Jersey and Guernsey, Governors were directly appointed by the English monarch to ensure royal interests were properly represented. In the early years, this meant jurisdiction over much of Jersey's civil affairs as well as ensuring that the Island remained firmly held for England. As local government institutions developed in the centuries following 1204, responsibilities for most legal and financial matters gradually passed from the Governor's hands into those of Islanders, leaving defence as their main responsibility. For this, and to ensure Islanders' loyalty if necessary, Governors could call upon the services of a garrison of English soldiers, the number of which would grow or contract according to the perceived level of threat. This military role clearly meant the position of Governor (or more frequently the Lieutenant Governor as the Governor was often absent), was suited to military men, a tradition that is maintained to the present time. The thaw in relations with France in the years following the Napoleonic Wars along with the development of Jersey's own government institutions saw a reduction in the Lieutenant Governor's responsibilities however. By 1914, his function had become mainly ceremonial in many matters or had changed to being the intermediary in Jersey's relationship with the British Government, which had taken over direct responsibility for the Island from the British sovereign by then. As a Crown Dependency, Jersey was free to make its own laws, although they still required the assent of Britain's Privy Council to come into force. Formal communications on such matters came through the Lieutenant Governor, who also acted on behalf of the Home Office, the British Government department with responsibility for the day-to-day relationship with Jersey in 1914. As a result, all official correspondence between the Island and Britain passed across his desk. But when it came to defence, the role of the Lieutenant Governor in 1914 remained very much an active one. As the senior military officer in Jersey, he was the commander-in-chief of local forces. During peacetime, this meant dealing largely with inspections, exercises and parades. In wartime, as Islanders were to discover, the Lieutenant Governor's responsibilities and interest assumed a far wider remit however.

The second important role to evolve after 1204 was that of Bailiff. In common with the Governor, Bailiffs were appointed to the position by the English monarch. Unlike the Governor, they were not men with military backgrounds but were selected from someone who had risen through the ranks of the Island's legal system. Among the Bailiff's more important duties was to hold sessions of the Royal Court, which administered justice in the Island on behalf of the monarch. The Royal Court also created the laws prior to the establishment of a separate government assembly, giving Bailiffs considerable power that some would take advantage of over the years. This gradually disappeared during the eighteenth and nineteenth centuries as executive power passed from their hands to those of Jersey's government, leaving many of their duties largely ceremonial, like their Lieutenant Governor counterpart. Yet the Bailiff remained a pivotal figure in 1914, as chief judge, president of the government assembly and the Island's foremost citizen. He also remained responsible for protecting the Jersey's constitutional rights and privileges, something that would come under considerable pressure during wartime.

Both the Lieutenant Governor and Bailiff were members of the Island's govenment, the States of Jersey. The States had developed from the sixteenth century onwards, gradually taking over responsibility for the running of local affairs. In 1914, the States assembly, which sat in a purpose built chamber overlooking St Helier's Royal Square, consisted of fifty-three Members present by virtue of one of four distinct positions. There were twelve Jurats chosen from the Island's notable citizens. Twelve Constables were present as the heads of each of Jersey's ancient parishes, St Brelade, St Clement, Grouville, St Helier, St John, St Lawrence, St Martin, St Mary, St Ouen, St Peter, St Saviour and Trinity. Also present were the Rectors from each parish, while the remaining group were seventeen elected Deputies, six from the most populous St Helier and one each from the other eleven parishes. The other Members of the States were two non-voting officers, the Attorney General and Solicitor General, who were appointed by the British Government to give advice on legal matters. The Attorney General was also head of the Island's Police force, which at that time consisted of a small group of paid policemen in St Helier and a much larger and voluntary Honorary Police Force. Presiding over them all was the Bailiff, who had the role of States' president and speaker. Although unable to vote in normal circumstances, the Bailiff had the status to strongly influence debates and their outcomes, and held the casting vote in the event of a tied ballot. The Lieutenant Governor had no vote in the States, but could and did speak from time to time on matters that they saw as their concern, and retained the power to veto any legislation believed to be incompatible with the interests of Britain.

If this was the leadership and system of government at the start of 1914, what can be said about the Island and the people who lived there? Demographically, this largest of the British Channel Islands was a quite different place in 1914, with a population of around fifty-two thousand, a number that is approximately half those living in the Island at the present time. A smaller population understandably meant less developed land, and therefore more green space in between the buildings and settlements. Such an arrangement also helped create a far clearer demarcation than found today between the town, which principally existed in the parish of St Helier, and the country, which filled just about every other parish in the Island.

Turning to the people of Jersey in 1914, one also finds some considerable differences to the situation that now exists. Political, economic and social changes experienced by the Island during the nineteenth century had led to the presence of three distinctly different population groups, each of which possessed its own heritage, customs and even language. The first to consider were those who had been there the longest and who constituted the largest group. The native Jerseymen had been present for centuries, descended from whatever peoples first came to the Island and made their homes there. In common with other island races, they had grown hardy and resilient during that time, developing a natural resourcefulness that comes from generations of isolation and hardship. They had also understandably become passionately attached to their Island, and fiercely proud of the rights and privileges obtained over the centuries in return for loyalty to the British Crown. This in turn had helped engender a strong sense of independence and a firm belief in the right to decide their own destiny. While loyalty to Britain and its sovereign was not in doubt, particularly among the local ruling class, there was also no doubt that the first and foremost loyalty of the majority was to Jersey.

Centuries of isolation had also given native Islanders their own unique customs, superstitions, foods and festivals, and allowed the development of their own language. Jèrriais, or Jersey-French, had its origins in old Norman-French, the dialect of William the Conqueror and his people, brought to the Island when it became part of the Duchy of Normandy in 933. It had been the

Islanders' everyday spoken language for centuries, although largely not written down – proper French was used for anything recorded, which in 1914 most native Islanders could also understand and speak. By that time, Jèrriais was a language sharply in decline, along with many other aspects of this traditional Jersey life however. One of the main reasons for this trend was the second major group population group present in 1914.

British settlers had been coming to Jersey since the end of the Napoleonic Wars. The first had been ex-army officers, pensioned off after 1815 and looking for somewhere to live with a milder climate and lower taxes than Britain. They came with their families and gradually established themselves among the upper echelons of Island society, which soon began adopting British customs and the English language as a result. Following these early immigrants there was another much larger group arriving in the 1830s and 1840s that soon began to have an even more profound effect. A range of civil and military building projects, including a massive naval harbour built in the east of the Island, required large numbers of workers for their construction. Jersey also had flourishing shipbuilding and fishing industries at that time, both of which needed considerable numbers of imported labourers in order to operate. Workers from Britain therefore arrived in large numbers to fill the demand, many also bringing their families with them. By the middle of the nineteenth century, they were helping to push net immigration into Jersey to five hundred people per year. Such a trend soon began to tell on the overall composition of the population, with the 1851 census revealing that 27 percent of people in the Island were not born there.

Most of these newcomers came from Britain and chose to make their home in the town of St Helier. At the start of the nineteenth century, it had been just a modest settlement, centred on the parish church and nearby market square, and still competing with St Aubin to the west for the status of the Island's chief port and commerce centre. Yet in the hundred years that followed, the town expanded considerably as its immigrant population grew, spreading out across the low-lying lands to the north, east and west of the towering hill named Le Mont de la Ville. At the start of the twentieth century, St Helier's population had reached almost twenty-eight thousand, a number that represented just over half the entire population at that time. Most were firmly British in character and English speaking, with the native Islanders and their customs and language now pushed into the outlying parishes. Despite a steady decline in British immigration after the 1850s, it was an irreversible change. After establishing a firm foothold, English progressively became more and more widely spoken, replacing French in most newspapers and as the official language of the States from the start of the twentieth century. And by then it had also become the language of choice for most Islanders, even those living in the country parishes.

A cause for the decrease in British immigrants coming to the Island had been the decline of Jersey's shipbuilding and fishing industries, which had contracted in the 1860s and then virtually disappeared. At the same time, an improving relationship with France meant less British Government money going into building and maintaining the Island's defences, so that requirement for labour had dried up too. Fortunately, following some worrying economic times for Islanders, a new and highly successful industry was emerging during the second half of the nineteenth century. Like its predecessors, agriculture also required a large number of imported workers to function. These would not come from Britain, however, but France, and they were arriving in growing numbers during the closing decades of the nineteenth century. They and their families were to constitute the third – and most contentious - of Jersey's three population groups in 1914.

There had always been a resident French community in Jersey that grew or contracted depending on the prevailing political or economic situation across the water in France. Some had come as refugees fleeing one or other regime in France. The most famous of these was the writer Victor Hugo who lived in Jersey between 1853 and 1855 after being exiled from his country. This occurrence had continued throughout the nineteenth century as various individuals and groups left France for political or religious reasons. While many would return home in due course, others decided to stay and make Jersey their home – for the immediate future at least. Among them were several religious educational orders that established themselves in the Island to continue the work they had considered to be under threat in France. The most prominent of these in 1914 were the Jesuits who opened a number of institutions in Jersey including Notre Dame du Bon Secours, a boarding school for naval cadets, and Maison St Louis, a theological college.* Both staff and pupils of these institutions largely kept themselves to themselves, with students and novice priests arriving to take up their studies and leaving the Island once they were completed.

Generations of French nationals had also come to Jersey in search of work, which may have been available on a permanent or seasonal basis. At the end of the nineteenth century some of them found employment in the Island's recently established tourism industry, working in hotels, restaurants or public houses. Visitors had been coming to Jersey in growing numbers from the second half of the nineteenth century as regular steamship services started to connect the Island with the south coast of England. Most French immigrants came to work in agriculture, however, which had changed greatly in the years leading up to 1914.

* Today the buildings of these two institutions house Highlands College and the Hotel De France respectively.

Agriculture had always been an important part of Island life, both as a means of local food production and the provision of goods to export. From the 1830s onwards, its importance had started increasing as overseas demand for two particular Jersey products began to rise. The first was the Jersey cow, a local breed that was small and relatively docile but capable of producing large quantities of protein-rich creamy milk. Such qualities made it highly sought, particularly in parts of the British Empire and in the Americas where Jersey settlers had first taken their animals. An official herd book to protect the breed was established in 1866, by which time Jersey cows were being sold at unprecedented prices to overseas buyers while returning excellent profits for their owners. The second product was the Jersey Royal Fluke, a variety of potato that first appeared in 1878 after a local farmer discovered an unusually large tuber from which he produced a heavy crop of distinctive tasting kidney-shaped potatoes. Other farmers began growing the new variety of potato and then exporting them to Britain where a strong demand for Jersey Royals (as they were branded) soon developed. It was not just the taste that drove sales, but also the fact that Jersey's fertile soil and mild climate produced an early crop that could be on British tables sooner than potatoes grown in that country.

As overseas demand grew for Jersey Royals, so too did the revenues that were flowing back into the Island. It was not long before the majority of agricultural land was given over to potato cultivation. Particularly prized were the sheltered sloping fields facing south and west as they grew the earliest crop, which in turn commanded the highest market prices. In 1907, admittedly a bumper year, local farmers had produced over seventy-seven thousand tons of Jersey Royals for export, which generated a value of £377,256. In 1914, the last crop before war broke out produced a lower total weight of just under fifty-five thousand tons, but with an increased monetary value in return of £481,993.[3] Such numbers made the potato crop an enormously important contributor to the Island's finances. In 1914, the total value of all goods and services exported by Jersey was £900,369, with the Jersey Royal crop representing just under 54 percent of that.[4] Given this, it's understandable that farming had assumed a dominant position in Jersey, and farmers now acquired a dominant role in running the Island. In 1914, a high number of States Members were either current or ex-farmers, who were understandably determined to do all they could to sustain and protect their industry. The policy would have significant consequences for the Island, both before and during the First World War.

Potato farming on the scale seen in Jersey was a labour intensive activity, especially when crops were being planted or harvested. At these times, there was a need for a temporary labour force willing to put in long hours of hard toil, ideally for a low wage in order to maximise profits. With insufficient numbers of such people in the Island able or willing to take such jobs, farmers looked for alternative sources. The answer was to be found in France, and in particular in Brittany and Normandy, the two nearest French *régions* to Jersey. In the late nineteenth century both of these predominantly agricultural regions were experiencing economic hardship leading to a shortage of work and low pay for those jobs available. Jersey, which was only a short sea journey away from the ports of Saint-Malo, Granville and Saint-Brieuc, offered the chance of work at a time it was scarce at home, even if the wages were low and the living conditions sometimes abysmal. Working in small gangs, the imported labourers were essential help during the potato planting and harvesting seasons. Their life in Jersey was extremely hard, with long hours in the fields and accommodation found in sheds and outbuildings for those who were fortunate, or under a hedge for those who weren't. Food was often just the potatoes that they helped plant and harvest, with the rough local cider to drink. It was not just French men enduring the deprivations as whole families would come, with women and children sharing the same work and living conditions.

Poor accommodation and hard work clearly did not deter French agricultural workers from coming to Jersey, or some deciding to subsequently make the Island their home. What had started as a seasonal arrangement soon began changing as some of those who came to work decided to stay. Renting meagre accommodation and small parcels of land from local farmers, they began growing crops of their own. Such arrangements allowed families to settle in the Island, with some men bringing their wives over from France while others married local girls. The number of French children present in Jersey grew correspondingly. Within a few decades, a French community, or colony as it was officially referred to, had established itself. The official figures at the time clearly reflect this. The 1911 census, which was the last taken before the war, reveals that of the 51,898 people then living in the Island, no fewer than 5,610 – or 11 percent of the population – gave France as their place of birth. Another report puts the number of French people present at that time even higher, suggesting that there were 10,088 present, of which 6,480 were permanently resident while the remainder were there for the potato season only.[5]

The increase in the number of French nationals living in Jersey was unintentional, and a cause for considerable concern among Islanders and their leaders. Unlike the English immigrants, who had largely confined themselves to town, the French community was putting its roots firmly down in the Island's countryside, and threatening to undermine the remaining bastions of traditional Jersey way of life still to be found there. Alarmed by this prospect, in 1906 the States commissioned a special report to look into the matter of French immigration and its impact on Jersey. Among its conclusions was that, 'the

Island is beginning to be swamped, and assimilation [of the French population] is becoming more and more difficult.'[6] Among the concerns highlighted by the report was that the children of French families living in the Island were being brought up with a distinct identity that was neither Jersey nor British. They spoke French at home (or Breton in many cases), they attended local French schools to be taught by French-speaking teachers, and they worshipped in one of the French-run Catholic churches that had sprung up across the country parishes since the 1870s. Most worryingly, the report concluded, was the threat that in due course the Island's French community would come to dominate Jersey's political system, with untold consequences for the centuries old relationship with Britain. 'The municipal government of each parish is still carrying on under Jersey influences…but each year sees numbers diminish and the number of landowners of foreign origin increase,' it stated. 'Once the municipal government of the parishes has changed hands, the representation of the parishes in the States will fall into the hands of a majority of foreign origin.'[7]

The presence of so many French people, the report concluded, will eventually lead to a marked reduction of the purely Jersey and British presence locally. The Island was in danger of losing its identity, and with it, the rights and privileges granted to Jersey over the centuries. Alarmed by that prospect, the States decided to introduce a number of policies to prevent this occurrence. Among them would be tighter controls on immigration from France, supposedly to ensure that those wanting to come to Jersey were of good character, but in reality to make it less easy to come to the Island. Steps were also taken to ensure that all school teachers in the Island were of Jersey or British origin, while a new education policy insisted that children had to be taught in English not French, and nor for that matter Jèrriais. To counter the perceived threat of French influence, the States had inadvertently set about hastening the decline of its own native language and customs. These deliberate moves to assimilate the local French community at the beginning of the twentieth century would hasten the unintentional changes that had commenced with the arrival of the first British settlers almost one hundred years earlier. Anxious to protect its identity and ancient rights and privileges, Jersey had decided to further develop and reinforce the importance of its relationship with Britain.

The changes were taking place at a time when Britain was also re-evaluating its relationship with the Island and reassessing the strategic importance of Jersey in view of the situation in Europe. German unification in 1871 following the Franco-Prussian War had upset the balance of power that had existed on the Continent since the end of the Napoleonic Wars. To counter the threat of a militaristic and aggressive Germany, France and Russia had become allies in 1894 with an agreement to come to each other's aid if either were attacked.

PEACE, PROGRESS AND PROSPERITY

Germany had already secured allies of its own by then, forming the Triple Alliance with Austria-Hungary and Italy that also established a series of mutual defence treaties to protect against attacks by a hostile power. Britain remained aside from these arrangements for a while. Since the Battle of Waterloo in 1815, it had pursued a policy of avoiding direct involvement in Europe's wars unless they directly threatened Britain's interests. Attention was focused on building a global trading empire instead, and success in achieving this was evident by the size and value of its overseas possessions by the end of the nineteenth century. Following the unification of Germany, this position had gradually begun to shift however.

Alarmed by the growing German domination of the Continent, Britain reassessed its policies towards Europe. Most threatening was the powerful navy that Kaiser Wilhelm II had begun constructing. Britain's links to its empire relied on control of the seas, and the Royal Navy was the strongest in the world to ensure that remained the case. The rise of Germany's navy along with the stated aims of the Kaiser to acquire a global empire of his own was perceived to be a direct threat to Britain's maritime dominance. As a result, the country had embarked on a warship construction programme to ensure it maintained an advantage over Germany. It also developed increasingly close ties with France, culminating in the signing of the 'Entente Cordial' in 1904, an agreement that formally ended centuries of animosity. The agreement also marked the start of a military alliance between the two countries, an arrangement that Britain extended in 1907 to include Russia too. Jointly, the three countries now constituted the Triple Entente, which opposed Germany and its Triple Alliance.

The changing circumstances in Europe also led Britain to review its military plans for an overseas war and to review the nation's home defences. These included those of the Channel Islands, which had been increasingly neglected as the threat of war with France declined during the nineteenth century. Yet the growing likelihood that the British Army may become involved in a war on the Continent once more, together with the threat of a powerful German Navy at large in the Channel led to a reassessment. The strategic military value of the Channels had begun to rise once more. Jersey would need to ready itself for a possible war.

On 28 June 1914, just seven months after the hopeful evening's celebrations in St Helier's Royal Square, the first shots in that war were fired. On a far-off Sarajevo street, a young assassin had confronted the Archduke Franz Ferdinand with a revolver and shot dead both the heir to the Austro-Hungarian Empire and his wife Sophia. Although few realised it at the time, the First World War was only five weeks away.

2 CALL OUT THE GUARDS

Jersey's defences, defenders and the mobilisation of the Militia on the eve of war

In July 1914, while Islanders and their holidaying visitors were enjoying a glorious summer in Jersey, tensions were rising in the capitals of Europe. The murders in Sarajevo had presented the enraged Austria-Hungary with an opportunity to settle a score with its troublesome Serbian neighbour. Relations between the two countries were already strained following the Balkan Wars of 1912 and 1913 during which Serbia had emerged as a threat to Austro-Hungarian ambitions in the region. When it was discovered the assassin, Gavrilo Princip, had links to Serbia, the Austro-Hungarians responded with a number of demands calculated to provoke a conflict with Serbia. Russia now intervened, warning Vienna against taking any aggressive action towards Serbia, which it had traditionally supported. In response, Germany countered with whole-hearted support for its Austro-Hungarian ally. Despite diplomatic efforts to calm the situation, as July came to a close, there was a growing resignation in European capitals that neither side was prepared to back down. What had appeared at first to be a localised Balkan issue had steadily grown into a rift likely to cause a general European war. On 28 July, the first hostilities broke out when Austria-Hungary declared war on Serbia. That same day Britain, which had been leading efforts to find a peaceful solution to the crisis, took steps to prepare for a possible war. Among them was the dispatch of a telegram to Jersey informing its Lieutenant Governor that he should, 'adopt the precautionary measures laid down in the Jersey Defence Scheme.'[1]

Major General Sir Alexander Nelson Rochfort, KCB, CMG, had been Jersey's Lieutenant Governor since June 1910. The sixty-four-year-old, whose impressive height and trim stature still lent an imposing appearance, had preceded this appointment with a distinguished military career in the British Army. First commissioned in the Royal Artillery in 1871, he had spent his early years of military service on home duties. It was at a time when the British Empire was at its height, and ambitious young army officers would have sought overseas service where they could hopefully gain promotion and earn a reputation fighting in one of Britain's far-flung colonial wars. By 1882, therefore, Rochfort's military career had taken him to India, serving on the staff of the Viceroy there. In 1885 he was in the Sudan taking part in the

Mahdist War and by 1899 in South Africa where he fought and was wounded in the Second Boer War. Further colonial service then followed in Somaliland before returning to Britain in 1904 to become the Inspector of Royal Horse and Royal Field Artillery. For any army officer harbouring ambitions to have a more restful role in their later life, it was a first class record and a well-rounded career. The role of Lieutenant Governor in Jersey demanded just such a military record, along with a wide range of social skills, a clear grasp of the intricacies of diplomacy and an understanding of the cut and thrust of politics. Fortunately, given the period in which he would be Lieutenant Governor, Rochfort appears to have possessed the right blend of attributes for the job. 'He knew how to rule firmly without making an overt show of authority,' one commentator noted, and that he was a fair man with, 'a genial disposition, who endeared himself to all who came into contact with him.'[2]

It was also fortunate that when war did break out, Rochfort had been Lieutenant Governor for four years. It was a time that gave him a chance to learn about Jersey, its people and leaders, and to develop important relationships both locally and with the British Government ministers and civil servants in London responsible for the Island's affairs. Through this, he seems to have grasped an understanding of the balance required to maintain the relationship between Britain and an independent-minded Island. In the years of peace, this balance must have been relatively easy to preserve, with both sides going about their business without much interference from each other. Yet with a heavy heart, Rochfort must have realised that the War Office telegram he received on 29 July meant this balance was going to be challenged in the months ahead. It also meant an end to any restful aspirations. Aside from his political and diplomatic role, the Lieutenant Governor was firstly the Island's military Commander-in-Chief and responsible for its defence in wartime. Now, for the first time in almost one hundred years, the order had arrived to prepare those defences for a possible war. First on the list of steps to be taken was for Rochfort to issue an order of his own mobilising the Jersey Militia.

While the exact origins of the Jersey Militia may be uncertain, for most of its existence the purpose had been very clear. Following the split between England and Normandy in 1204, there arose a need to defend Jersey against the now hostile French. While King John and his successors built the formidable Mont Orgueil Castle on the Island's east coast and filled it with a garrison of English soldiers for this purpose, local men were expected to show loyalty to their sovereign by fighting in defence of their Island if required. Although the principle of militia service, which was the temporary calling up of local men for home defence in time of war, may have existed in Jersey before 1204, it is possible that its formal organisation began at that time. What is certain is that

Thomas de Ferrers, who was Warden of the Isles, received orders in 1337 from King Edward III to raise the men of Jersey in readiness for war. In response, De Ferrers formed companies of local men to aid in the Island's defence, an action that may represent the foundation of the Jersey Militia. If so, it was a principle that was to remain in place for almost seven hundred years.

By the sixteenth century, the Militia had become integrated into the Island's parochial system. Documents from 1545 record that the Island's then Governor, the Earl of Hertford, ordered each parish to appoint a captain for its 'Company of Trained Bands'. This was at a time of frequent French raids and invasions, including one that took place in 1549 at Bouley Bay on the Island's north coast. On that occasion, these trained bands were recorded as being instrumental in helping defeat the invaders and sending them fleeing back to France. In the years that followed the Militia continued to evolve, and by the mid-seventeenth century, the trained bands had become three distinct regiments, titled the West Regiment, North Regiment and East Regiment. The Militia has also grown to include an artillery component possessing twenty-four cannon by then, with two allocated to each parish and stored along with other weapons in the parish churches, which were also the designated muster points in the event of an enemy threat. It was under these arrangements that the Militia took part in the defence of the Island during the English Civil War, although not against the traditional enemy of France. With Jersey actively supporting the Royalist cause, a Parliamentarian fleet landed a strong force of soldiers in St Ouen's Bay on the west coast of the Island on 22 October 1651. They faced limited resistance from a dispirited Militia with divided loyalties that was tired and wet through. It was soon dispersed after putting up only a limited defence, leaving the invaders free to overrun the Island and lay siege to Mont Orgueil Castle and the more recently constructed Elizabeth Castle situated on an islet off St Helier. Both castles would surrender after short sieges.

During the eighteenth century, the structure of the Jersey Militia changed once more. By 1730, there were five infantry regiments, all of which raised their men on a parochial basis. The 1st (North-west) Regiment was formed from the men of St Ouen, St Mary and St John; the 2nd (North) Regiment from Trinity and St Martin; the 3rd (East) Regiment from St Saviour, Grouville and St Clement; the 4th (South Regiment) from St Helier and St Lawrence; and the 5th (South-west) Regiment from St Brelade and St Peter. Each regiment had a single infantry battalion with the exception of the South Regiment, which possessed two battalions drawn from its increasingly populated part of the Island. There was also a regiment of cavalry by then, and a regiment of artillery armed with twenty-five cannons.

These were the preparations in place on 6 January 1781, when Jersey and its Militia would face the sternest test for centuries. In the early hours of that morning, a French force landed unopposed on the Island's south-east coast under the cover of darkness. Led by adventurer and soldier of fortune, Phillippe de Rullecourt, it quickly marched on St Helier while most local people were still in their beds. The Island's Lieutenant Governor, Major Moyse Corbet, was surprised in his town house and was taken prisoner. Through a combination of threats and bluff, de Rullecourt obtained a signed surrender from Corbet and an order for the Island's defenders to lay down their arms. It was ignored by the commander of Elizabeth Castle, who fired on the approaching French, and by Major Francis Peirson who was the officer in command of the Island's British Army garrison. Peirson, who had been left in charge while more senior officers returned to Britain for Christmas, ordered all available troops to assemble. The force, which included both regular British soldiers and Jersey's Militia, advanced into St Helier to confront de Rullecourt and his men. In the short battle that followed, the French were totally defeated, although the twenty-four-year-old Peirson heroically died at the head of his troops. Wounded in the fighting also, de Rullecourt survived only to succumb to his injuries the next day.

In recognition of the part it had played in what is now known as the Battle of Jersey, and for the commitment shown over the long years of the Napoleonic Wars that followed, the Militia was honoured in 1831 with a new title: The Royal Militia of the Island of Jersey. Then, to mark the one hundredth anniversary of the Battle of Jersey in 1881, it was further permitted to add the battle honour 'Jersey 1781' to its colours. By that time, its structure had changed once more. Four years earlier, in 1877, the Militia's five infantry regiments were reorganised into three, each of which contained roughly five hundred men, and now known as the 1st (West) Regiment, the 2nd (East) Regiment and the 3rd (South or Town) Regiment. The Militia's artillery now had 280 men organised into three field gun batteries and one company supporting a British Army unit operating a number of coastal defence guns in the Island. The cavalry regiment had disappeared by this time, while six purpose-built arsenals, in St Helier, St Lawrence, St Peter, St Mary, St Martin and Grouville, had been added in the 1840s to house the weapons and equipment previously stored in the parish churches.[*] Irrespective of organisation and facilities, by the end of the nineteenth century the Militia had become far more than just a defensive force in Jersey; it had become a pillar of the Island establishment.

The declining threat from France during the latter half of the nineteenth century had presented a welcome opportunity to focus on the ceremonial

---

[*] Those in St Lawrence, St Peter, St Martin and Grouville and St Helier remain to this day and are used for housing and as offices in the case of St Helier. St Mary's Arsenal was demolished after the Second World War.

aspects of soldiering. Militia parades and grand balls become splendid society occasions, complete with extravagant dress uniforms, regimental silver and military bands. The numbers of officers, almost all of which were exclusively from Jersey, grew to nearly two hundred, drawn from the Island's upper and middle classes. Training and standards declined, with a greater emphasis on inter-unit competitions rather than on preparations to fight against an enemy that now no longer appeared to exist. It was not to last however. Britain had begun a process of army modernisation even before events on the Continent forced it to reconsider the policy of remaining detached from European Wars. Attention eventually fell on Jersey and its defences, leading to a situation widely known at the time as the 'The Militia Question'.

Experiences in the Crimean War and during the 1857 Indian Mutiny had shown up considerable shortcomings in the British Army's capabilities. At the same time, there was a realisation that the organisation and staffing arrangements under which the army had fought the Napoleonic wars were increasingly out of date. As a result, from the 1860s onwards, successive British Governments had instigated and overseen a series of major reforms designed to modernise the army and give it a more professional establishment. The goal was to create a force of regular full-time soldiers capable of being deployed overseas should the need arise while ensuring adequate trained and equipped forces remained at home to defend the country. There also needed to be sufficient troops available to garrison and protect the Empire. The Boer War that started in 1899 showed the new arrangements still needed further attention, particularly with the readiness of the part-time soldiers who were expected to supplement the home defences after most of the regular army had departed.

A question over the effectiveness of Jersey's part-time Militia had already been raised in the years immediately preceding the Boer War. At that time, the British Army maintained a garrison of regular soldiers in the Island consisting of a battalion of infantry and a company of artillerymen. In the event of an overseas war, these men were to be withdrawn and replaced by less experienced reserve soldiers. In this case, the Jersey Militia would become the Island's principal defenders. To ensure that it was up to the task, the War Office wanted the Militia to modernise, to bring local forces into line with the new revised standards of the British Army. The view was that years of peace had left the Militia unsuited to the demands of modern warfare, and it needed to adapt if it was to fit into the wider scheme of national defence. It had become, in the words of the Island's Lieutenant Governor at the time, a force that was no longer efficient.[3]

The changes demanded by the War Office were an enlarged Militia operating under a different structure that more closely aligned to that used in Britain. Militiamen also needed to undertake an extended training regime that for many would include spending nine days each year on exercise in a military camp. Regular British Army officers would take of command of all the major Militia units, contentiously replacing the Jersey appointed officers who had led them previously. At the same time, other British Army officers and senior non-commissioned officers would join to assist with administration and training. What's more, Jersey would have to pay for these outside appointees, along with the general running costs of the entire Militia. The total cost could be up to £6,500 per year – a considerable sum in those days. To show how serious Britain was on the matter, the War Office had threatened to withdraw the regular army garrison if the proposed modernisation was not implemented.

Some States Members agreed that such changes were necessary. In the words of one during a debate on the matter in 1905, the claim was that, 'The Militia under the old system were looked upon as playing soldiers.'[4] Most others felt strongly that it was not right for Britain to tell the Island how to organise and run an institution that had been established for seven hundred years. Not solely because of the principle of political independence at stake, Militia service was also unpopular with many local young men. Jersey, and its neighbour Guernsey, were the only places throughout the British Empire to have compulsory military service. A considerable number of young Islanders were already leaving from the Island at this time, moving to Britain, Australia, Canada and elsewhere in the world in search of a better life. There were fears that making Militia service even more onerous would not only drive more young men to immigrate but deter those who may consider moving to Jersey to replace them. Attempts by the States to water down the changes led the War Office to do what it had threatened. In 1904, the British Army garrison battalion departed and was not replaced. The Militia Question had become a serious one. The garrison's withdrawal meant not only a diminishment in defence, but, in many ways more importantly, it also meant the loss of valuable army service and supply contracts. Under pressure, the States relented and passed the Militia Law (1905), which set out the terms under which Islanders were required to do their duty, and established the units in which they would serve. This would be the structure under which the Militia would mobilise in July 1914 and the one in place during the First World War. The 1905 Law maintained the overarching principles of Militia service. First, that it was compulsory between the ages of sixteen and forty-five. Second, that it applied to all men born in Jersey, or whose father was born Jersey, and to British subjects living in the Island for more than two years and who owned property there. Third, that Militia service was undertaken gratuitously - that is without pay – except for those days spent fully on training. Anyone failing to comply with the law faced a fine, with a 'Militia Vingtenier' appointed in each parish (two in St Helier) for enforcement. The only acceptable reasons for exemption from service were by failing a medical examination, being employed in a designated important role such as lighthouse keeper, schoolteacher or member of the Police Force. Members of the Society of Friends (Quakers) were also exempted on the grounds of their religious beliefs. For everyone else, as from 1905 there were three categories of Militia service:

1. The Preparatory Service: undertaken from the age of sixteen to twenty-years-old, although recruits aged eighteen and over who were considered ready for active service could be upgraded at that point. Service consisted of not more than forty compulsory drills per annum, none of which would start until after five o'clock in the afternoon so as to minimise disruption to employers.
2. The Active Militia: for men from eighteen until the age of thirty-five, although no one had to serve for more than ten years in this category. Thus a man who started service in the Active Militia at the age of twenty would complete his term on reaching thirty. The Law established the number of men in the Active Militia as 1,800, exclusive of commissioned officers. Training consisted of nine consecutive days in a summer camp per annum, although only one thousand men chosen by ballot had to take part each year, while all had to attend eight other non-consecutive days for rifle and gun practice, field days or reviews. The camps were mainly held either on a large area of open ground at Les Quennevais in the west of the Island, or near to Fort Regent on its eastern glacis, an area of land also known as Mutton's Field.
3. The Reserve: consisting of the First Reserves, formed from those men up to the age of thirty-five who had completed their time in the Active Militia and who now had to undertake four training days per annum, and the Second Reserves formed from men between the ages of thirty-six and forty-five who had to undertake just two training days per annum.

For administration, recruitment and training of these men, the 1905 Law divided the Island into three military districts:

> The Western District, consisting of the Sub-district of St Ouen and St Mary based at St Mary's Arsenal, the Sub-district of St John and St Lawrence, based at the St Lawrence Arsenal and the Sub-district of St Brelade and St Peter, based at St Peter's Arsenal.

The Eastern District, consisting of the Sub-district of St Martin, Trinity and the Maufant area of St Saviour, based at St Martin's Arsenal and the Sub-district of Grouville, St Clement and the remainder of St Saviour, based at Grouville Arsenal.

The Southern District, consisting of St Helier. Following a damaging fire at the Town Arsenal which had occurred in 1900[†], it also used the Queen's Assembly Rooms in St Helier's Belmont Road, pending the construction of a new Town Arsenal that was being built at Rouge Bouillon on the town's eastern outskirts but which would not be completed until 1917[‡].

The Militia was restructured into a single infantry regiment, the Royal Jersey Light Infantry (RJLI), and a regiment of artillery, the Royal Jersey Artillery (RJA). The RJLI was composed of three battalions aligned to the military districts, the 1st (West) Battalion, the 2nd (East) Battalion and the 3rd (South) Battalion. They were commonly referred to as the West Battalion, East Battalion and Town Battalion, however, which are the names that shall be used from this point forward. The battalions, which were commanded by a lieutenant colonel, were divided into six rifle companies drawn from the Active Militia, designated A to F, with the total number of men present in each dependent on the population size of their District. On the outbreak of war, for example, the West Battalion had twelve officers and 385 other ranks, the East Battalion thirteen officers and 349 other ranks while the Town Battalion had fifteen officers and 547 other ranks. They wore the standard British Army uniforms of the day, with Jersey Militia cap badges and shoulder flashes, although some units were still equipped with some older items of clothing and equipment in 1914. The infantry were armed with Lee Enfield rifles and Maxim machine guns. True to British Army doctrine, there was great emphasis placed on shooting practice at the Militia's rifle ranges at Crabbé on the Island's north-west coast, Les Platons in Trinity and Grouville Common in the east. To help develop marksmanship, a close association also existed between the Militia and the Jersey Rifle Association, which had been founded with the military in mind to improve the standard of shooting in the Island. The 1905 Law retained this principle, with the States paying for shooting competition prizes.

The RJA comprised two batteries and two companies. A (West) Battery and B (East) Battery were mobile field artillery units equipped in 1914 with horse-drawn Ordnance BLC (breech-loading converted) 15-pounder guns, while C Company was a heavy mobile unit equipped with 4.7-inch QF (quick-firing) guns mounted on carriages. The final D Company was attached to the British

† The old Town Arsenal was in St Helier's Nelson Street, with the current site occupied by the Parish of St Helier as an administration building.

‡ Converted into the police and fire brigade headquarters after the Second World War.

JERSEY'S GREAT WAR

Army operated coastal defence batteries protecting St Helier Harbour. The total number of men from the Active Militia serving in the RJA at the outbreak of war was 12 officers and 281 other ranks. The artillery practiced firing their guns at coastal locations around the Island, with shots ranged out to sea, this subject to providing prior notice to fishermen and sailors of course. In addition to the infantry and artillery regiments, from 1905, the Militia also had an Engineer Company with one officer and 118 other ranks, and a Medical Company of five officers and 85 other ranks. While the cavalry had disappeared from the order of battle, there was now a cyclist company drawn from across the infantry battalions.

This force had to be paid for, and the 1905 Law clearly set out responsibilities. The States paid for the Militia salaries and allowances, the running costs of arsenals and other Militia facilities including the rifle ranges, fuel and rations, transport costs, and the general administrative costs of running the Militia. The British Government in turn paid for the uniforms, weapons and equipment. Thus reconstituted, equipped, trained and paid for the Jersey Militia became acceptable to the War Office as an integral element of Britain's home defences. And the very day after the States had passed the new Militia Law in October 1905, the then Lieutenant Governor, General Gough, announced that a regular British Army battalion would return to the Jersey District for garrison duty with immediate effect.

The Jersey District was the army headquarters in direct control of all the units stationed in Jersey including the Militia, and responsible for the Island's defence. Under the overall command of the Lieutenant Governor, it had a small headquarters staff located in an elegant house named Beau Sejour[§] on St Helier's Rouge Bouillon. In 1914, responsibility for the day-to-day administration of the garrison was in the hands of Brigadier General John Godfrey, a sixty-three-year-old Jersey-born professional soldier who held the position of Assistant Adjutant-General. Along with Godfrey, there were other officers responsible for overseeing the local artillery, engineers, supplies, medical facilities and so forth. In addition to the Militia, the District's Headquarters was also responsible for the garrison of regular British Army units, which in 1914 still consisted of an infantry battalion, a garrison artillery company and a number of minor supporting and administration units.

The infantry battalion was the 1st Battalion of the Devonshire Regiment, which had arrived in 1911 to replace the 2nd Battalion of the King's Own Royal Lancaster Regiment. Its men were housed across the Island in barracks dating back to the nineteenth century. The largest of these was St Peter's Barracks, a sprawling army camp located in the west of the Island on land above St Ouen's

---

§ Today the house is the Savoy Hotel.

Bay¶, with smaller barracks at Grève de Lecq, Bonne Nuit and in Rozel Bay. The main accommodation was in Fort Regent, however, a massive Napoleonic era fortress built on St Helier's Mont De La Ville and which was at the heart of a large military complex covering much of its surrounding district. Within this area were married quarters for families in nearby Green Street, a military hospital, a prison, a gymnasium, a garrison school and an engineer barracks. Elizabeth Castle also remained in military hands at that time, and was home to the 20th Company, Royal Garrison Artillery, whose role was to operate the Island's remaining coastal artillery guns. To protect the approaches to St Helier Harbour the South Hill Battery had two fixed 6-inch B Mark II guns while two 4.7-inch QF guns were emplaced at the Lower Keep Battery on Elizabeth Castle.

Along with the infantry and artillery, there were small units of other specialised troops in the Island including detachments from the 34th Field Company, Royal Engineers, from No. 6 Company, Royal Army Medical Corps, from the Army Ordinance Corps and from the Army Service Corps. As well as army units, Jersey's pre-war military forces also consisted of two Royal Navy operated 'Port War Signal Stations', one on Fort Regent and the other at Gorey Harbour. A third station was provided at Ronez on the Island's north coast after the war started.

There was a further military unit in Jersey in 1914 which would have a role to play in the Island's defence. One of the nineteenth century British Army reforms had centred upon improving the quality of the officer corps. With universities and public schools seen as ideal institutions to produce officers, a number had established military cadet units to undertake the training of young men interested in army careers. In 1908, as part of the reforms instigated by Secretary of State for War Richard Haldane, these early cadet forces were integrated into the Officer Training Corps (OTC). Jersey's Victoria College had established a Cadet Corps in 1884 that was aligned to the Militia's Town Battalion. In 1908, this now became the Victoria College OTC and lost its association with the Militia. Training subsequently took place locally and in army summer camps held in Britain. Many of its former members would go on to serve with the British armed forces during the First World War, along with hundreds of other ex-boys and a number of masters from that school.

These were the forces in Jersey when the Lieutenant Governor issued his order to mobilise the Militia on the evening of 29 July 1914. As the news had spread through the Island, there was an unprecedented night of fevered speculation as people tried to make sense of it. The order was for the men of the Active Militia to report for duty at 2.00 pm on the following day, 30 July. Most struggled to comprehend the reason why. While the newspapers had

¶ St Peter's Barracks were demolished in the 1960s to allow the expansion of Jersey's airport.

reported the assassinations in Sarajevo and the subsequent diplomatic activity, stories from closer to home had kept the growing crisis out of the headlines. In the absence of firm facts on the matter, there was plenty of rumour and no shortage of excited speculation over possible motives and likely outcomes. Some assumed the mobilisation was an exercise, designed to test the readiness of the Militia just in case there was a need for a real mobilisation. Others held the opposite view, believing that war must be imminent and that once assembled, the soldiers were going to be immediately sent for overseas duty. The only people who knew the reason were senior Militia officers and members of the Lieutenant Governor's staff, and they were not saying anything. Their focus was on the next day, working tirelessly throughout that night and into the next morning preparing for the mobilisation. Everyone else would have to wait until two o'clock to learn what was happening.

As the appointed hour approached on 30 July, the Militiamen had gathered at pre-determined assembly points throughout the Island. They were wearing their uniforms and equipment, and had brought an extra blanket with them as ordered, although there was some uncertainly as to why it was needed. At two o'clock, after the men had paraded, the reason became very apparent. 'At the outset I wish you to realise that this was not merely a test mobilisation, as supposed by some, but a serious mobilisation ordered by the War Office,' announced Lieutenant Colonel Gerald McKenzie to the assembled men of the Town Battalion. 'You have been called-up as soldiers, and I expect and know you will behave as such. How long it will last, I cannot say, but all ranks must understand that they are under military law until demobilisation takes place.'[5] The official reason given for their mobilisation was, 'in view of the state of feeling among European powers'. This meant little to most Militiamen as they lined up to draw their rifles, ammunition and rations before marching away from the barracks and arsenals under the command of their officers. Their duty henceforth would be to guard the Island's coastline against an enemy attack. The extra blanket was needed because most would be sleeping in the open, or if fortunate, in temporary accommodation.

Bemused Islanders watched as the Militiamen took up station at various points around the Island. In town, armed soldiers established checkpoints on the main thoroughfares into St Helier from the east and west, with their military camps of pitched tents set up on the wide grassy lawn of People's Park in the west and along the seafront near St Luke's in the east. Militiamen watched over ships coming to and going from St Helier Harbour, stood on duty in the Royal Square and guarded the railway terminal near the Island's potato export weighbridge, with the men posted there at least fortunate to have the first class carriages made available to sleep in. Elsewhere men found places to bed down wherever practical, which in the countryside often meant under a hedge, behind a wall or in the shelter of some trees. The luckier ones were offered a shed or outbuilding by considerate locals, some of whom also brought out hot coffee and warm food for comfort. Despite the less than ideal conditions, and the shock of unexpected mobilisation, the men were reportedly in good spirits as they set about the task of defending their Island. 'Everyone seemed satisfied that the need was urgent, and the men marched off to their different stations very cheerfully,' wrote one reporter. 'In many cases the [mobilisation] notices had been delivered very late. A St Ouen's man told me he received his well after one o'clock, but the inconvenience was accepted without a grumble…'[6]

By 31 July, the Militia were firmly in place in their wartime stations. Their mobilisation had gone smoothly, which was a reflection on the good planning undertaken by the Jersey District staff before the war. The Militiamen's bearing and professionalism was widely complimented upon, which was taken as being a credit to the modernisation activities undertaken since 1905, with Rochfort singled out for his part in this. The Militia occupied both military facilities and requisitioned civilian buildings throughout the Island. The West Battalion had its headquarters at St Peter's Arsenal, with a detached command at Grève de Lecq Barracks. The East Battalion took over St Martin's School and the adjacent Public Hall for its headquarters, with detached commands at Fort Henry on Grouville Common, at Bonne Nuit Barracks and at Rozel Barracks. The Town Battalion had its headquarters at the old Town Arsenal buildings and yard in St Helier's Nelson Street and also occupied the nearby Halkett Place School. The RJA had its mobile batteries in the east and west of the Island at St Peter's Arsenal and Grouville Arsenal respectively, while the heavier guns of C Company were located at the Town Arsenal with a detached unit at Springfield Showground, an expansive agricultural facility located on the northern outskirts of town. The gunners of D Company took over responsibility for the South Hill Battery and its harbour defence guns. Finally, the Engineer Company and Medical Company both had their headquarters in the Engineer Barracks at La Collette, which stood on the St Helier foreshore south of Fort Regent, and sent detachments to the Eastern and Western Districts.

As matters in Jersey settled down on that day, there remained a small hope that war could still be avoided as calmer heads among European governments sought to find a diplomatic solution to the crisis that had arisen over the deaths of the Austro-Hungarian Crown Prince and his wife. In Berlin and St Petersburg, there was a growing clamour for war however. In response to the Austro-Hungarian declaration of war on Serbia, Russia had ordered a partial mobilisation of its army to demonstrate a determination to support the Serbs, and then a full mobilisation after Germany threatened to intervene. It was at this point that the series of alliances in place to help ensure peace in Europe became the cause for a potentially far wider war. To counter the potential of having to fight both Russia in the east and France in west at the same time, Germany had developed an innovative military strategy. The Schlieffen Plan assumed that war would start with France and Russia at the same time, but that it would take the less advanced Russian Empire longer to mobilise its forces and attack Germany. During that time, calculated as being at six weeks, the German Army would concentrate the majority of its forces against France and aim to defeat the French comprehensively before the Russians could start their offensive. Thereafter, Germany would concentrate its forces in the east and deal with the Russian threat. At the heart of the Schlieffen Plan was that fundamental assumption that war would start against France and Russia concurrently. When the Russian Czar ordered his armies to mobilise on 31 July 1914, this assumption, and the subsequent timetable for war, was in danger of being lost. Unless, that is, a war with France was started at the same time.

On 1 August, Germany sent a provocative ultimatum to the French government asking for a guarantee that France would remain neutral in the event of a war against Russia, and demanding territorial concessions as an assurance. In France, there was no intention to accept German demands. Under pressure from its Russian ally to declare war, and from its own army commanders to prepare for what was seen as being inevitable, on 1 August 1914, the French government ordered the mobilisation of its armed forces to begin at midnight. And that included Frenchmen then living or working overseas, including in the British Channel Island of Jersey.

3 POUR LA PATRIE

Jersey's French community responds as France prepares for war

Scenes of jubilation in Paris greeted the news that France had ordered the mobilisation of its armed forces on 1 August 1914. For over forty years, the French nation had been living with the shame of defeat, and the consequences of a humiliating peace treaty. To many French people, therefore, the prospect of another war with Germany was the opportunity to settle an old score.

There had also been celebrations in July 1870 at the start of the Franco-Prussian War. Emperor Napoleon III, the ailing and less talented nephew of the great Napoleon Bonaparte, had rashly declared war on Prussia and ordered his French Army into battle. Having been deliberately provoked by Prussia's 'Iron' Chancellor, Otto von Bismarck, into a conflict that it was far from ready for and left isolated from any potential allies, France and its army were soon found to be seriously wanting. It quickly became obvious that any cause for public optimism was misplaced. There was chaos as troops from all over the country assembled for war, many lacking their weapons, supplies and even their officers. There was confusion as to who was in overall command and what exactly the French military strategy was. It was clear that any pre-war reputation that France and its army of 1870 had for military prowess had arisen from past glories rather than present capabilities. Within six weeks of the war starting, most of Napoleon's army were either prisoners of war, hopelessly besieged or dead on the field of battle. With the Emperor himself captured following the Battle of Sedan, the Second French Empire that had ruled France since 1852 soon disintegrated. The republican regime that now replaced it vowed to continue waging the war, holding Paris against the investing German armies and raising new forces in the provinces. Their efforts came too late however. It was not possible to rectify French military deficiencies and put aside political differences in the time available. Pitted against of one of the most formidable armies ever created, France's defeat was inevitable. On 18 January 1871, the King of Prussia was crowned Kaiser Wilhelm I of a unified Germany in a glittering ceremony at the Palace of Versailles. A few days later, the Franco-Prussian war ended with the conclusion of an armistice. The ensuing peace treaty completed France's humiliation, with the former '*grande nation*' of Europe stripped of the eastern province of Alsace and part of Lorraine, made to pay enormous reparations, and forced to endure a German army of occupation.

Defeat and the shame of defeat had galvanised the new French Third Republic into making efforts to rectify the military shortcomings of the Bonapartist regime it replaced. High on the list of priorities of the new government was reforming the country's army. Despite the scale and nature of the recent defeat, there was a widespread desire in France to gain revenge through a future war. Yet the country now faced a united Germany with a larger population that was growing at a faster rate than that of France. Translated into possible numbers of soldiers available in wartime, it was becoming obvious to any observer that France's position would only weaken over time while that of Germany grew stronger. If it were to improve the chances of victory in a future war, France needed to take steps to strengthen its military capabilities.

One solution was to seek allies against Germany, something that had been sadly lacking in 1870. Germany had initially sought to continue France's isolation through a series of leagues and treaties, which had served their purpose for a number of years. Disagreements between Germany and Russia gave France the opportunity to conclude an alliance with the Russians, which came into place in 1894. Signing the Entente Cordiale with Britain in 1904 had further strengthened the French position. This agreement initially dealt with colonial matters, removing some of the points of global contention between the two countries. Following a German intervention in Tangiers in 1905, and the diplomatic crisis that followed, Britain and France agreed to extend their relationship to a military alliance as well. It meant that in the event of war, Britain would send an army to fight on the Continent alongside France.

While the commitment of British troops was welcome, France still needed to mobilise sufficient numbers of men to have a chance of meeting Germany on equal terms in a future war. The second solution to the question of military manpower was therefore to ensure that the maximum number of French soldiers possible were trained, equipped and ready to fight at the outbreak of a future war. Efforts to improve matters had started almost immediately after the Franco-Prussian War. A shortcoming of the French Army in that conflict had been the lack of trained reservists to replace those men lost in the opening battles. It followed that among the first acts of the French Third Republic was the introduction of a new Military Service Act in 1872 that permitted the conscription of all eligible young men into the army. The implications of the move were profound for the population, yet was seen as being necessary by politicians, including the prominent Republican firebrand Leon Gambetta who, in a speech made in 1871, had said, 'let it be understood that every boy born in France is born a soldier as well as a citizen.'[1] That obligation extended to those French citizens who had left to live and work abroad, including those in the Channel Islands.

Jersey's French community had been steadily growing since the 1840s, driven by the need of the Island's burgeoning agricultural industry for a large and low cost labour force. From just over two thousand in 1851, the number of Jersey residents who had been born in France had doubled by 1871. Thirty years later, in 1901, that number had grown again to just over six thousand, which was roughly 11 percent of the total population. Furthermore, it was not just new migrants swelling the numbers; the 1901 census shows that 30 percent of all children born in Jersey had fathers who were born in France.[2] The majority of those arriving in the Island came from Brittany and Normandy, the two nearest French *régions* to Jersey. Within these, there were two principal sub-divisions, or *départements*, from which many of the migrants came. In Brittany, it was the Côtes-du-Nord *département**, which lies in the north of the region between the ports of Saint-Malo in the east and Lannion to the west. In Normandy, it was the Manche *département*, which broadly encompasses the Contentin Peninsular with Cherbourg at its northern tip down to Mont Saint-Michel in the south. Both Brittany and Normandy were predominantly agricultural regions at this time, and economically poor compared to other parts of France. With limited work opportunities and low levels of pay for those who found it, both Côtes-du-Nord and Manche had seen a considerable number of their inhabitants leave to seek work elsewhere in France or overseas in the second half of the eighteenth century.

Although some of these migrants would chose to live and work in Jersey, the majority who did also wished to remain French nationals, and were thus subject to the laws of France and its institutions. Representing French interests in Jersey was a Consulate, whose office in 1914 was located in St Helier's Church Street. On arrival in the Island, French workers registered with the Consulate to retain connections with France and in order to obtain documents such as passports. Here they also registered any children born to them while in the Island. Although these children had British citizenship through the location of their birth, the parents were obviously anxious that they should not lose their French nationality. Some may have also wanted to ensure an exemption from the Jersey's Militia Law, which applied only to British nationals. By being registered as a French national, it meant that when they were old enough, those children would become liable for compulsory military service in France.

Subsequent law changes following the Franco-Prussian War would tighten the terms under which men undertook their military service. Up until 1905, a national ballot decided who had to serve and there were considerable opportunities for those selected to claim an exemption. In 1905, there was a significant change with the introduction of the so-called 'two-year's law', which

---

* Today renamed Côtes-d'Armor.

extended the principle of compulsory military service to all and removed the majority of the options previously available to avoid the call-up. The new law specified that the obligation for military service commenced in the year that a man reached twenty years of age. Each year, the military authorities in France issued a notice of impending military service by posting up lists of the men who would become eligible. This year was known as their *Classe de Recruitment* (Recruitment Class). Those named had to appear before an inspection board, which would decide whether there were any grounds for a man's exemption from military service, typically for medical reasons. At a time when France was striving to increase its number of men available on the outbreak of a war, few of those appearing before the board could have expected a complete exemption. Those cases where a man's height and weight were found to be below general expectations usually meant his entry into the military was delayed a year to allow more time to grow in stature. The majority were passed as fit for service, however, and sent home to await their formal call-up, which would take place on 1 October in the following year. The year in which this happened was known as the *Classe de Mobilisation* (Mobilisation Class).

In Jersey, the Consulate's register of local French citizens allowed them to maintain a record of men in the Island who were approaching the age when their military service should begin. All those due to reach twenty in a given year were notified and formed into a local *Classe de Recruitment*. At the same time, notices placed in local French language newspapers announced the formation of a new *Classe*, and requested any eligible twenty-year-olds who were not registered with the Consulate to come forward. Each *Classe* was identified by the name of the year in which it was formed, thus a man born in 1890 would be a member of the 1910 *Classe*. For each member of the *Classe*, the Consulate completed an initial form that included the man's personal details, a brief description of his appearance and noted any skills or experience that may help place him within the army. Could he ride a horse or bicycle, for example, drive a car, play an instrument or did he have the experience of keeping pigeons. With the information in place, the *Classe* was sent on to France for medical examination, and then returned to Jersey while waiting for the call-up as a member of the following year's *Classe de Mobilisation*. This meant that the majority of Jersey-Frenchmen in the 1910 *Classe* would begin their military service in October 1911, at the age of twenty-one.

Where they undertook their military service and with which branch of the military they served depended upon a number of factors. Prior to the Franco-Prussian War, there was a practice of preventing French soldiers from serving in military units based near their home. The principle dated from the French Revolution, which had swept away traditional links between the regiments of the *Ancien Régime* and provinces of France because of fears that soldiers might refuse to supress uprisings by people with whom they had previously lived. Despite some continuing misgivings, the French Army was reorganised in the years following 1871 to make regiments more strongly associated with individual *départements* of France. The affiliation helped foster a strong sense of unity between the army and the population, many of whom had soldiers living permanently in their midst as new barracks and training centres were constructed throughout the country. The revised arrangements also meant that many men reaching eligible age could do their military service in a regiment near to their home. It was not a universal rule, however, due to among other things the different population levels of the various *départements*. Thus a man from Brittany could do his military service with a regiment based in a location that was short of the required number of recruits.

In peacetime, France's army was distributed throughout the country, with major headquarters stationed in a *région* and controlling a number of smaller units based in the surrounding *départements*. In the event of war, these units would come together and form the armies to confront Germany. In peacetime, they were responsible for training the soldiers who would have do the fighting. The nearest major headquarters to Jersey was that of the *10e corps d'armée* (10th Army Corps), which was stationed in the city of Rennes. It controlled a number of subordinate units distributed throughout two *départements* of Brittany, Côtes-du-Nord and Ille-et-Vilaine, and the Manche *département* of Normandy. These were the *2e régiment d'infanterie (RI)* based in Granville, the *25e RI* in Cherbourg, the *41e RI* in Rennes, the *47e RI* in Saint-Malo, the *48e RI* in Guincamp, the *70e RI* in Vitré, the *71e RI* in Saint-Brieuc and the *136e RI* in Saint-Lô. In the event of mobilisation being ordered, each of these would form a second 'reserve' regiment with its number being created by adding two hundred. Thus, the *2e RI* formed the *202e RI* and the *47e RI* the *247e RI* and so on. Also stationed in these *départements* were a number of artillery, cavalry and engineer regiments along with the *1e régiment d'infanterie coloniale (RIC)*, which was based at Cherbourg as part of France's *troupes coloniales* (Colonial Army). It drew many of its soldiers from settlers and natives living in France's North African colonies, but retained an affiliation with *départements* of metropolitan France.

Given the predominance of immigrants from Brittany and Normandy in Jersey's pre-war French community, many men from the Island would have undertaken their compulsory military service with one of these units following their call-up as part of the *Classe de Mobilisation*. Generally, they were sent to the nearest unit to their home, although there remained a rule against permitting someone to serve with a regiment that was actually stationed in their home city or town. Most joined the infantry, but those who had declared experience or expertise in riding or working with horses were likely to find themselves in one of the artillery or cavalry regiments, while those with technical backgrounds might have joined the engineers. Whichever unit it was, a new soldier's time in the army would have commenced with four months of basic training, carried out in or near the regimental barracks. Once this was complete, a man moved on to more advanced training such as route marching to improve his stamina, learning field craft skills and extensive shooting practice. Each year his acquired skills were thoroughly tested when the army gathered in the autumn for large scale manoeuvres. Once his military service was complete, it was a return to civilian life for the men of one *Classe* as another group arrived to take their place in the barracks. A man's service in the French Army was not yet over however.

The 1905 law had specified that, after completing two years of full-time military service, each man would remain liable for a further twenty-three years of service as an army reservist. During this time, men were obliged to return to their regiments for periodic refresher training and for full recall in the event of war. In 1913, however, there was a further change in recognition of a growing German military strength. Starting with the 1911 *Classe*, which was then already serving, every man had to start his training from an earlier age and remain as an army reservist for twenty-eight years. The 'Three-Year Law' of 1913 required that after joining the army, each man should now spend three years in full-time military service instead of two, and it established the *Classe de Mobilisation* as twenty-years-old rather than twenty-one. A man starting military training in 1913 could therefore expect to serve three years in full-time service with the 'active army'. This was followed by eleven years as part of the 'active army reserve', which included an obligation to return for forty-nine training days each year and an immediate recall in the event of war. After this, men would transfer into the 'territorial army' for a further seven years, with less stringent training demands, and they would finally spend seven years in the 'territorial army reserve'. The changes meant that from 1913 an average Frenchman could expect his military service obligation to continue until he reached the age of forty-eight.

The new terms for military service increased the number of French soldiers who would be immediately available in the event of war. The further year of full-time military service also provided each man with the benefit of additional training, which was expected to raise the overall quality of the 'active army'. French generals and politicians knew that this was essential to improve the chances of meeting Germany with equal numbers of well-trained soldiers at the outset of any war. Through their Consulate and from contacts with home, Jersey's French colony, as it was termed, would have been fully aware of the changes to the military service system in the years leading up to the First World War. They had little choice but to accept them, and continue with life as normal. Despite the stretch of water between Jersey and the French mainland, the obligations to serve their country remained. Like their Jersey Militia counterparts, they just hadn't expected those obligations to come into force in the summer of 1914.

Although the mobilisation of the Militia on 30 July had no effect on the majority of the French community, it would have served to underline the seriousness of the growing crisis in Europe. Anxious for news of events outside the Island, crowds had already been gathering in St Helier's Charles Street where the offices of the *Evening Post* newspaper regularly displayed in their window the latest updates reaching the Island. From 30 July, the numbers present there increased, among which there were many French nationals who were waiting for any sign of an army mobilisation order. Between that day and 1 August it seemed that any chance for a positive solution to the crisis was slipping away with each news item posted. The only glimmer of hope as the crowds dispersed on the evening of 1 August was that there had still been no French army mobilisation order arriving in the Island. Perhaps there was still a chance war could be avoided. This was not to be.

The formal notification of France's decision to mobilise its armies reached Jersey late in the evening of 1 August via a telegram to the French Consul. Having been in the role since 1910, *Monsieur* Auguste Jouve was a familiar figure in the Island and widely respected. The duty that he had to undertake that night would have been one of the most painful of his life. Fully understanding the importance of what needed to be done, Jouve immediately began enlisting help to spread news of the mobilisation order throughout the Island. Jouve contacted the parish Constables to ask for the help of their Honorary Police forces to distribute the news throughout the farming communities in the countryside and among the cafés and hotels where French seasonal workers were known to be widely employed. He asked that the newspaper officers, St Helier Town Hall and the cafes and shops in St Helier's Hilgrove Street, which was widely known as 'French Lane' because of its popularity with the French community, to display notices announcing the mobilisation. As the next day was a Sunday, he also informed the Catholic clergy, who solemnly announced the mobilisation news to their congregations during morning mass. The notice was plain: the French government had ordered the mobilisation of its armed forces in preparation for war and all eligible reservists must return to their regiments. For those living in Jersey, this required a passport and a boat ticket to be issued by the Consulate.

Gradually the news circulated to French families and individuals throughout the Island. The result was that a large crowd started gathering outside the Consulate's office from early on the morning of Sunday, 2 August. Despite the seriousness of the situation, there was reportedly an excited atmosphere, partly fuelled by the presence of many local people who had decided to spend their day off witnessing the dramatic events. It all presented, 'a spectacle which will not be readily forgotten by those who saw it,' wrote one commentator. 'Young and middle-aged Frenchmen, filled with the fire of enthusiasm, all anxious to rejoin the colours and, if necessary, to fight for the honour of their country had assembled there.'[3] In batches, the men were admitted into the Consulate offices to collect passports and the necessary travel permits. By two o'clock that afternoon, the staff had processed 620 men, with hundreds more still waiting outside for their turn. While some of these returned home to complete preparations to leave, others went straight from Church Street to the nearby St Helier Harbour from where the London and South-West Railways steamer SS *Laura* was due to depart for Granville at midday.

On the following day, 3 August, there were further sailings to Carteret, Granville and Saint-Malo planned, from both St Helier and Gorey harbours, with hundreds of French reservists waiting to depart. They and their families gathered on the piers to await the men's turn to board ship. That day being a bank holiday it meant that there was also a large crowd of curious spectators present, who had come to see what the *Evening Post* had described as 'touching and pathetic scenes'.[4] The interest and size of the crowd seems to have taken the harbour authorities by surprise. Barriers had been placed across the piers to permit entry only to those with travel permits, and Police posted along them zealously prevented anyone else from passing through. The crowd built up against the barriers, jostling departing men and their families as they tried to say their goodbyes. Conditions for such difficult, personal separations were far from ideal. 'Many pathetic scenes were witnessed on the quay,' wrote one reporter, 'in several cases a man had to say goodbye to wife and family, or the aged parents dependant on him, and these partings were of such a tender nature and were accompanied by so much emotion, but that few of those in the crowd could watch them unmoved.'[5] Notwithstanding the private and often highly emotional moments of individual separation and departures at the quayside, there remained an excited and strongly patriotic atmosphere at the harbour that day. As each ship departed through the pier heads, there were shouts of 'vive la France', and choruses of *La Marseillaise* sung by those on board and those now left behind.

Some three hundred French reservists sailed on 3 August to join those who had already departed the previous day. Hundreds more left on each of the days that followed after they had settled their affairs in Jersey or in accordance with predetermined mobilisation instructions for their *Classe*. There was no option but to follow instructions, since anyone failing to return after the mobilisation order had been promulgated would face harsh prison and punishment sentences when caught. If there was any comfort it was that the Military Service Act and its obligations applied equally to all Frenchmen; there was no general distinction made on the basis of class, profession or education. This was apparent to anyone watching the reservists depart from Jersey, as one local commentator recalled noting that on board the ships, 'Well-groomed Frenchmen occupying good positions…rubbed shoulders with their less fortunate, ill-clad and rough-mannered compatriots…'[6] Some of those who had left in the initial mobilisation were well-known and respected businessmen, among them bootmaker Jean Boudin who had premises in St Helier. The forty-year-old closed up his shop and put a notice in the window to say that anyone who had boots or shoes in for repair should collect them immediately as he did not know when he would be back. Also among those departing were many of the priests who had announced the mobilisation order on the previous Sunday morning along with teachers and students from the local Jesuit institutions. France's military service laws made no distinction between the obligations of churchmen and their congregations.

In total, it appears that some two thousand men left Jersey to join the French Army and French Navy during those first few weeks of August 1914. By the middle of 1915, this number had risen to a reported 2,457, or around 38 percent of the pre-war French population.[7] This is greater than the average for France as a whole, which mobilised around 22 percent of its male population between 1914 and 1918.[8] Jersey's higher number can be attributed to the proportion of males working in the Island, many of whom were from younger age groups. After they had gone, the only Frenchmen who were left behind in the Island were those too young or old to serve, those deemed medically unfit or men with six or more children. It represented an extraordinarily high number of men for the local community to have to give up, with obvious consequences for the Island's agricultural industry in the months ahead. A more pressing concern for the departing men was trying to arrange for the welfare of their families once they had left. The French government had agreed to pay an allowance to the wives of reservists living in Jersey of one shilling a day plus five pence per child, but it was uncertain when payments would commence. As the Consul had pointed out, during the Franco-Prussian War a similar arrangement had been promised but it had taken a considerable time to materialise. In many French families, women would now have to take up the work formerly undertaken by their husbands wherever possible and to rely on the compassion and generosity of Islanders in order to survive.

JERSEY'S GREAT WAR

As the reservists from Jersey made their way to barracks in Brittany, Normandy and across France, they joined hundreds of thousands more heading back to join their regiments. In contrast with the disorder of July 1870, the French Army's mobilisation in August 1914 was a meticulously planned and well-executed affair. The first men required to return to duty were those in the youngest age groups who would have most recently completed their military service in the 1900 to 1910 *Classes de Recruitment*. They joined the current full-time soldiers in the 'active army' regiments in order to bring them up to full strength. The next group were older men allocated to newly mobilised 'active army reserve' regiments formed on the outbreak of war. The next group that was required to return were men of the 1896 to 1899 *Classes*, who would have been aged between thirty-five and thirty-eight-years-old. They would join the regiments of the 'territorial army', whose planned role on the outbreak of war was to undertake secondary duties such as protecting the army's lines of communication. Despite the original intentions of the French military commanders, many of these territorial soldiers would be quickly drawn into the fighting. Replacements for 'territorial army' casualties were drawn from the final category of army reservist to be recalled, the 'territorial reserve' formed from those men between the ages of thirty-nine and forty-eight. Depending on their physical fitness, some of these men would end up joining their younger comrades in both the 'active' and 'reserve' regiments as the demand for soldiers increased.

After arrival at their regimental barracks, each reservist received his army uniform and boots. In contrast with the British Army (and Jersey Militia) who wore khaki and the Germany Army clad in field-grey, most French infantrymen went to war wearing bright red trousers known as *le pantalon rouge*, clad in a heavy blue overcoat and with a cloth kepi cap on their head (all sides made only limited use of steel helmets before 1916). French cavalry regiments went into battle with steel breastplates and wearing magnificent helmets complete with sweeping horsehair tails. It was all very reminiscent of some former military age, but it would prove to be hopelessly outdated when faced with an enemy armed with modern weapons of war: long-range rifles, machine guns and heavy artillery. Each soldier also received a knapsack to hold his belongings, mess equipment, including a bowl, spoon and fork, field dressings and a small amount of tinned or wrapped food. Among the indispensable items issued was a small coffee grinder and coffee tablet, together with a water bottle, often used to hold the rough but precious red wine known as 'pinard', a quarter of a litre of which was distributed to each man per day. Adding to the considerable weight of equipment, infantrymen were issued with an 8mm Lebel rifle, a reliable but outdated weapon of a design dating back to 1886. Cavalrymen received a carbine rifle and a sword, or a lance if they were in a dragoon regiment. For artillerymen, most would serve the renowned '*soixante-quinze*', a highly mobile quick-firing 75mm gun that equipped most of the French Army's artillery regiments in 1914.

Once armed and equipped, the reservists boarded another train along with those men who had been undertaking their military service when mobilisation was ordered. As they left, further reservists filled the barracks behind them. Most were destined to assemble along the country's northern and eastern frontiers in readiness for war. There was a sense of euphoric patriotism and optimism among the soldiers, sentiments shared by much of France's civilian population at the start of the war. They saw it as the longed for opportunity for revenge, to redress the defeats of 1870, to recover the lost provinces of Alsace and Lorraine and to demonstrate France's superiority over Germany. It all seemed so straightforward to those who scrawled '*à Berlin*' on the sides of railway carriages, or who studied maps of Germany rather than maps of France. The only thing missing following the mobilisation order was the actual declaration of war. There was not long to wait.

Despite hastily arranged meetings among diplomats and a spate of frantic telegrams between European capitals, the chance for peace had all but disappeared by the time France had responded to German threats with its mobilisation order. On that same day, Kaiser Wilhelm II had declared war on Russia and, under intense pressure from his military commanders, taken the first aggressive steps to fulfil the requirements of the Schlieffen Plan by invading Luxembourg. On 2 August, the German presented an ultimatum to Belgium demanding free passage through that country in order to invade northern France. The German Army's long-planned and meticulous timetable for war was in motion and there was no turning back. On 3 August 1914, Germany declared war on France. The stage was almost set; the only player yet to declare its intentions was Britain.

JERSEY'S GREAT WAR

Pre-war Jersey: an Island family enjoys a day out at Grève de Lecq in 1909

Pre-war Jersey: the popularity of the Jersey Royal had led to a community of more than six thousand French nationals in the Island, many of whom worked in the agricultural industry

Pre-war Jersey: marching soldiers were a familiar sight in the Island, such as these men of the East Surrey Regiment arriving in 1905 to take over British Army garrison duties

Sir William Venables Vernon, Jersey's Bailiff since 1899 and civilian leader between 1914 and 1918

The Militia mobilises on 30 July 1914: men of the Town Battalion armed and ready to take up guard duties in St Helier

French reservists departing from St Helier harbour to rejoin their regiments at the start of August 1914

JERSEY'S GREAT WAR

French soldiers returning to the Island on leave were a familiar sight between 1914 and 1918

'Our noble army of standbacks': some of those who had previously managed to avoid Militia service but who were called up in September 1914 to increase the number of men available to guard Jersey

'Kitchener volunteers' arriving in St Helier for training in Jersey with the South Staffordshire Regiment

JERSEY'S GREAT WAR

South Staffordshire Regiment volunteers engage in bayonet practice on People's Park, St Helier

Officers of the South Staffordshire Regiment outside of St Helier's Grand Hotel, which was requisitioned in 1914 to house 750 soldiers

Société Jersiaise

Members of the Victoria College Officer Training Corps (OTC) played a part in the Island's defence by taking over a section of coastal defences every one night in five

4 AN ENTRENCHED CAMP

Preparing to defend Jersey as the enemy approached in 1914

For Islanders, it must have seemed that for a few days in the summer of 1914 there was barely time to draw breath. From 29 July, the Island had experienced a number of momentous events in rapid succession. Yet in comparison to the Militia mobilisation, which was totally unforeseen, and the departure of the French reservists, which had been a surprise but half expected, the third momentous event was accepted with almost muted resignation. On 4 August 1914, Britain declared war on Germany.

It had not been a foregone conclusion that Britain would enter the conflict on the side of its allies, despite the German declarations of war on Russia and France. The treaties with those countries were less about binding agreements and more focused on general areas of mutual interest. Under pressure from its allies to join and under pressure from Germany to remain out, the British Government had hesitated to commit either way on 3 August. What was really needed was a cause behind which British politicians and the public could unite. News that Germany had invaded Belgium on 4 August following the Belgian Government's rejection of a request to allow the German Army free passage across its territory offered just that. Belgium was a country whose neutrality and independence Britain had guaranteed by a treaty in 1839. In line with its obligations, Britain demanded an immediate German Army withdrawal from Belgium, threatening war if it did not happen. Understandably, given that it was now fully committed to the military actions laid down in the Schlieffen Plan, Germany refused to withdraw its troops and pressed ahead with the invasion. As a result, from eleven o'clock on the evening of 4 August, Britain - and therefore Jersey - was at war with Germany.

The news had swiftly reached Jersey and was quickly circulated, with Islanders anxiously trying to make sense of the situation and struggling to comprehend what would happen next. In the absence of radio and television, the only real sources for the latest public information from the outside world were the newspapers. Such a monopoly led to the press gaining a greatly respected status in the years before the war. It also meant that circulation and readership was considerably higher than it is today, which in turn permitted a far larger, and therefore a more competitive, market for the daily and weekly publications. Islanders had a choice of three principal newspapers in 1914: the English language *Evening Post* and the *Morning News*, both of which were published from Monday to Saturday, and the weekly French language *Les Chroniques de Jersey*. Together with those national newspapers that arrived by ship, the local papers were keenly awaited, and at no time more so than in August 1914 as people anxiously sought news on the progress of the war and events taking place in the wider international setting. Demand quickly rose. As a temporary measure, the *Evening Post* even began publishing a supplementary edition that came out at half past seven each evening to cover any new information arriving in the Island after the afternoon's edition had gone to print.

Despite the best efforts of local newspaper editors and their staff to meet the increased demands and expectations of Islanders, the reality was that the latest news about the war was in the hands of others and was strictly controlled. While local reporters could cover Island events, what was happening beyond Jersey's shores came from the official news agencies who distributed their dispatches through the international telegraph network. On the outbreak of war, these agencies had attempted to send correspondents to the front and report on the events they saw there. The British Army and Government were uncomfortable with the idea of independent reporters commenting on their actions at the front and decided to put a stop to their activities. War news became tightly controlled and heavily censored to ensure the actions of Britain and its allies were not presented in an unfavourable light. Local newspapers therefore had little choice but to present what they had received and offer usually favourable editorial comment on what appeared to be happening. Through other news agencies, the local newspapers also received and printed reports from enemy news sources as well, which often contradicted British and Allied statements. Such a situation left readers wondering what the actual situation was, and whether they were being told everything. Helped by plenty of rumour and hearsay, in the opening days of the war, many Islanders drew their own conclusions as to what was going to happen next.

Early concerns centred on a public fear that the Germans would find a means to attack the Island – why else had the Militia been mobilised after all? Admittedly, this enemy was further away from Jersey than had been the case in most previous wars, while the French and British armies would stand between German Army and the Channel coast. Yet there were other means to reach Jersey, some Islanders reasoned. German warships, for example, could break out of the North Sea to arrive and bombard the Island. News that the French Navy had intercepted and captured a German vessel off the Channel Island of Sark on 5 August would certainly have helped lend substance to that theory. The fact that it turned out to be just a small coaster carrying a cargo of corn and a crew who were probably unaware that war had broken out did not fully allay fears. There was due celebration when the vessel and its cargo were claimed as a prize of war, however, and therefore represented an easy victory for the Allies in Channel Islands' waters.

More worrying for some was the threat of an attack from above. Aircraft had been occasional visitors to the Island prior to the August 1914, but there was an increasing awareness of their potential as machines of war. More sinister still were Germany's much vaunted fleet of airships, the infamous cigar-shaped Zeppelins, which were capable of ranging over hundreds of miles. People anxiously scanned the skies for any sign of the enemy, whether in a plane or an airship. Militiamen were equally nervous about the threat of attack from the air. So much so that orders were issued instructing men not to fire on any plane that was spotted over the Island until its country of origin was established, and definitely not to fire on any airship until an officer had confirmed it as hostile.

In addition to these external threats, there were also fears that something more sinister was occurring in the Island. Could there be enemy spies and saboteurs operating in Jersey? People walking along the seafront at St Helier's La Collette in early August certainly became concerned when two suspicious figures were spotted on a rock surrounded by water some distance from the shore. They appeared to be signalling to someone onshore and someone else further out to sea. After dark, flashing lights were seen emanating from the same location. When the tide had receded later that night, an armed Militia patrol made its way out to the location of the suspicious signallers and discovered a man and a boy coming in the opposite direction. Their story was that the incoming tide had cut them off, and the signalling from the rock was to the boy's father on the shore to say that they were safe. The Militiamen, and a crowd who had gathered to witness the incident, seemed less than sure about the explanation, however, even though the man claimed to be a captain in the Militia Reserve. The Police were summoned and in view of the circumstances, and apparent hostility of the crowd, the man was escorted to the local Militia headquarters while checks were made. It turned out that George Mauger, the man in question, was indeed a Militia captain who claimed that he and the boy had been studying rocks in the area when cut off by the rising waters. In view of the circumstances, he felt compelled to write to the *Evening Post* to state his case, claiming that the crowd's hostile reaction was, 'only an error caused by excess of zeal that was quite excusable under the present circumstances.'[1]

Those 'present circumstances' were the cause of a number of spying incidents in the early months of the war. In such a charged atmosphere, it was all too easy to view a seemingly innocent activity with suspicion, particularly if someone foreign was involved. In the absence of facts, any such incidents were quickly blown out of proportion. A man – said to be recently arrived in the Island – was detained for allegedly putting suspicious markings on a wall in Georgetown, although no evidence to support such claims was subsequently found. A farmer denounced his cowman as being a German spy, despite the man having worked for him for thirty years. Shots were reportedly fired over the heads of two men seen acting suspiciously on a St Helier beach after dark, although it turned out they were only fishing for sand eels. Most concerning of all was the rumour that a spy had been caught putting poison into a local reservoir, although quite where the story came from was never established.

The mobilisation orders, the departure of the French reservists and the declarations of war, as well as the perceived threat of enemy warships, Zeppelins and spies, helped fuel a general sense of anxiety in the early days of the war, which, at times, bordered on panic. The *Evening Post* called for calm, saying, 'The suspense of the last few days has, we admit, been difficult to endure in serenity, and in addition other causes have contributed to the feverish excitement that prevails…but while our hearts are moved we must see to it that we keep our heads, remembering that under the circumstances patience and self-control are the first essentials.'[2] There were also more worrying matters to be concerned about, the newspaper pointed out, such as the rapidly increasing cost of food and fuel, coupled with the potentially shrinking stocks of both in the Island. Certain shopkeepers and merchants, it appears, had taken the opportunity to raise prices at the outbreak of war in view of potential shortages, an action roundly condemned by commentators. 'We had a right to expect a little patriotism in the crisis,' one newspaper editor admonished, 'but in some cases greed has won an easy victory over conscience…'[3]

On 5 August, the States met for the first time since the crisis had begun, having been summoned to the chamber to discuss the contents of a letter from the Lieutenant Governor to the civilian authorities. Drawing the Members' attention to the gravity of the situation, Rochfort announced that a number of special measures needed to be implemented immediately in order to ensure the security of the Island and its people.

- First, it was necessary to prohibit the export of any food or fuel from the Island, in order to retain whatever there was for both civilians and the military.
- Second, to take steps to ensure food and fuel could continue to be imported – the Island did not grow enough to feed itself – and to take control of local distribution and prices if necessary.
- Third, to remove anyone temporarily residing in the Island who was not essential and anyone deemed undesirable to the Island's well-being.
- Fourth, to prevent anyone landing in the Island who had not come on business or for reasons of necessity.

'Under these circumstances I think it my duty to request the States to take such precautionary, preventative measures as may be thought necessary for provisioning the Island generally and the military forces under my control,' Rochfort stated, 'and I would suggest that legislative and administrative measures should be considered by the States.'[4] There were laws passed in 1803 and 1900, he reminded them, that gave Lieutenant Governors the extraordinary powers needed to take such steps in wartime. Rochfort was sure, however, that the States would see the necessity for such measures and consent to put them in place without the need for his intervention.

The Lieutenant Governor's request that the States agree to make the changes rather than have them imposed by the military authorities was the appropriate course to follow. It underlined the British Government's deference of the Island's right to self-government, even under the very straitened circumstances of the time. There was no real question over whether or not a patriotic States of Jersey would support the proposals. The measures were wholeheartedly accepted, although some Members did appear somewhat conflicted by self-interest. The Constable of St Saviour, John Perrée, who by his own admission possessed one of the Island's largest herds of Jersey cows, hoped that the ban on exports would exclude cattle, particularly those that had already been sold to America. They were milking cows, he argued, and would therefore be no use for food. His argument found few supporters, however, and plenty of critics. Understandably, the Constable's amendment was defeated forty votes to seven. The States then set about implementing the agreed measures.

There was one very important person absent from the chamber that day. Sir William Vernon, the Island's Bailiff, was not present, indeed he was not even in the Island. In fact, no one knew exactly where he was, and when – or whether – he would return. This was because on 20 July, Vernon had accepted the invitation of an old acquaintance to join him on a cruise and had left the Island for his holiday. Trusting that the developing quarrel between Austria-Hungary and Serbia would remain a regional affair, and with no obvious pressing matters at home, he had judged it a suitable time to get away. By the beginning of August, however, the unforeseen consequences of that decision became clear as Europe - and Jersey - mobilised for war at a time that Vernon was sailing through the Suez Canal towards the Red Sea. It was somewhere off Port Said that a small launch drew alongside his vessel bearing a telegram from Jersey that simply said, 'Return – urgently needed'. Vernon had already made up his mind to return before the telegram arrived, and was arranging to go ashore to find a way back. Caught up in the confusing melee that accompanied the outbreak of war, he made his way across the Mediterranean, narrowly missing two German warships sailing in the opposite direction. Intercepted by the

French Navy, Vernon's ship had been escorted to Marseilles. Unable to return to Jersey by train due to the wartime situation in France, he was forced to make the journey by sea, travelling back via Gibraltar and Portsmouth before arriving in Jersey on 18 August, exhausted and without money following the general freezing of bank accounts. He was ready, however, to resume his position as Bailiff as Jersey faced its most serious threat in one hundred years.

For one of Jersey's most notable recent leaders, William Henry Venables Vernon's links to the Island, prior to becoming Bailiff, are surprisingly tenuous. Although he was born in the parish of Trinity, his paternal family were only comparatively recent arrivals in the Island from Derbyshire. In common with other land-owning families at that time, they had chosen to leave Britain in the wake of the economically damaging Corn Law repeals of the late 1840s. Vernon's grandmother, whose late husband Henry fought and had been wounded at the Battle of Waterloo, arrived with her only son, Edward Vernon, a serving naval officer, who later married Louise Charlotte de Joux, the daughter of a local church minister. On 1 January 1852, she gave birth to a son whom they named William. Tragedy struck a few years later, when Edward died in 1856 from wounds received while serving in action leaving Louise widowed and her four-year-old son William fatherless. When Louise decided to remarry, young William was left in the care of his paternal grandmother and other family members.

These arrangements meant that Vernon spent the early years of his life moving between a number of different homes in Jersey, Derbyshire, France and even a castle near Heidelberg in Germany. The experience of these different countries, peoples and cultures seems to have given him a love of travel and an appreciation of the wider world – something that would stand him in good stead later in life. It also led him to choose a career in the diplomatic service after completing his education. Before setting out on that path, however, he returned to Jersey to arrange the sale of his late grandmother's property, a move that brought him into contact with a number of influential members of the Island's legal profession. The Bailiff of the time, Jean Hammond, persuaded Vernon to remain in the Island and become an advocate. His sharp and enquiring mind soon gained him a reputation within the legal profession, and among prominent Islanders. Vernon's attention subsequently turned to politics and he was elected to the position of Constable of St Peter in 1875, at the age of twenty-three. A year later, he became the Judicial Greffier, a government role with responsibilities for legal and legislative record keeping. It was the start of a career climb through the ranks of local government posts, which culminated with his appointment as Bailiff on 2 May 1899.

When the war broke out in August 1914, Vernon was sixty-two and had been Bailiff of Jersey for just over fifteen years. He had certainly learnt much about the Island and its people by then. In return, Islanders had learned much about him and generally, it seems, they liked what they saw. In public, Vernon was a keen conversationalist, always happy to find time to exchange a few words - in English, French or Jèrriais - with the people that he encountered. He enjoyed sharing his considerable knowledge with anyone willing to listen, especially on matters to do with dogs, sailing, cattle breeding and travel, all of which he counted among his interests. Yet in private there was a different side to Vernon. He appears to have been something of a solitary figure, enjoying his own company and having few close friends. Although he had married Julia Gosset in 1880, they had not had children and, reportedly, no real home life existed between them in later years. He preferred to spend a lot of his leisure time walking alone in the countryside, usually wearing worn and shabby clothes, perhaps to ensure some anonymity. When in the States chamber, however, he displayed a further side to his character. He presided over the assembly with a firm hand, employing a natural talent for public speaking to tactfully but determinedly control debates. And whether inside the States or out, Vernon doggedly stood up for the rights of Jersey and its people, often in the face of considerable pressure from the British Government. 'Never did the Island have a better, abler and more determined fighter in her interests,' wrote one commentator, 'than Bailiff William Vernon.'[5]

As soon as he returned to Jersey after his travel adventures in August 1914, Vernon set about acquainting himself with what had already taken place up until then. What he found must have been quite astounding to him. Having left a peaceful Island enjoying a warm and thriving summer, he returned to find one that had become in his own words, 'practically an entrenched camp.'[6] In the official War Office terminology of the day, the Island had been designated as a 'Defended Port', but the meaning was much the same. This status meant the first priority at that time had become Jersey's defence, responsibility for which was in the hands of the Lieutenant Governor. The Island's civilian government, led by the Bailiff, were expected to offer him their full support, which included accepting such draconian measures as those that had been presented to the States on 5 August. In the meantime, the Lieutenant Governor had focused much of his attention on preparing the Island's defences and defenders. Ironically, during August 1914, Rochfort had to watch the departure of Jersey's most experienced soldiers and sailors.

The first group left immediately after the outbreak of hostilities. Britain's declaration of war had resulted one further exodus of men from Jersey. There were more emotional scenes at St Helier Harbour as British army and naval reservists said goodbye to their families. In common with the French Army,

AN ENTRENCHED CAMP

Britain's armed forces in 1914 required men who had completed their military service to return and fill out the ranks in a time of war. In contrast with the armed forces of France, the British reservists were all volunteers however. Alone among the European great powers – and different to Jersey for that matter - Britain had no compulsory military service law prior to the First World War. Although there had been a degree of obligatory military service during the Napoleonic Wars, Britain had relied on volunteers for its army and navy throughout the remainder of the nineteenth century. The approach had produced the men needed to meet the demands of a British foreign policy that focused on building a global empire rather than becoming entangled in European wars. A small professional army was adequate for fighting limited colonial wars and for maintaining order in distant possessions once the fighting was over. Moreover, with Britain able to rely on the protection of a powerful Royal Navy, a system of volunteering produced enough full-time and part-time soldiers to provide for home defence as well. By the start of the twentieth century, however, the approach was coming under scrutiny as Britain became increasingly committed to supporting France with plans to send a force of soldiers to the Continent in the event of war with Germany. Nevertheless, as the British Army prepared to do just that in August 1914, it remained firmly wedded to the principle of voluntary rather than compulsory military service.

Under these arrangements, a man who decided to join the British Army before the First World War would sign-up for a fixed term of twelve years' service. This consisted of seven years of regular service followed by five years as a reservist, although some would chose to spend the whole term in the army. On completing their regular military service, army reservists would leave the army and return to civilian life where they would be paid for undertaking a number of days training each year. They were also obliged to rejoin the army in event of war. Similar arrangements existed for men who volunteered to join the Royal Navy. In August 1914, the British Army recalled thousands of reservists to fill out the ranks of those regiments earmarked for service on the Continent, among them the men who had left from Jersey. At that time, many of the naval reservists were already with the ships, having been taking part in fleet exercises during July. In view of the deteriorating situation in Europe, the British Admiralty had taken the prudent decision to retain them once the exercises where complete.

Men from Jersey who had joined the British Army and Royal Navy before the war were scattered throughout many regiments and corps and serving on numerous warships and naval bases. In the army, there were clusters of Jerseymen in the Hampshire, Dorsetshire and Devonshire Regiments, all of which recruited on the south coast of England and thus were closest to the

Island. Significant other numbers were found serving in those regiments that had been on garrison duty in the Island before the war, such as the East Surrey Regiment. There were also many men in the more specialist branches of the army, the Royal Engineers, Royal Artillery, Royal Army Medical Corps, and so forth. In the Royal Navy, Jerseymen served on all sizes and types of vessels, from the battleships and battlecruisers that formed the backbone of Britain's fleet, to smaller cruisers, destroyers and submarines. They were also present at Royal Naval bases throughout Britain and elsewhere across the Empire. The exact number of Jersey army and naval regulars and reservists in 1914 is unclear, but an official 1915 estimate suggested the total as 1,460 men, with 910 in the British Army and remainder serving in the Royal Navy.[7] This number appears to have included the army and navy reservists recalled or retained with their units and ships on the outbreak of war.

For the army reservists who rejoined in August 1914 it meant a return to regimental depots across Britain to receive their uniforms and weapons in anticipation of a move together with their regular comrades to planned wartime stations. They all wore thick woollen khaki tunics with pockets to hold personal items and a medical field dressing, army trousers with puttees around the ankles and lower leg and a stiffened peaked cap on their heads. Men serving in Scottish Highland regiments still wore the traditional tartan kilt although with a khaki cover to make them less conspicuous on the battlefield. Their ammunition, water bottle, mess tin, entrenching tool, bayonet, haversack and backpack were carried using a system of straps and belts made of cotton (or leather) called webbing, which was fastened to the uniform at the shoulders. Infantrymen were armed with the Lee-Enfield Mk III rifle, a reliable, accurate and fast-operating weapon. Cavalrymen were issued with the same rifle and also a heavy sabre. Artillerymen served on a number of different types of weapon, although most were in Royal Field Artillery batteries equipped with the 18-pounder gun or 4.5-inch howitzer.

Thus equipped and armed, the majority of Britain's regular and reserve soldiers were destined for service in the British Expeditionary Force (BEF). Britain could commit this army to the Continent in the event of a European war, to fight alongside the French Army under the broad terms of the Entente Cordiale. By comparison to the French Army, and the German Army it would face, Britain's contribution was minuscule. While compulsory military service in France and Germany created armies more than one million men strong for the war's opening battles in August 1914, Britain's contribution to the Allied order of battle was just eighty thousand men, grouped into four infantry divisions and one division of cavalry. Nonetheless, they were a contribution warmly welcomed by France, which also gained the protective power of the

Royal Navy's Grand Fleet in the North Sea.

Between 12 and 18 August the BEF, under the command of Field Marshal Sir John French, had crossed the Channel to assemble at Maubeuge in France, close to the Belgian border. Alongside to its right, five French armies had moved into position ready to begin a planned offensive against the gathering German forces. The far greater number of French and German soldiers meant the front line stretched all the way from Mons to the Swiss border. On 23 August, after crossing into Belgium in support of the general French offensive, the BEF encountered an advancing German army around the small mining city of Mons. By comparison with later battles, the Battle of Mons was a small affair, although casualties still included 1,600 British soldiers killed, wounded or missing.

The Battle of Mons and those fought by the French armies in the opening month of the war are collectively known as the Battle of the Frontiers. Although the British had fought well at Mons, and the French armies attacked with all the courage and determination they could muster, the Germans emerged victorious almost everywhere. Neither Belgian resistance nor the French offensive had failed to significantly disrupt the timetable of the Schlieffen Plan. Its next stage was for the German armies to advance south from Belgium and capture Paris before turning east to crush the remaining French armies. Pouring over the Belgian border, the German Army soldiers marched towards the French capital, the Allied armies falling back before them in retreat. With every step of that retreat, the war and German Army came closer to Jersey. The departure of the French government from Paris to Bordeaux on 3 September was an ominous sign of the seriousness of the situation. Britain began making contingencies for a possible further retreat deeper into France or, if the necessity arose, the evacuation of its army from the Continent.

It is easy today to regard the First World War as a trench-bound stalemate fought mostly in northern France and Belgium, and a long way from Jersey's shores. While this was indeed the case for much of the war, the situation had appeared quite different during the late summer and autumn of 1914. Battles were fought in the open as the opposing sides advanced and retreated, at times over considerable distances. At the beginning of September, there was a very real prospect of the French Army abandoning Paris and retreating south, perhaps as far as the River Loire. That would have almost certainly meant a German advance into Normandy and Brittany, which would have brought the enemy to within twenty miles of Jersey's coast. This would occur in June 1940, when Hitler's armies defeated the Allies in northern France. Then, the British Government decided to abandon the Channel Islands to the enemy, who duly arrived after the islands surrendered. But twenty-five years earlier, Britain took the opposite decision; if the Germans approached, Jersey would be defended.

The motivation for doing so was not simply due to some patriotic sense of duty to protect British citizens and territory, although that would have been a factor. Far more importantly, as far as Britain was concerned, the strategic position of Jersey and the other Channel Islands took on a new importance. If an Allied retreat to the Loire proved necessary, the Island's value would have increased considerably as the lines of supply for the BEF moved further south. To fight on the Continent, the British Army would depend on secure lines of communication. Soldiers, weapons and supplies required to be transported across the English Channel to France and then deployed to wherever the army was fighting. Seriously wounded men needed to be evacuated in the opposite direction. The ports chosen for the BEF after it crossed the Channel in August 1914 were Boulogne in the Pas de Calais region, Le Havre at the mouth of the Seine River, and Rouen some sixty miles further up that river. They were well placed to support an army operating in northern France, but once the retreat from Belgium began after the Battle of Mons and the BEF fell back towards Paris, these ports became less secure. As the Germans moved closer, there was a growing possibility of them falling into enemy hands. On 29 August, the decision was made to move the depots established at Boulogne, Le Havre and Rouen to more secure locations south of the Loire, with Saint-Nazaire in southern Brittany chosen as the principal port. To reach it, ships from Britain would need to pass the Channel Islands. Far better then, for Jersey and Guernsey to be in British hands than those of the enemy.

So the War Office decided that Jersey was to remain fully defended, although not by the British reservists, who had been recalled to colours at the start of August. Nor by the British Army garrison either, which was the second group of experienced soldiers Rochfort had to watch leaving the Island in August 1914. The 20th Company Royal Garrison Artillery had been the first to go, leaving Jersey at the start of August. Then on 21 August, the 1st Battalion of the Devonshire Regiment left from St Helier Harbour. The men's wives and children followed them back to Britain a few days later while the regimental silver was placed in a local bank for safekeeping. The 'Devons', as they were known, had made many friends during their time in the Island and a crowd of well-wishers had turned up to see them off. Islanders would eagerly follow their progress in the war – in the early months at least. After a brief period spent guarding the BEF lines of communication, the 'Devons' would fight their first battle in September 1914 near the Aisne River to the north-east of Paris. Their losses in this and subsequent actions were sadly heavy, with Island newspapers reporting the casualties and printing pictures of some of those killed or wounded to much local dismay.

The garrison's departure from Jersey in the event of war had been a planned part of the deployment of the BEF. The British Army soldiers who arrived on 9 August 1914 to take the 'Devons' place were very different from those who were departing however. The 4th Battalion of the South Staffordshire Regiment was a reserve unit whose role in peacetime was training soldiers in preparation for regular service. Early in August, under the command of Lieutenant Colonel Edward Bulwer and with a Jerseyman, Captain William Jervoise Collas, as regimental adjutant, the battalion had left its barracks in Lichfield for Jersey, bringing six hundred newly recruited soldiers with it. The first challenge presented to the military authorities by its arrival was to find suitable accommodation for the men.

At the time the South Staffordshire Regiment arrived, the 'Devons' were still in residence at Fort Regent and at the other army barracks around the Island. With the Militia having taken over almost every other available military facility, accommodation was in distinctly short supply. The departure of the 20th Company Royal Garrison Artillery had freed space at Elizabeth Castle, and some of the newly arriving soldiers went there. For the rest the only remaining option was under canvas – for the immediate future at least. A large tented camp was set up on the east glacis of Fort Regent, which had been ground used for Militia camps and training before the war. A second camp was established at the Springfield Showground, which stood on the north-eastern outskirts of town. This site had already been requisitioned by the Lieutenant Governor at the start of the war for a possible use as prisoner of war camp, but was now put to use as a home for British soldiers instead. The nearby St Mark's Church became the location for military church services, while a number of clubs were opened in the area to provide recreation facilities for off-duty soldiers. In October 1914, as the number of South Staffordshire Regiment men in the Island grew, the Grand Hotel on St Helier's Esplanade was requisitioned and converted into accommodation for 750 officers and men.

The second challenge was to equip and train the new recruits, whose number quickly grew to nearly 2,500 men – more than double the normal strength of an infantry battalion. There were so many present that a second South Staffordshire Regiment unit, the 11th Battalion, joined the 4th Battalion in Jersey to accommodate the additional men. While the new recruits' spirits were high, uniforms and weapons were in short supply as British industry struggled to keep up with the increased wartime demand. So the soldiers paraded, marched and trained in mainly civilian attire, almost universally topped off with a traditional working man's flat cap. It all presented quite a spectacle to curious Islanders, who turned up to watch the recruits take physical exercise on the beach and carry out bayonet practice at St Helier's People's Park.

Yet what was obvious to any onlooker was that the majority of the South Staffordshire recruits required a considerable period of training before they were ready for battle. This meant that the Island's defence, should the Germans reach the French coast opposite, was largely in the hands of the Jersey Militia. For the purposes of that defence, each of the Militia's three battalions were allocated a stretch of the Island's coastline. The West Battalion had responsibility for guarding the longest sector of around twenty-three miles, west from Ronez Point on the north coast around to Beaumont on the south. The East Battalion's sector went in the opposite direction from Ronez round to Green Island that lay to the east of St Helier, giving it responsibility for around seventeen miles of coast. The Town Battalion had the remaining five miles to guard, but also the responsibility for defending the town. Each battalion's defence sector was further divided into small sub-sections. In the sector of the West Battalion, for example, the No. 1 Sub-section stretched from Ronez Pier to Plemont Beach, No. 2 Sub-section from Le Pulec Slipway below Les Landes along St Ouen's Bay to Petit Port Beach and No.3 Sub-section from there round to Beaumont. Areas considered as potential enemy landing points were fortified by digging trenches along the shoreline or adapting existing structures with sandbags. Machine gun emplacements were constructed at locations considered particularly vulnerable, the wide St Ouen's Bay possessed five for example. Wherever possible, existing military fortifications and structures were pressed into use as headquarters for each sub-section, giving a new lease of life to many of the old granite round towers that studded the coastline. And in each battalion sector, a force of reserve troops was held back at headquarters and other strategic locations, along with detachments of artillery, engineers and medics ready to reinforce any threatened point.

Those men stationed at the coastline had their duties strictly set out in a document entitled 'Outpost Regulations'. Duty commenced at three o'clock in the afternoon and lasted for twenty-four hours. The men had to be fully equipped and armed, carrying one hundred rounds of ammunition each. At night or in foggy weather, men had to leave their defensive positions when the tide was low and patrol the beach down to the water's edge. Anyone or anything regarded as suspicious had to be loudly challenged, to ensure they were heard. There were potentially serious consequences for persons not responding to the challenge as sentries had orders to shoot at anyone who they believed was going to directly attack them, or who was doing damage to the facility or location being guarded, or who having been seen to do damage ran away after having been challenged. Furthermore, boats approaching the shore at night or in foggy weather were considered legitimate targets. Such serious orders did result in concerns that someone would be accidentally shot. Young boys who reportedly thought it amusing to play pranks on the Militiamen by pretending to be spies did not help matters. To avoid any such mistakes, the military authorities repeatedly put notices in the newspapers warning Islanders to stop immediately if challenged by a sentry and for boat-owners to take extra care if out after dark or in the fog. Thankfully, the warnings appear to have worked, with no reports of injuries caused by accidental shootings.

As well as gaining the attention of young boys and other curious Islanders, Militiamen on duty soon had to contend with the boredom and discomfort of military service once the excitement of mobilisation faded. Those who had to serve on outpost duty found the experience particularly trying at times, especially given the usually rudimentary living conditions that were slow to improve. 'At first the men slept anyhow and anywhere, but mattresses are now provided,' commented one militiaman. 'Some of the mattresses leak – mine generally did – and as the straw works out, the things degenerate into veritable skeletons of mattresses.'[8] The accommodation was not necessarily better for the men serving in the reserve positions, particularly in the arsenals that were not built to accommodate large numbers of soldiers. A report by the Militia's Senior Medical Officer in August 1914 found that the arrangement at St Mary's Arsenal far from satisfactory for example. 'At present the arsenal and grounds are occupied by fifty-eight men, the only latrine for this number is an old pit latrine which I was informed had not been cleaned out for eight years or more,' he noted. 'The smell from it is horribly offensive and the accommodation is quite insufficient.'[9]

To improve the conditions of military service, groups of Militiamen had been allowed to return home in the daytime from the start of the mobilisation. The system soon became formalised into a rota system, with men serving one week at a time on duty – divided between time on outpost duty and time in reserve - followed by a week off. This not only eased the burden of service on the men, but also allowed the Island to continue functioning. To ensure that the defences were not diminished, however, the number of men available for service needed to rise. Within days of mobilisation, the military authorities busily set about finding the extra soldiers.

The first group called to service was the Militia Reserve, which had not been mobilised on 29 July. Under the terms of the Militia Law, the Lieutenant Governor could only call-out the Active Militia in an emergency; it required additional arrangements involving the King to summon the Militia Reserve for duty. At the beginning of August, when it had become obvious that war was imminent, there had been an exchange of correspondence between Rochfort, Henry Le Vavasseur dit Durell, who was the Island's Attorney General and the War Office to confirm what exactly was required. It was resolved by an

'Order-in-Council' and a 'Proclamation' signed by King George that were sent from Britain, the former to be registered in the Royal Court and the latter to be read out in St Helier's Royal Square and then posted up throughout the Island. Following this promulgation, which took place on 6 August, the Militia Vingteniers delivered individual notices to each member of the Militia Reserve in accordance with agreed procedure, stating where and when they should report for duty.

The move added a further 1,483 men to the number available for the Island's defence.[10] From another source there came a smaller but well intentioned group. Members of the Victoria College Officer Training Corps (OTC) had volunteered their services on the outbreak of war, and were accepted by the Lieutenant Governor. Attached to the Militia's East Battalion, the cadets led by their headmaster and captain, Arthur Hardy Worrall, took over a section of coastal defences every one night in five, with forty or fifty boys on duty at a time. As a result, one biographer noted, Victoria College gained the almost unique distinction of being the only independent school having its OTC on active service during the First World War.

Even with the additional numbers provided by the Militia Reserve and the OTC, it was apparent there was still a need for more men. The departure of French and British reservists had drastically reduced the available manpower in the Island, while the Militia's mobilisation was placing a heavy demand on the workforce that remained. With little prospect of an immediate return to normal peacetime conditions further measures to raise available numbers would follow in September 1914. A combing-out process of men who had avoided Militia service up until that time produced nine hundred new recruits from St Helier alone. Some had been previously exempted from service because of their health, while others had managed to slip through the net for one reason or another. Regardless of the reasons or excuses for not having undertaken Militia service to date, those identified came in for harsh criticism by one newspaper editor. 'Our noble army of standbacks looked well at Grève d'Azette Camp yesterday afternoon and they will look better still after a month's hard drill. For years they have jeered and gibed at the men who were doing their duty; they have considered themselves very clever fellows for getting out of it. Now they have been roped in it is our turn to laugh and their turn to work.'[11] The Militia vingteniers were also vigilant, checking departing passengers at the harbours for any serving militiaman trying to avoid their obligations by leaving the Island, and by questioning anyone of military age not in Militia uniform.

As a result of these measures, it became possible to establish a fixed pattern of Militia service that balanced the Island's defence with the need to ensure daily life could continue with some semblance of normality. To further ease the situation, employers were also permitted to apply for exemptions from military service for men who held jobs deemed as essential for the economy and the well-being of Islanders. All other off-duty Militiamen were aware they could be instantly recalled to duty, the prearranged signal being two cannon shots fired in quick succession. In anticipation of this many of the men wore their uniforms when going to work or out and about in the Island – despite orders for them not to. It meant that the Island remained awash with khaki, at the fortifications and barracks, around the coast and in day-to-day life as deliverymen, tradesmen, retailers and in fact most other male workers went about their business in their uniforms.

Across the sea in France, during the first two weeks in September 1914 the battles to determine the fate of France and the outcome of the war were being fought near Paris. Stretched by their relentless advance from Belgium, the German armies pursuing the retreating French and British had not taken Paris as the Schlieffen Plan had intended but swung to advance to the east of the capital instead. There, along the Marne River, the Allies had halted their retreat, and then begun a counter-attack. At the same time fresh French forces that had gathered around Paris also launched an attack of their own against the now exposed flank of the advancing German armies. For a few days the outcome of the Battle of the Marne, in which men from Jersey fought in both the British and French armies, remained uncertain. On 9 September, the Germans gave way and began to retreat however. Exhausted by their advances, apprehensive of the resurgent Allies and concerned over an early Russian offensive in the east, they fell back to regroup along a line of hills above the Aisne River where the advancing Allies would attack them later in that month.

The Battle of the Marne and a German withdrawal lessened the chance of an enemy breakthrough into Normandy or Brittany. Consequently, the perceived threat to the Channel Islands declined as did Jersey's strategic value with the BEF lines of communications moved back to Le Havre and the other northerly ports once more. Despite this, Britain was not yet prepared to lower its guard in the Channel Islands, and so the Militiamen remained firmly at their posts and doing their duty. One can only speculate as to what that duty may have entailed if events in September 1914 had gone differently for the Allies. Had they lost the Battle of the Marne, the British and French would have had to abandon Paris and try to retreat further south. In that situation, Germans almost certainly would have reached the Normandy and Brittany coast and captured Cherbourg, Granville and Saint-Malo. As in 1940, Jersey and the other Channel Islands would have made tempting prizes to capture and so the probability is the Militia would have been called upon to defend the Island against invasion. Unlike 1940, however, the Germans had no airpower as such and with its fleet bottled up in the North Sea by a more powerful Royal Navy, crossing the short distance to the Island would have been a challenge. So perhaps the Militia would never have been tested in a battle to defend their Island – it is impossible to say. But they were prepared to stand and fight - an act worthy of remembering to this day.

While Islanders were full of praise for the commitment shown by the Militia in the opening weeks for the war, there had also been some questions asked over whether the men would have been more useful serving in France than in Jersey. They were trained soldiers after all, and Britain was clearly going to need as many soldiers as possible on the battlefield if it were to emerge victorious. The German retreat from Paris after the Battle of the Marne had brought this question to the fore. In the light of what was going on in Britain and elsewhere in the Empire at that time, it was asked, should not the Island be doing more for the war effort? Kitchener was calling for volunteers by then; in such momentous times, where were the Jersey Pals?

5 YOUR ISLAND NEEDS YOU

Kitchener's recruitment campaign and the response of Jersey's volunteers

There were two significant lessons that Britain learned from the opening battles of the First World War. First, it was manifestly clear that despite the many optimistic assumptions and wishful forecasts, the war would not be over by Christmas. And second, that if Britain was to play a meaningful part in that war, and ensure that it emerged on the victorious side, the country would require an army that was many times larger than that with which it had gone to war.

Britain's Secretary of State for War, Field Marshal Earl Kitchener of Khartoum, had been forcefully making both of these points to the British Government from the very start of the conflict. Kitchener, whose military exploits had made him a widely respected public figure, had joined the Cabinet on the outbreak of war to bring military experience into the government. He quickly made it his mission to expand the British Army from its small pre-war size into a force numbering several millions. It was an unprecedented move, but one that he deemed vital to ensure victory. On 6 August 1914, the British Parliament approved Kitchener's plan to raise five hundred thousand volunteers for the army and notices calling for an initial one hundred thousand men to enlist for the duration of the war appeared in the national newspapers immediately afterwards. To the surprise of most, the response was instantaneous and almost overwhelming. Throughout the country, eager volunteers in their thousands came forward to fill army recruitment offices while outside long queues formed as men patiently waited for their turn to join up. Even Kitchener had not anticipated such a response. In almost no time, the first target for volunteers was reached and then passed

Soon, the numbers of men swamped the existing army recruiting offices, leading to temporary new ones being opened to help cope with the demand. By mid-September 1914, the number of 'Kitchener volunteers', as the men were called, exceeded the original target of five hundred thousand, with the rate of enlistment continuing strongly. The recruitment campaign, immortalised today by the famous 'Your Country Needs You' poster featuring Kitchener's face and pointing finger, was a resounding success. As well as attracting volunteers, it also served to unify the country and invigorate the war effort. Newspapers got behind the campaign, urging men to come forward, publishing lists of volunteer's names and reporting on the progress of recruiting throughout Britain. Local civic authorities began taking an increasing role in the campaign as even the expanded army recruitment facilities struggled in the face of such numbers. Enthusiastic committees were formed to encourage enlistment, taking over rooms in town halls and other public buildings up and down the country as their recruitment centres. Some came up with novel ways to report success. In Birmingham, for example, the campaign included a huge barometer hung on the Town Hall to show the growing number of volunteers from that city.

It was from this civilian participation that the concept of the 'Pals Battalions' emerged. As an encouragement to volunteer, men received assurances that they would be permitted to serve together in the same unit along with others from their town or city, or from the same university or who were working in the same profession. The army was happy with the arrangements; they not only increased recruitment but also created a strong sense of pride and camaraderie in the new units. The Pals concept quickly took hold, with rivalry between competing locations for the honour of being the first to raise the required one thousand men to form an infantry battalion. Liverpool emerged as the winner, but many others were not far behind. Among them was Manchester, which would go on to raise seven Pals Battalions and Bradford, which managed to raise three. There were four from Salford and no fewer than eight from Tyneside, divided equally into four Tyneside Irish and four Tyneside Scottish Pals Battalions. The small East Lancashire town of Accrington formed one of the best known, called the Accrington Pals. The port city of Hull raised four battalions, calling them the Hull Commercials, the Hull Tradesmen, the Hull Sportsmen, and - for want of a better name - the Hull T'Others. Across the country, there were similar results.

The response to the appeal for volunteers and the Pals concept was not limited to the British mainland. In Ireland, where the question of Home Rule had divided the country prior to the war, both Nationalist and Unionist communities had responded to the call. And in the British Dominions of Australia, Canada, New Zealand and South Africa, men came forward in their thousands after the declaration of war on Germany to join locally raised units destined for overseas service. Even Newfoundland, which at that time was a separate self-governing British Dominion, raised a full battalion for service overseas from its two hundred and fifty thousand inhabitants.

The situation was very different in Jersey at this time. While there was full awareness of Kitchener's recruitment campaign in Britain and an understanding of what was happening elsewhere in the Empire, there were no official actions being taken to encourage volunteering in the Island. As the German threat had receded in September 1914, the question increasingly being asked was why Jersey was not playing its part in these momentous events. Since their mobilisation, a number of Militiamen had been expressing a desire to be allowed to leave and to take part in what was seen by many as a great adventure. Under the Militia Law, however, they had to remain and defend the Island. As Kitchener's campaign took hold in Britain, and with the then still widely held view that the war would be over by Christmas, agitation grew for a change in policy. Initially, the War Office remained adamant that Jersey should continue to be fully defended, particularly in view of its growing strategic importance following the BEF's retreat from Mons. There followed a change of heart early in September, with a concession allowing individual Militiamen to leave the Island and enlist in the British Army. But they had to join the Regular Army, which meant committing to the usual twelve years rather than the terms of service offered to Kitchener's volunteers in Britain, which were namely to serve for the duration of the war only. It was all rather confusing, and there was frustration given the lack of clarity over Jersey's involvement and Kitchener's campaign. 'One might go further,' remonstrated one local newspaper editor, 'and say that the red tape and the so-called etiquette of the military have largely contributed to an impossible position.'[1]

Behind the scenes wheels were slowly turning however. The Lieutenant Governor and the civilian authorities were determined to do something about the matter. On 16 September 1914, Rochfort wrote to the War Office to offer a contingent of Militiamen for overseas service. It would consist of two full companies of soldiers, a machine gun detachment and stretcher-bearers - in total around five hundred officers and other ranks. 'The men are of a good stamp,' he wrote, 'shoot well, and with a month's special training would be very useful on the lines of communication.'[2] The response that came back nine days later swiftly extinguished hopes that the Island may be able to play a more active role in the war at that time. The War Office reply declined the offer, stating that, 'it would be inadvisable at the present juncture to reduce the military strength now available for the defence of Jersey by withdrawing any of the trained personnel from the Royal Jersey Militia.'[3] Jersey was not to have a Pals unit of its own – at least not at that time.

Given the military situation in France in September 1914, the War Office had reasonable grounds for not accepting a Jersey Contingent at that point. Even after Allied victory in September's Battle of the Marne and the subsequent German retreat, the fighting in France and Belgium remained fluid throughout October and November. Britain would not have wanted to weaken its 'Defended Port' through any wholesale reduction in the strength of the Island's garrison. There may have also been another factor contributing to the decision to leave the Militia in place. Kitchener was known to have a disdain of part-time soldiers, having seen them in action during his various military campaigns where he had not been impressed with their performance. This view appears to have coloured his decision not to use Britain's part-time Territorial Force (TF)* when it came to training or commanding his volunteers. Instead, he created new formations for the Pals Battalions and other units raised at this time. Termed the 'New Army', they would train and serve outside the pre-war 'Regular' and 'Territorial' structure. While much of the Regular Army had joined the BEF in August 1914 for service on the Continent, Kitchener's preference – in the early months of the war at least – was for the TF battalions to remain at home or serve overseas on garrison duties. He may well have decided that Jersey's part-time Militia firmly fitted into this same category.

Kitchener did not dismiss the idea of individual TF soldiers going to the front if they volunteered to serve in either the Regular or the New Army. At the end of September, the same option was at last extended to Jersey. It remained limited to individual Militiamen, however, who could join up now for the duration of the war. Within days, the first men were on their way to Britain, among them St Helier brothers Louis and Maurice Béghin who left the Town Battalion and Royal Jersey Artillery (RJA) respectively. Twenty-four-year-old Louis would serve as a sergeant in the Royal Army Medical Corps while Maurice, who was aged twenty-one, joined the Royal Fusiliers as a private. Others soon followed, including eight officers who resigned their Militia commissions in mid-October to take up appointments in various army regiments. Other senior Militia officers left in ones and twos along with a number of senior non-commissioned officers to take up equivalent roles in the British Army. Yet it was a steady stream of volunteers rather than a torrent, with around sixty men leaving in October and another twenty in November.[4] Many others were said to be holding back in the expectation that a Jersey unit would be formed at some point, with rumours swirling round in October and November that the War Office had agreed to accept one from Guernsey. As disquiet grew, there was unofficial news in late November that, finally, Jersey was about to be allowed to send one too.

Behind the scenes, Rochfort appears to have continued to lobby the War Office to allow a representative Jersey unit and at the beginning of December 1914, it finally relented. On 5 December, a notice appeared in the Gazette section of the *Evening Post*. The War Office, it announced, had now consented to meet the desire of the inhabitants to be represented overseas by a contingent raised from the Jersey Militia. Depending on the numbers coming forward, it went on to say, the volunteers would either form half of a joint Channel Islands'

---

* Renamed the Territorial Army in 1920.

battalion or be attached as a company to a battalion in Kitchener's New Army. For half a battalion, the number required was at least five hundred men; for a company, around two hundred and fifty were needed. Guernsey received the same terms. Volunteers would have to meet the standard criteria of the New Army, which required men that were between the ages of nineteen and thirty-eight, at least five feet and three inches tall and who had a minimum chest size of thirty-four and half inches. They had until 9 December to come forward and report to their commanding officers.

The notice stirred the newspapers into offering their wholehearted support. 'Jersey has been given the opportunity of practically demonstrating the reality of that loyalty and patriotism which forms an important part of her traditional heritage,' the *Morning News* enthused. 'Past generations of Jerseymen displayed a devotion to Crown and country which has never been questioned. It will shortly be proved whether their present day descendants are animated by the same spirit.'[5] There was a widespread view that the Island would easily raise the five hundred men required for the half battalion, with some claiming Jersey should set its sights even higher. 'Jersey has a chance of taking its part in the war which would see the world free,' proclaimed the Dean of Jersey who was the Island's senior church leader. 'I pray that we have not five hundred,' the Very Reverend Samuel Falle told his parishioners,' but one thousand volunteers.'[6] Both the newspaper editors and the Dean were to be sorely disappointed, however, when it became known that little more than one tenth of the Dean's prayed for number had actually come forward by the end of the deadline day for volunteering.

The date by when Militiamen had to volunteer was now put back until 12 December, while their commanding officers assisted by the Militia Chaplain, the Reverend Carey Walters, applied pressure to encourage more to give their names. Rumours that Guernsey had reached and exceeded its quota added to a growing sense of disappointment – among public figures at least – over the apparent lack of loyalty and patriotism. There had long been good-humoured rivalry between the two largest Channel Islands; it was inconceivable to some that the smaller neighbour was upstaging Jersey. Yet not everyone felt the same. 'When I read the address of the Dean of Jersey and the Reverend Carey Walters…it seemed to me that they would not be sorry to see every male inhabitant of the Island enrol themselves as recruits,' one commentator wrote in a letter to the *Morning News* on 14 December. 'Is it logical to reduce [the Militia's] efficiency by depleting it of some hundreds of men to form a "contingent" for duties outside the Island – entirely foreign to the terms of its constitution?'[7] Clearly, the States thought that it was logical. After the 12 December deadline came and went without any appreciable rise in volunteer numbers, it was time for the States to act. The Island's reputation was at stake.

In a special sitting on 15 December, the States met to debate the matter of recruitment for Jersey's contingent. The assembly started with the reading of a stirring proposition:

> Proud of its traditions and of its past steady and loyal attachment to the throne of England, and determined to bequeath to generations to come the glorious heritage of British patrimony; confident in the patriotism of Jerseymen, and resolved to incur any sacrifices to help the Mother Country and her allies to throw back and conquer the common enemy on foreign soil; the States have unanimously decided to appeal to the Island, and especially to the Royal Jersey Militia, in order to be able to provide a contingent of trained Jersey volunteers for the service of the Crown…[8]

Member after member stood to speak up in support of the proposition. The Constable of St Helier, John Pinel, 'wished that the whole of the Militia had been asked to go…at a time when the Colonies in all parts of the world were sending of their best to save the Empire, Jersey could not, dared not, stand aside, and there must be no hesitation.'[9] Deputy Middleton agreed, adding that, 'Jersey now had the splendid opportunity of placing another glorious page on the historical record of the Island…If we refused then there would be such a blot on our escutcheon as would wipe out all our past splendid achievements.'[10] 'No one should hang back,' Deputy Cory told his colleagues, 'because our success demanded more men.'[11] With no dissenters willing to speak against, the Bailiff swiftly interceded to summarise what had been said and asked the States to vote. 'The youth of the Island now had a glorious opportunity,' Vernon announced, 'to show that they as Jerseymen feared neither death nor the enemies of the country.'[12] The proposition was passed unanimously.

The outcome of the States debate and proposition was a recruitment campaign that started on 17 December and that continued until the end of the month. Politicians, church leaders and army officers were all involved, making appeals to Militiamen directly and Islanders generally. As well as lectures at the barracks and arsenals, they spoke during the intermissions of public theatre performances and picture shows. Specially convened meetings took place in parish halls, church halls and other community centres throughout the Island. An extra effort went into taking the message to the country parishes, from where the lowest number of volunteers were known to have come forward since the appeal began. The new deadline was set at 31 December, with the campaign continuing right up until the last moment. Medical examinations for those who had come forward began on 29 December. A few days later, the much anticipated final number was released. There was widespread relief among those championing a Jersey contingent that 330 men had volunteered, mixed with frustration on finding out that only 250 of these volunteers had been passed as medically fit for active service. It was still enough, however, to form a single company of soldiers: Jersey would have its contingent – just.

Any lingering sense of disappointment that the campaign had not encouraged more Militiamen to come forward was tempered by the news that Guernsey too had only just managed to find enough volunteers to form a company. There was also a conviction that the response would have been different if only the War Office had accepted Jersey's original offer of a contingent back in September 1914. The eighty men who had left the Island as individual volunteers to join up in October and November 1914 would surely have made a difference to the final number, it was argued. Nevertheless, at the start of January 1915, Rochfort must have felt some relief at being able to write to the War Office with the offer of a contingent of volunteers from the Jersey Militia for overseas service. They would, he hoped, be attached to one of the New Army battalions then being raised, and be permitted to bear the name the 'Jersey Company' in order to maintain a sense of separate identity and a clear link to their Island.

With the dispatch of the letter, it was possible to put aside the fractious recruitment campaign and the questions over Jersey's commitment to the war effort – for the present time at least. Yet even as the authorities and Islanders rallied round the newly formed Jersey Company in preparation for its expected departure, there was lingering disquiet over one aspect of the campaign. Irrespective of the number who had actually come forward, there was no disguising the fact that the final count showed a marked disparity between the response of the town and that from the country parishes. Just under three quarters of the volunteers were from St Helier, whereas only seventy-three men in total had come forward from the West and East Battalions.[13] From some country parishes there had barely been a response. Of the volunteers that were accepted, only one came from St Mary, admittedly a small parish, while seven other parishes contributed less than ten men each.[14] In some ways, this was understandable. St Helier accounted for a little over half the Island's population at the start of the war. Furthermore, the departure of the French reservists had denuded the country parishes of resident labour and there was hardly any expectation that many seasonal workers would be available in 1915. This left the burden of farm work on local men already stretched by the need to fulfil their Militia service obligations. Under such circumstances, some argued, it was completely reasonable that men in the country parishes had not come forward in the numbers anticipated. When the matter was discussed by the

States, there was strong support shown towards those who decided to stay and work the land rather than volunteer for the army. 'They must all realise that the men who were planting their crops were serving their country,' one member argued, and, 'were just as patriotic as those who took a gun in their hands.'[15] But there was also the opposite view that some people were putting the needs of Jersey's farming industry above the need to support Britain. It would become a recurring theme, and one that would trouble the Island for the remainder of the war.

For the Jersey contingent volunteers preparing to leave for overseas service, the subject of town versus country was an irritant rather than a cause for concern. In early February, they learned which regiment they would join and where they would have to travel in order to join it. The War Office had decided to place Jersey's volunteers, who had become known as 'Our Contingent' or simply 'Ours', with the 7th Battalion of the Royal Irish Rifles, which was then training in the south of Ireland. It was a somewhat surprising choice given Jersey's closer links with regiments on the south coast of England or with those who had supplied the Island's garrison battalion before the war. The matter was dismissed, however, on the basis that the War Office must know best and from that time forward, Jersey's contingent would become the Jersey Company, 7th Royal Irish Rifles. The reality was that the choice of an Irish regiment was clearly little to do with association and was almost certainly due to the recruiting difficulties experienced by a number of New Army battalions in Ireland, particularly those in the Nationalist areas, the inhabitants of which felt little loyalty towards Britain. Similarly, Guernsey's contingent now joined the 6th Battalion of the Royal Irish Regiment while a second group of volunteers raised by that island later became part of the 7th Battalion, Royal Irish Fusiliers for the same reason.

On 2 March 1915, the Jersey Company volunteers paraded in the Royal Square in front of a large group of family, friends and well-wishers. They totalled 224 men, numbers having declined from the original 250 who were passed fit for active service through illness and withdrawals. It was the first time that they had come together as a complete company, an event according to one newspaper editor that was, 'a red-letter day in Jersey annals.'[16] Under the command of Major Walter Stocker, a forty-seven-year-old originally from Yorkshire who had been a lieutenant colonel in the East Battalion but accepted a reduction in rank to lead the volunteers, they came to attention and marched smartly off the square. Led by a band and flanked by the Bailiff and Brigadier General Godfrey from the Jersey District's staff, the volunteers made their way to the harbour's New North Quay where the Great Western Railway steamer SS *Ibex* was tied up alongside. Further dignitaries, including the Lieutenant

Governor and the Dean of Jersey, were waiting there to shake each man's hand as he stepped up to board the ship. At 7.30 am, the *Ibex* pulled away from the quay and sailed out through the pier heads. A crowd of thousands cheered and sang as the ship departed, while cannon blasts from Fort Regent echoed around the harbour in tribute.

Apart from the Jersey Company, there was only one other attempt during the First World War to form a unit for overseas service with identifiable Island connections. At the end of December 1914, officers of the RJA had endeavoured to form a heavy artillery battery, to be called the 'Jersey Battery'. They needed at least 198 volunteers to come forward from the 550 or so Militia artillerymen under their command. If that target could not be achieved, then there was the option of forming a joint Channel Islands' battery with Guernsey. By February 1915, however, the number of volunteers for the planned Jersey Battery remained disappointingly low, leading to the idea being quietly dropped and leaving those Guernseymen who had volunteered to form a unit on their own. Thereafter no further official or unofficial attempts were made to form Jersey units from volunteers, leaving men free, as before, to join the British Army individually. This they did, even as recruitment for the Jersey Company was in full flow.

By mid-December 1915, the Jersey District Office could report that 1,016 officers and men had volunteered and been accepted into the British Army, a figure that included the original 224 members of the Jersey Comapny who left the Island on 2 March. During the same period, 128 men had joined the Royal Navy, while a further 272 volunteers had been turned down on medical grounds.[17] These figures only covered men who had enlisted in Jersey and not those who joined up in Britain or elsewhere. It meant that in total, just over 1,500 men from the Island would have volunteered for military service between the start of the war and the end of 1915. They continued to join up as 1916 began.

What had motivated men to come forward in such numbers, particularly in an Island where many of them could reasonably claim they were already doing their bit towards the war effort by serving in the Militia. The passage of time and a lack of first-hand written accounts by Jerseymen who served in the First World War make it difficult to say with any certainty what made individuals decide to volunteer. It is possible to generalise, however, based upon an understanding of comparable recruitment campaigns in Britain and elsewhere. This suggests that the motivation for the majority of the Islanders who volunteered in the early years of the war fell into three broad categories.

The first would have been straightforward patriotism. The decades leading up to the First World War saw the British Empire reach its peak in terms of expansion, achievements and acceptability. For many people, this was a great cause of pride in the nation's accomplishments, creating in turn a powerful sense of duty towards Britain and its monarch. Reinforcing this, there was a strong set of values prevailing in Edwardian society that instilled a clear sense of right and wrong. When it came to war, the moral situation was simple: Britain was in the right, and therefore Germany in the wrong. Newspaper reports of German atrocities against civilians in Belgium helped confirm this, enflaming a sense of outrage and a desire for retribution. The widely held belief that the war would be over by Christmas further helped drive early patriotic enthusiasm, while news of British military setbacks also swelled the volunteer numbers as patriotically minded men rallied to the nation's cause.

A second reason for men volunteering was simply that they had felt under pressure to do so. In some respects, this was an indirect pressure. The fact that family members, friends and colleagues had decided to join up led to many men deciding to do the same thing, especially if it meant that they could serve together in the same unit. The sound of a military band and the sight of marching soldiers stirred the consciousness of some men. Having more than two thousand men, all volunteers, of the South Staffordshire Regiment training in the Island from August 1914, for example, must have exerted a subtle pressure on Islanders. In some cases it would have led to an impulsive decision to visit the recruiting office straight away, in others started a slow fuse that would eventually only be put out by joining up later. In many other respects, the pressure to volunteer was brought to bear far more directly. There was no shortage of clergy lecturing their congregations, politicians addressing gatherings and Militia commanding officers reminding parades on why it was a man's duty to serve the King and their Island by joining-up. Then there were official campaigns run from time to time. As already noted, the lack of volunteers for a Jersey contingent had led to a formal campaign at the end of 1914. In early October 1915, another official recruitment drive led by the Lieutenant Governor directly appealed to Militiamen, encouraging them to join-up in the most forthright terms.

After patriotism and pressure, the last reason for men to volunteer arose from their social and economic backgrounds. For some, joining up meant escaping the dull routine of life in Jersey, even if the expectation was for a short time only. Many of the men who volunteered worked long hours often doing mundane and laborious jobs. Some lived in cramped and dilapidated housing, especially in the poorer parts of St Helier, or in humble dwellings in the country. The only prospect on their horizon was for more of the same. Joining the army or the navy offered a chance to experience something different, and escape the Island. It was a chance not to be missed - even if it meant leaving behind a wife and children. In the ranks of the Jersey Company, for example, around one third of the men were married, with about half of these having children.

The armed forces also presented men with the chance of economic betterment. Kitchener's New Army offered a shilling a day to privates, two shillings and four pence for sergeants. Trained and experienced soldiers could supplement this with proficiency pay after completing training, while married men and fathers were entitled to claim separation allowances: nine shillings a week for a wife only, rising to eighteen shillings and sixpence for a wife and four children. For men working for a low wage in Jersey at the time, pay rates such as these, along with the prospect of regular meals and a uniform, must have been a strong enticement. Moreover, as trained soldiers – albeit part-time – former Jersey Militiamen would have been welcome additions to Kitchener's New Army battalions, which had mainly men without any previous military experience. So the opportunity existed to gain an even higher rank, and to receive commensurately higher pay.

Each man had his own particular reasons for volunteering, which may have fallen into one of these categories. Yet whatever it was, most who volunteered decided not to join the Jersey Company, which may have seemed the logical choice for them.

After leaving Jersey in March 1915, the Jersey Company travelled to the town of Buttevant, set among the green hills of County Cork in Ireland for a period of initial training. In September, they would then move to Aldershot to undertake further training in preparation for departure to France that took place in December 1915. During that time, a further ninety-six men from Jersey joined the original volunteers, bringing the total number to 320. The additional recruits came about through the efforts of the Jersey Company, however, whose members took every opportunity to encourage Islanders to join their ranks. There was no official drive from the Island's authorities to reinforce the only formed military unit they had sent for overseas service.

Although Jersey may have recruited and sent off its contingent, there seems to have been little thought given to establishing a method for maintaining its strength with replacements and reinforcements. It would prove to be tragic oversight. While 320 men were more than enough to form a company in peacetime, it was too small a number for a fighting unit. Losses through enemy action and illness were bound to reduce its ranks over time. Without a means to recruit and train reinforcements from home, the Jersey Company was destined to weaken and ultimately disappear. Moreover, if the Island's authorities failed to provide any replacements, there was a marked reluctance among most Islanders to volunteer for the Jersey Contingent. 'There can surely be no serious reason,' wrote the editor of the *Morning News* about the lack of new recruits, 'for what seems on the face of it, to advocate a certain prejudice against Major Stocker and his men.'[18] Yet there clearly was. It may have stemmed from the Lieutenant Governor's original offer of a contingent in September 1914. At the time, Rochfort had made it clear that he thought that Militiamen would be very useful *on the line of communications*, in other words used for guard duties in the rear areas rather than actual fighting at the front. Such a prospect had put some men off joining the Jersey Company. Moreover, rumours and mischievous gossip also exacerbated the problem. It was said that there was no opportunity for promotion within the Jersey Company, or that the men were not fit enough for active service. Complicating matters was that the 7th Royal Irish Rifles, to which the Jersey Company was assigned, was part of the Sixteenth (Irish) Division, a formation whose constituent units had struggled to find enough recruits. While other New Army divisions formed at the same time had already gone to the front, it remained behind with many observers speculating it would never be allowed to serve overseas. It led to a widespread belief that no one who joined the Jersey Company would ever see active service. The stigma persisted up until December 1915, when the Jersey Company eventually arrived at the front and went into the trenches shortly after. Whatever the actual truth, it was enough to dissuade the majority of the Island's volunteers from enlisting in the Royal Irish Rifles and the Jersey Company. In the end, it would only attract one in six of all Jersey's wartime volunteers. Most Jersey volunteers would therefore not serve in the Royal Irish Rifles.

Like their pre-war Regular Army counterparts, the majority of Islanders who volunteered joined one of a wide variety of regiments and corps of the British Army. A number of factors appear to have influenced their choice of which exactly. Their role in the Jersey Militia would have determined where some went, with a number of those serving in the RJA logically joining the Royal Artillery, for example, while some members of the Militia Engineer Company would have opted for the Royal Engineers. Others had personal reasons for choosing a particular regiment or corps, perhaps because a friend, work colleague or family member was already serving with that unit. There were some who felt compelled to join a unit to which they felt an affiliation, such as a number of local postmen who chose to join the 8th Battalion of the London Regiment, which was widely known as the Post Office Rifles. These, and a variety of other individual reasons, account for perhaps half of the choices made by Jersey's volunteers. The other half served in a small number of units that were logical choices for men volunteering in Jersey. The Jersey District Office recruiting staff appear to have placed many volunteers with no particular preference where they served in regiments with an affiliation to the Island through garrison duty, such as the East Surrey Regiment, or which were located close by on the south coast of England, such as the Hampshire Regiment.

As well as those who volunteered to join the British Army, it is also important to remember that a considerable number of men who had family ties to Jersey served in the overseas contingents of Britain's Australian, Canadian, New Zealand and South African Dominions. By the start of the First World War, these important colonial territories had all achieved Dominion status within the wider British Empire and had their own leaders, governments and armed forces. The original reason for developing the Dominion's armed forces had been to provide for home defence and permit Britain to deploy its regular soldiers in less secure parts of the Empire. In the years before 1914, these forces had the time to develop, evolving their own institutions and identity separately from the British Army. After the Dominions joined the war on Germany in August 1914, their governments immediately took steps to form military units that could serve overseas.

In common with the situation in Britain, the Dominion armed forces that existed at the start of the war were comparatively small and consisted mainly of part-time volunteers formed into regional militia units. The first call to serve overseas was made to these men, and in common with Britain, the response was instant and very impressive. With many people living in the Dominions at that time first generation immigrants, the sense of affinity and loyalty towards Britain remained extremely high, and so the response was understandable. In Canada, for example, over thirty thousand volunteers responded to an appeal by mid-September 1914. There was a similar response in Australia where over fifty thousand men had come forward and been accepted into the army by the end of 1914. Caught in the wave of enthusiasm were many men formerly from Jersey who had left the Island and Europe behind over the previous two decades in search of a more prosperous life. Between five and six hundred would cross the Atlantic between 1914 and 1918 for service with the Canadian Expeditionary Force, as it was known. More than one hundred Jersey immigrants would also serve in the Australian Army and a few in the fledgling Royal Australian Navy. Smaller numbers – around thirty in each – joined the New Zealand and South African expeditionary forces.

After training in Britain, the Canadians went on to serve in France and Belgium, where the majority of the other Dominion troops eventually joined them following campaigns at Gallipoli and in Africa. For Islanders who had chosen a new life on the other side of the world, the war would bring them close to their Island once more. Many would to return home during periods of leave or when convalescing from wounds, much to the delight of families and friends who would have assumed that they might never see them again.

The experience of a Jerseyman volunteering for the army would have been much the same wherever enlistment took place. He would report to a recruitment centre to join up – in Jersey this was located at the Jersey District Headquarters in Rouge Bouillon – and undergo a medical inspection to establish whether he was fit for military service. He would also have to confirm his age. Officially, the army only took volunteers between the ages of nineteen and thirty-eight, although in the heady enthusiasm of the early Kitchener campaigns many recruitment centres were happy to accept men who didn't quite measure up to the criteria. There were among the Jersey Company volunteers, for example, men of forty-four and lads as young as fifteen. One of the latter was Arthur Mallet who had stated that he was nineteen-years-old when joining-up in July 1915 to serve alongside his elder brother Charles. When Charles was killed in July 1916, their mother wrote to the army, trying to 'claim' Arthur back. Enclosing his birth certificate, she wrote, 'You will see that the boy joined at the age of fifteen years and eleven months, and is under age being only sixteen years and nine months…I gave my only two sons to the army and one had made the great sacrifice and the other one, who is only a boy, has played a man's part and bled for his country.'[19] By that time, however, the army was reluctant to let any of its men – or lads – go. Arthur Mallet, who had been wounded in the head by then, would remain in the army until the end of the war.

Once the enlistment procedures were complete, and with a first week's pay in hand (hence the well know phrase to 'accept the King's shilling'), men were sent from Jersey to join their chosen regiment or corps. Armed with the necessary travel warrants, they had to report to the regimental depot, in Winchester for the Hampshire Regiment, for example, or Dorchester for the Dorsetshire Regiment. There they typically remained for a few days, and may have received some basic training and been issued with a uniform and equipment. Many volunteers soon found that the euphoria associated with enlistment now disappeared amid draughty and often cramped accommodation blocks. From the depot, the men were sent off in groups to an army camp for basic and then advanced training prior to despatch to the front. Some of these camps were pre-war establishments, complete with permanent barracks and other facilities. Others were temporary, constructed to help accommodate the mass of recruits drawn in by Kitchener's campaign. For those volunteers who left Jersey in 1914 and found themselves in one of these camps, it may have been an uncomfortable first winter living under canvas. Like the South Staffordshire Regiment volunteers they had left behind in the Island, most of the early volunteers would lack uniforms, equipment and weapons while food remained in sporadic supply, and what was available was often barely palatable.

Fortunately, the accommodation and facilities gradually improved in 1915, as the army replaced draughty tents with heated wooden huts. At the same time, the flow of uniforms, equipment and arms began to accelerate as British industry got into its wartime stride. It meant that Kitchener's volunteers could at last begin looking like soldiers – with training they would be ready to go to the front.

In common with many other aspects of Kitchener's New Army, the training received by the volunteers was somewhat rudimentary at first, but soon improved as the British Army expanded to cope with the new recruits. Most Jersey volunteers would have spent about six months in training, although the period was longer for some and often depended on how ready their unit was to go overseas. The original Jersey Company volunteers, for example, spent just over nine months in training before leaving Britain for France. Given that the majority of Jersey volunteers would have already completed their Militia training, it must have been frustrating at times to serve alongside men who were completely new to military service. Starting with basic army skills, such as standing to attention, saluting and parading in a straight line, each soldier progressed to learn entrenching, bayonet-fighting and field craft skills along with many hours spent on the rifle range and on route marches. In the latter stages of their training programme, infantrymen acquired specialist skills such as machine gunners, bombers and scouts. Artillerymen studied gun-laying, loading, and signalling if they served on the guns, or handling teams of horses if their role was a driver. Engineers learned to build bridges and construct field fortifications, and so forth.

For new officers, the demands of training was even more challenging than that of the men they found themselves commanding, and certainly more daunting. They not only had to master the skills of soldiery, but also to acquire the leadership skills needed to command a unit of men, many of whom were older than themselves, and most of whom had been civilians until recently and therefore unaccustomed to receiving orders. Experience gained from previously serving in an Officer Training Corps (OTC), such as that found at Victoria College, would have been a great help for many new officers. Ex-Jersey Militia officers would have had an even better advantage, which must have been appreciated by commanding officers of the units to which they were attached. Fortunately, the willing and enthusiastic nature of the volunteers also helped new officers settle into their new roles, and together they set about the job of becoming effective soldiers.

When Kitchener had proposed his New Army there had been considerable misgivings expressed by many senior military figures. The prospect of turning a mass of civilians into trained soldiers in the timeframe proposed was simply unimaginable. To do so with facilities designed for a small regular army seemed impossible. Yet Britain succeeded in doing just that. In mid-1915, the first New Army divisions were ready for service overseas. By mid-1916, thirty had left Britain for service active overseas, including within their ranks many of the 1,500 volunteers from Jersey. Well motivated, they arrived at the front armed, equipped and trained. Unfortunately, as they were soon discovered, their training was only partially effective. Once there, men now had to adjust to life in trenches and learn the deadly skills of the new type of warfare found there, something for which no amount of training in camps back in Britain could prepare them.

Back home in Jersey, meanwhile, those Islanders the volunteers had left behind were having to make adjustments of their own as the impact of the war took a progressively tighter grip on their lives. For some, the new wartime rules and regulations would come as a very unpleasant shock.

6 NEW RULES AND REGULATIONS

Jersey's people and politicians adjust to wartime conditions

The first few months of the war had been a time of mixed contrasts for Jersey's civilian population. After the excitement, anxiety and emotion of the opening weeks, daily life had gradually settled back into a more orderly pace and routine after September 1914. The threat of enemy attack had clearly lessened following the German retreat after the Battle of the Marne. Then in October and November, renewed fighting appeared to further diminish the chance as the Allies and Germans 'raced to the sea' in a series of battles that moved northwards towards the Channel coast and ended in stalemate around the small Belgian city of Ypres. At sea, the outlook was also promising for Islanders. Apart from venturing out of port for raids and minor actions, the German High Seas Fleet had not dared to openly challenge Royal Navy supremacy in the North Sea, leaving the English Channel free of enemy surface warships. Even the much feared Zeppelins has not yet made an appearance over Britain, never mind the Channel Islands. With the question of Jersey's involvement in Kitchener's recruitment campaign apparently settled and the expanded Militia adapting to its routine of service, it appeared that Island life could begin returning to a semblance of normality. Yet even the most thick-skinned of Islanders could not completely forget that they were at war. From its very start, the conflict had begun changing people's lives, sometimes in a way they barely noticed, at other times in the most dramatic of fashions.

It was also impossible to forget there was a war on given the constant visible reminder of the changed circumstances that it had brought about. Despite the diminishing enemy threat, after September 1914 Jersey remained an island full of soldiers. They were to be seen everywhere. The coastline and key locations remained steadfastly guarded by armed Militiamen with their orders still to shoot anyone thought to be acting in a threatening manner. Off duty Militiamen went about their daily business wearing uniform. Busy staff officers from the Jersey District in car or on horseback hurried between their headquarters and Fort Regent, up to Government House, and out to the country arsenals and barracks. And the men of the South Staffordshire Regiment, who became increasingly uniformed as Britain's war industry stepped up production, paraded, marched and trained throughout the Island.

By the start of October 1914, there were also the first members of another, far more thought-provoking group of soldiers present in the Island. Many of the men who had been lightly wounded during the early battles of the war had been granted a short spell of convalescent leave before returning to duty. A number chose to return home and spend their few days back among family and friends. While their arrival and subsequent presence was greeted with some excitement, the experiences and appearance of some were a sobering reminder – if one was needed – of the war's potentially shattering effects. One of the first back was *Soldat* Jean Du Prat in early October 1914. He had left on the outbreak of war to rejoin the *6e Régiment d'Infanterie Coloniale* stationed in Lyon, then going into action with it during the opening Battle of the Frontiers. Wounded in the fighting, there was some surprise that Du Prat had been sent home on leave still wearing his original uniform, now torn and bloodstained – an occurrence that says much about France's attitude to its soldiers. Another French reservist, Constant Variallon, who had been wounded in the fighting at Maubeuge, arrived with a bandaged head and arm and an injured foot. Still clearly unwell, he was fortunate to receive medical support from a local woman, who had also taken in Variallon's heavily pregnant and penniless wife after he had rejoined his regiment in August 1914.

There were British Army soldiers among the early returnees too, including some men who had fought in August's Battle of Mons. Private Frank Vallois of the Lancashire Fusiliers was one of the earliest, arriving in the Island on 10 September – just short of three weeks after the battle had been fought. As a British Army reservist, he was one of those men who had left on the outbreak of war to rejoin their regiment, which in the case of Private Vallois meant travelling first to its depot at Bury. From there he departed for France and took part in a series of forced marches to reach the battlefield near Mons in time to join the fighting. Wounded in the ankle by shrapnel, he was helped by a Jersey comrade, Private Jack Le Riche, to crawl to safety when the Germans threatened to overwhelm his unit. After treatment in Rouen and Le Havre, Private Vallois was evacuated across the Channel to a hospital in Cambridge before being allowed to return home to Jersey for a short period of leave.

The returning soldiers, along with stirring newspaper accounts of heroic battles fought by Britain and its allies, helped to start and sustain one of the first and certainly the longest running civilian responses to the war. Almost from the outset, there had been an expressed desire to find a way to 'support the troops'. The first campaign to do so had commenced within days of war being declared. The Jersey branch of the Young Man's Christian Association (YMCA) had started collecting books, magazines and newspapers for Militiamen to read while on duty in their barracks. A military committee for the local YMCA branch had already existed before the war, having been formed in 1908 to provide a recreation tent and then later a hut for Militiamen taking part in the annual summer training camp. As the pattern of militia and army service settled down in September 1914, the organisation stepped up its efforts by opening canteens and rest rooms or tents at the various arsenals and barracks and at Fort Regent. In 1915, the YMCA, which had the Dean of Jersey, the Very Reverend Samuel Falle, as its president, would also strongly support the Jersey Company by providing bibles and gifts to the departing volunteers and posting weekly newspapers and regular 'comfort' parcels to the men at the front. This idea of 'comforts' for the troops quickly took hold. The YMCA or another organisation would launch an appeal for blankets, socks, soap, tinned food, writing materials and anything else that they thought serving soldiers might appreciate. Once collected, the items were sorted, parcelled and despatched to Jersey soldiers serving overseas. They enlisted the newspapers to help in the appeals, and they responded wholeheartedly to the campaigns. In November 1914, the *Morning News* started one of its own called 'Smokes for Our Troops'. For a donation of just sixpence, readers could ensure a Jersey soldier received enough smoking materials to last him one week.

In October 1914, the Jersey Branch of the British Red Cross Society, started the most ambitious appeal so far. They asked for financial donations towards the cost of buying and running a motor ambulance for the British Army in France. The army had gone to war with mostly horse-drawn vehicles that had soon proved to be of limited effectiveness in the often broken and muddy conditions found at the front. The estimated cost of a motor ambulance was between £400 - £500. Islanders responded generously; so much so that over £1,000 was raised and before the end of the year, two Jersey ambulances were on their way to France. Christened *The Duke of Normandy* and *The Jersey*, they reportedly did excellent work in the Dunkirk area carrying 109 and 117 wounded respectively in December during their first week in action. By the end of the war, four more Jersey funded ambulances had joined them at the front.

While the attention of many public appeals was focused upon the men in the armed forces, there was also a swift realisation that members of Jersey's civilian population also needed assistance. As early as 7 August 1914, an appeal began towards providing financial assistance for the wives of French reservists, who had been largely left to manage after their husbands had departed. With many French families already living in deprived conditions, the need was obvious. A committee set up by the *Société Française de Bienfaisance* (French Benevolent Society) opened a collection and distribution office in St Helier's Beresford Street where members of the public could leave donations and needy families request assistance. The Lieutenant Governor was one of the first to donate, Rochfort giving five pounds to the appeal. In the weeks that followed, however, the campaign broadened its remit to include the families of British

Army reservists also – there being some reluctance expressed to giving money to a fund that solely supported French families.

The families of British and French servicemen could also appeal for financial aid from their parishes, whose Constables had established 'War Relief Committees' to assist those in difficulty. As a system of parish-based welfare already existed, this move made sense although it increased pressure on the level of property rates collected from parishioners to fund the additional assistance. One way of securing additional funds for relief efforts was for parishes to launch appeals of their own, with the most popular choice being a 'flag day'. From October 1914 until the end of the war, flag days were a regular feature of Island life with all manner of causes promoted and collected for through the public sale of flags or other small mementos. One of the first causes collected for was the Belgium Relief Fund set up to help refugees from that country who had escaped to Britain after Germany overran most of their homeland in the opening battles of the war. It was clearly a popular cause, raising £600 in a day. Thereafter, flag days supported appeals towards numerous other causes, among them the St Helier War Relief Fund, the *Croix-Rouge Française*, the YMCA Hut Day, the British Red Cross Day and even a Russian Flag Day. In March 1915, there was a St Patrick's Day Flag Day, in recognition of the Jersey Company's new links with Ireland, with shamrocks collected by the Jersey volunteers in County Cork and sent home to help raise money towards supporting both the contingent volunteers and other causes. Patriotic support for Jersey's soldiers was not just confined to the Island. The London Channel Islanders' Society had decided that from the beginning of the war it would suspend its usual entertainment programme in favour of arranging visits to wounded soldiers from Jersey and Guernsey in British hospitals.

While men in uniform were the cause of deserving the support of their community they were also the cause of changes to it, one of which in particular was not universally welcomed. One of the first changes to the daily life of some civilians was an amendment to the local licencing hours. Jersey publicans had enjoyed relatively relaxed licencing laws in the years before the war. They were permitted to remain open until ten o'clock in the evening all year round, with an hour's extension until eleven during the summer months in order to continue the hospitality provided to holidaymakers. Most of the Island's tourists had left on the outbreak of war, however, with little chance of them returning while the conflict continued. In their place were several thousand soldiers who, in the opinion of some, needed protecting from the temptation of alcohol. On 29 September, the States agreed a proposition requested by the Lieutenant Governor to move closing time forward by one hour to 9.00 pm. A move to retain 10.00 pm closing on Saturdays was briefly considered but soon rejected. One month later, in response to requests by the soldiers' commanding officers, Rochfort asked for closing time be moved forward again, this time to 8.00 pm. At the same time, all thought of extended hours in the summer disappeared. It may have been in line with similar British legislation that enabled the restriction of opening hours in public houses near army camps, but it would still cause financial woes for landlords, who would try unsuccessfully on a number of occasions to petition for longer hours. And it caused consternation among some Islanders, many of whom now had to change their drinking habits.

The stated position of protecting young soldiers against the evils of alcohol soon became somewhat incongruous however. In November, Islanders discovered that while all public licenced premises had to close at 8.00 pm, those run by the army were still staying open until 10.00 pm or even later. In the Grand Hotel, where the South Staffordshire Regiment was quartered, and at St Peter's Barracks, the military canteens and sergeants' messes continued to serve alcohol to soldiers and some invited civilians as late as 11.00 pm. After discovering what was going on, the Constable of St Helier, John Pinel, wrote indignantly to Rochfort in November saying that, 'It seems to me that this ought to be put a stop to, and that it is unfair to the civil population of the Island.'[1] The Lieutenant Governor responded with immediate effect: from 2 November, all military bars were to close at 8.00 pm. Soldiers and civilians were all in this together.

As well as a desire to keep soldiers from the perils of drink, the reduction in the opening hours of licensed premises was also part of a growing moral conviction that it was wrong for those at home to be enjoying themselves while other were fighting and dying on the battlefield. Crusades against alcohol and other excesses were nothing new at this time. Before the war, there had been a strong emphasis on abstinence and sobriety, led by church organisations such as the Salvation Army and other temperance movements. With the outbreak of war, support for temperance grew, driven by individual decisions to cease drinking while the fighting continued, by government initiatives from time to time and through the preaching of church ministers. In April 1915, following an appeal by King George for greater abstinence, the Dean of Jersey prayed that the whole Island should refrain from alcohol for the duration of the war. Fortunately, for those who continued to enjoy a drink, such a draconian policy never received official sanction from the States.

Those who enjoyed another type of entertainment were less fortunate, for a short time at least. In early August 1914, it became widely known that States were not planning to renew entertainment licences for St Helier's picture houses and theatres when they expired that month, meaning that all shows would cease from September. The States faced considerable public objection. 'It goes without saying that the best intentions lie at the back of this determination, but we seriously doubt the wisdom of this,' opined the *Morning News*. 'During the next few months life is likely to be depressing enough without being deprived of all opportunity for temporarily losing sight of our troubles.'[2] The authorities backed down and the idea of a complete closure was dropped on the condition that the venues finished their evening shows earlier and dropped matinee performances. The owners complied, licenses were issued and the shows went on. The matter of what was an appropriate level of entertainment during wartime was not dropped completely however.

In 1914, there were three main venues in St Helier, the Opera House in Gloucester Street, Wests in Peter Street and the Alhambra in nearby Phillips Street. All three put on a combination of film shows and live entertainment. And all three were popular and well attended, much to the disdain of some who believed that such distractions were also morally wrong during wartime. One of these was the Constable of St Helier, who seems to have embarked a crusade against so much public entertainment being available and in particular the need for town to have three venues. At the start of November 1915, he would insist on the Alhambra's closure, leaving just one venue in the east of town and one in the west. Despite a petition and in the face of employees losing their jobs, the closure went ahead resulting in just the Opera House and Wests open for business. The Alhambra would not be permitted to open again until the end of the war.

In addition to the official restrictions on public houses and places of entertainment, a host of other event cancellations from August 1914 onwards, including the annual Battle of Flowers and the Eisteddfod, had served to remind Islanders they were at war. There was serious consideration given to banning fireworks on 5 November, but the tradition of Bonfire Night was allowed when the War Office consented to it going ahead provided there were no rockets or other aerial fireworks. In some cases, the cancellations became permanent fixtures for the duration of the war, in others the actions taken were just a temporary measure, driven by the uncertainty of 1914. As the fighting settled into the stalemate of trench warfare in 1915, some public events such as garden shows began again, albeit with a more subdued tone.

While reducing public house opening hours and cancelling the Battle of Flowers had a highly visible impact on Jersey, far more profound and longer lasting changes were taking place, which were largely unnoticed by most Islanders. On 8 August 1914, the British Government had swiftly brought in a new Act designed to secure public safety and security during wartime and to allow the prosecution of the war to the utmost extent. The act, which was known as the Defence of the Realm Act or DORA for short, also gave the government and the military a number of wide ranging powers that were believed necessary for wartime. Once passed – which happened without debate – DORA was translated into a number of Defence of the Realm Regulations, which set out specific powers and offences under the Act. As a result of the new regulations, the military authorities gained sweeping powers to requisition, gain access to or even destroy private property if such an act was deemed necessary for the purpose of defence. The military could also order the removal of people who may interfere with that defence and arrest anyone refusing to comply. The DORA regulations forbade members of the population to obstruct the military, discharge a firearm near any military facilities, publish or communicate information that may be advantageous to an enemy and to take photographs of military installations or navy ships. The regulations gave the Police, acting under the direction of the military authorities, the right to arrest without warrant anyone suspected of committing an offence. Anyone found guilty of committing an offence under DORA could face a military court martial, with the maximum penalty allowed being death.

The Act was extended by the British Parliament on 28 August to encompass further regulations, including making it an offence to spread false information likely to cause discord or concern among the population and permitting the military to take over any factory or workshop engaged in making goods for the war effort. In September, DORA was extended again, and then amended a number of times throughout the war as more and more aspects of daily civilian life came under the control of the military.

Jersey's Lieutenant Governor and senior members of the States would have been aware of plans to introduce such measures as these in wartime. Britain's Committee for Imperial Defence, which had been formed in the early years of the twentieth century to consider the Empire's future military strategy and the associated defence policy for a possible war, had agreed the necessity for DORA and the initial Defence of the Realm Regulations in the years leading up to 1914. Jersey's senior government officials were privy to some of this important planning and so would have been aware of changes likely to occur on the outbreak of war. Nevertheless, how exactly DORA should be extended to Jersey was raised in a letter from the Home Office to the Lieutenant Governor on 18 August 1914. Referring to the new Act, the letter stated, 'I am directed by the Secretary of State…to say that he thinks that it would be desirable that the provisions thereof should be made applicable to Jersey either by registration of the Act and order by the Royal Court or by separate legislation by the States of the Island.'[3] It was polite language, but the message was clear: the provisions of DORA also had to apply to Jersey. After consultation with the Bailiff (who had only just made it back to the Island after his foreign adventures at that time), Rochfort signalled the Home Office that it was Jersey's intention to accept the Act and that regulations should come into effect in the same fashion as in Britain. There was no need for the States to pass new legislation; once issued by the Privy Council in Britain, the new Act and any subsequent changes would be simply registered in the Royal Court to come into force with immediate effect. There then seems to be have been a change of heart however. When the first regulations came before the Royal Court on 5 September, it was decided to refer them to the States for consideration. The assembly met on 7 September to discuss and agree a proposal that the DORA legislation should be extended to Jersey. The reality was that they had little choice in the matter. 'If the United Kingdom was prepared to submit to them, they, in Jersey, should be proud to follow suit as good patriots,' the Bailiff had stated to the Members. 'There is nothing in the regulations that could not be applied to Jersey; they certainly widened military powers, but everyone knew this was necessary in wartime.'[4] There was no dissent, only a question or two about whether anyone whose home was demolished by the military would receive compensation or not. Responding, Vernon rather vaguely assured Members all matters of compensation would be settled after the war – subject to Britain being on the winning side. They would have to put their faith in the Lieutenant Governor to act in the best interests of the people of Jersey, he announced, and in Britain's victory. With that matter closed, there was unanimous acceptance of the proposal.

As the Bailiff had stated, in accepting DORA, the Island's civil authorities, headed by himself, had handed over extensive powers to the Island's military authorities, led by the Lieutenant Governor who was designated as the 'Competent Military Authority' in the Island. It was of course the sensible act of any government in wartime, where defence and prosecution of the war understandably took priority over many aspects of established civil rights. For the States and the people of Jersey, it was not a step to take lightly however. The Bailiff had reminded States Members during the debate on 7 September that, despite the changed circumstances, 'they must be careful to defend their constitution and to preserve their right to initiate their own legislation.'[5] In the early days of early September 1914, with the war barely one month old, few would have given too much thought to the implications of military authority as opposed to civilian authority, or for that matter British interests set against those of Jersey. Yet from that point forward, civilian authority was subsidiary to that of the military; and Jersey's interests were secondary to those of Britain. Both were committed to the successful prosecution of the war, and to ensuring a respectful cooperation for its duration. But it did mean that the British Government and the States would on occasions be in dispute, and that invariably it was the States that came off worst. The introduction of the new rules meant that there would be challenging times ahead for both the States and individual Islanders. This became evident in the final days of 1914 when among the first to experience the full force of DORA was a baker's deliveryman from St Helier.

The first day of December 1914 had started out just like any other working day for Edward Single. The fifty-two-year-old, who was employed by Maison Rickett, had embarked on his normal round of customers in the parish of St Peter, dropping off bread and chatting to those that he encountered in his usual friendly fashion. Among the topics of conversation was the progress of the war. Having come from town, Single could be relied upon to bring the latest news. He reportedly mentioned to several people that he had heard that the Germans had captured Calais; apparently, the news was posted on a notice in the windows of the *Evening Post* office in St Helier. With his round complete, Single then went home and thought nothing more about the day. But the deliveryman's dramatic (but incorrect) piece of war news was passed on by some of those who had heard it, and it eventually came to the attention of someone with an official interest in such matters. On 29 December 1914, the Police went to Single's house in St Helier's Clairvale Road and placed him under arrest. He was handed over to the military authorities for trial by court martial, charged with creating alarm by spreading false reports in contravention of Article 21 of the Defence of the Realm Regulations. The maximum punishment for such an offence was death. If the people of Jersey had needed reminding of the extent to which the war was exerting its influences over their lives, then Edward Single's arrest on that day and subsequent trial certainly served the purpose.

Single appeared in front of a court martial convened at the Grand Hotel two days after his arrest. The court, with Major Hugh Johnston of the Royal Jersey Artillery as its president, opened with a number of statements from prosecution witnesses. Each claimed to have heard Single say that Calais had fallen to one hundred and fifty thousand Germans, and that the source had been a window poster in the *Evening Post* office. The majority stated that they had not believed or been concerned on hearing the news but when pressed by the prosecuting officer, one man admitted that the information had disturbed his wife. In his defence, Single claimed to have been told that the Germans were in Calais by one customer while on his round, and that it had been corroborated by others when he had repeated it to them. Nevertheless, he asked the court to take a lenient view because of his good character, and to release him from custody. After deliberation, the court martial found that Single was guilty as charged and it sentenced him to fourteen days' imprisonment, although sparing the additional punishment of hard labour.

The intent of the military authorities in bringing the prosecution against Single was clearly to set an example to Islanders. The deliveryman seems to have been the unfortunate 'sacrificial lamb' required to underline the seriousness of the new wartime rules and regulations. After all the evidence had been heard, the court president had even remarked that, 'the publicity given to that morning's proceedings through the medium of the press would be thought to be a sufficient deterrent to others.'[6] The fact that Rochfort commuted Single's sentence and freed him almost immediately suggests that by simply putting the poor man on trial the outcome was adequate. Edward Single's trial was clearly an effective deterrent since there were only a few subsequent prosecutions under the DORA regulations, although there were many threats of action if the military felt that their authority was being challenged.

As anticipated, the newspapers did report Single's trial although with little editorial comment. There was also surprisingly little public dissent over the matter – in the newspapers at least – which may have reflected a general realisation that offences against DORA would be taken seriously. This quiet may have also been a reflection of the pressure that was now being placed on newspaper editors to be careful as to what they were reporting. One of the earliest moves of the British Government had been to restrict freedom of the press when it came to reporting the war. DORA formalised this arrangement by introducing official press censorship for reporting events on the battlefield and on the home front also. The Lieutenant Governor was determined to ensure that those home front restrictions were extended to Jersey too. In November 1914 and again in January 1915, Rochfort wrote to the Attorney General, Henry Le Vavasseur dit Durell, enquiring whether there were grounds for prosecuting the editors of the *Evening Post* and the *Morning News* for their publication of material that he considered infringed the DORA regulations. In July, after receiving a complaint from the War Office, he went a step further. Citing an article in the *Evening Post* reporting the departure of a machine gun detachment of the South Staffordshire Regiment that he saw as a clear violation of Article 18 of the Defence of the Realm Regulations, the Lieutenant General demanded a prosecution of the newspaper's editor, Mr Walter Guiton. Rochfort underlined his complaint by providing a list of other alleged offences committed by the *Evening Post* since the start of the war. On 17 July 1915, Guiton duly appeared before a court and was fined one pound. As with the case of Edward Single, it seems that the act of prosecution rather than the punishment awarded was deemed a suitable deterrent.

Unlike in the case of Single and the newspaper editors, the implementation of DORA and its regulations affected most Islanders gradually rather than in a dramatic fashion. Among the first regulations to come into force was one closing down all private and experimental wireless systems. In August 1914, the Police received instructions to ensure any that existed in the Island were dismantled, and were given explicit guidance as to the aerial arrangements to look for if they suspected that anyone was continuing to use their equipment. Given the limited use of such apparatus at the time, the effect of such a rule was minimal, although it was a blow for the Jesuit community at Maison St Louis. They had been conducting specific meteorological and scientific experiments that relied upon a time signal transmitted from the Eiffel Tower in Paris. Unable to access the signal, their work had to stop and it would be 1919 before they could recommence.

Other forms of communication came under scrutiny, including some that were less sophisticated than wireless. In May 1915, a regulation restricting the ownership, transport and release of homing pigeons came into force, the perceived risk being that pigeons could carry illicit messages to and from the Island. The draconian measure – to their owners at least - was to confine all pigeons to their lofts for the duration of the war and to require owners to register their birds with the newly created post of Pigeon Officer. In addition to issuing permits, this official had the responsibility of monitoring the activities of the Island's four hundred or so pigeon fanciers. As the war continued, it would become a thankless task, with growing frustration among owners at a policy that they believed was ruining prize racing birds through a lack of exercise. The officer appealed to the Lieutenant Governor on their behalf, asking for permission to organise just one race to Jersey from Guernsey or Alderney. The answer was a polite but firm no; the requirements of national security as set out in DORA came before the well-being of pigeons and their owners.

While there may have been some questions over the rational for banning private wireless equipment and restricting the release of homing pigeons, these regulations and their implementation were reasonably straightforward. When it came to certain other DORA regulations, there was more ambiguity. One, for example, prohibited the photographing of military and naval installations, or creating images that may be beneficial to the enemy. In 1915, there were concerns raised in Britain that certain picture postcards might be contravening this regulation. Any that featured military ships or aircraft, or which showed fortifications, harbours and other prominent landmarks may have proved useful to someone gathering intelligence on Britain and its defences. As a result, the decision was made that it was necessary to check all postcards before they were published. The requirement also extended to the small picture cards included in cigarette packets. Merchants found to be selling any such products that broke the regulation risked having their stock seized and were likely to be prosecuted under DORA.

In Jersey, these new regulations on the sale of postcards proved to be a cause of confusion at the outset and remained so throughout the war, and not just among the shop proprietors. Soon after the regulation came into force, the commanding officer of the South Staffordshire Regiment found that it was necessary to ask whether the planned regimental Christmas card, which showed Fort Regent, was allowed or not. The local branch of Boots the Chemist asked for clarification as to what exactly was allowed and what was not after receiving a warning about the selling of prohibited photographs. 'As we are not quite certain which subjects to withdraw, we enclose a complete series of local view postcards and we kindly ask you to mark those that are prohibited.'[7] The response was ambiguous, although it was noted that Corbière Lighthouse, on the Island's south-western corner, should be considered a prominent building and therefore photographs of it should not be published. Boots were not alone in struggling to understand the rules, although the consequences for others could sadly be far more personal and distressing. Islanders regularly sent postcards to friends and relatives serving in the armed forces, and would receive the same in return. Those postcards found to show prohibited images were stopped from time to time and never reached the intended recipient. For some, it may have may have been the last communication that they ever sent or should have received.

Slowly but steadily, these and numerous other DORA regulations entered into and affected the daily lives of Islanders. Among them there were tighter controls on firearms and ammunition sales (including restrictions placed on the sale of guns to women), the storage of petrol was prohibited, shop opening hours were reduced, trading with the enemy was strictly forbidden. Travel became more difficult from 1 December 1915, with the introduction of a requirement for Islanders to have passports or permits to enter or leave Jersey. This caused considerable uproar because Islanders had traditionally not had been required to have passports when travelling to and from Britain. It was wartime, however, and such rules were pointed out as being necessary. Remarkably, some of the restrictions imposed remain in force today. Prior to the First World War, cocaine and opium were legal drugs and freely used for medicinal and recreational purposes. As part of the same drive to limit alcohol and other stimulants for soldiers and workers, DORA Regulation 40b banned the sale of cocaine, opium and other such drugs without a prescription. That legislation continued after the war ended, along with a number of other wartime restrictions much to the dismay of those campaigning for civil liberties.

While most DORA regulations only affected individuals and groups, there were some that had a far wider impact. One such regulation imposed restrictions on public and private lighting. Although air raids and blackouts are usually associated with the Second World War, they were an aspect of civilian life in the First World War as well. Before 1914, the world was well aware of Germany's Zeppelins, there having been no secret made over their development and potential use in wartime. While the Zeppelin threat may not have materialised in the opening weeks of the war, it had not gone away. The first effective attack from the air came on the night of 19/20 January 1915, when two Zeppelins dropped bombs on a number of Norfolk towns and villages, killing four civilians as a result. A few months later, London was targeted, and by the end of 1915, it had suffered twenty raids resulting in nearly two hundred deaths. Furthermore, Britain's towns and cities were not only under attack from the air. In December 1914, German warships had approached the country's east coast under the cover of darkness and bombarded the ports of Scarborough, Hartlepool and Whitby, causing considerable damage and leaving over one hundred dead.

After recovering from the initial sense of shock and outrage caused by these attacks, Britain had taken steps to protect against future raids. One of the preventative measures was the introduction of blackout regulations. These required that homeowners and organisations shade their lights from a specified hour in the evening and to cover any lit windows. Public street lighting was to be dimmed or turned off while the carriages of trains, trams and buses had to be fitted with window blinds. The new regulations were strictly applied in London, which remained the prime target for Zeppelin raids. Elsewhere, local authorities had flexibility as to what extent they implemented the regulations. In some locations, such as the east coast towns under threat of naval bombardment, the approach was to apply the regulations rigorously, while others adopted a more relaxed regime. In Jersey, much to the dismay of many Islanders, the Lieutenant Governor took the matter seriously when the new regulations had come into effect in March 1916.

DORA had already put in place a regulation against the showing of lights in the vicinity of a harbour, leading to Leswick Forbes of St Aubin being convicted and fined one pound for such an offence in August 1915. There had also been restrictions on public lighting put in place by that time, although not for reasons of security at first. Powered by gas extracted from stocks of imported coal, the hours that street lights were lit had been reduced following concerns over the continuing availability of fuel stocks. But from March 1916, in view of a growing Zeppelin and naval threat, Rochfort insisted upon further public lighting restrictions and extended it to lights in homes and other buildings. From then on, all lights that were visible from the sea and on the seashore had to be obscured or extinguished by eight o'clock each evening, except on Saturdays when an extra hour was allowed. One month later, the order was extended to all lights that reflected on streets or roads in the town of St Helier, and in the St Aubin, Georgetown, Millbrook, First Tower and Beaumont areas. Some people struggled to comply. The headmistress of the Ladies' College in St Helier, Phyllis Good, appealed to the Attorney General for advice. 'Under the new lighting regulations we are compelled to darken over fifty windows in this building and the cost of doing this will be very heavy…With regard to the dormitory windows which, after 8.00 pm, are lit up only for about twenty minutes…do you think the present system of hanging black screens over the gas globes would be sufficient?'[8] In another appeal, a local minister asked to be allowed to keep one outside light on after eight in the evening so that his parishioners leaving church could safely negotiate the steps leading down from the main door. The answer to all such enquiries was a regrettable no – if he allowed one appeal, Rochfort explained, he would have to consider all.

There was scrupulous investigation of any infringements of the lighting restrictions. Both the paid and Honorary Police approached premises seen showing lights after 8.00 pm and would instruct the occupants to cover the source. Reports of uncovered lighting were investigated, sometimes by means of a 'stakeout' while waiting for the offending light to reappear. Most cases appear to have been resolved with just a few words, although on at least one occasion an uncooperative person spent a night in the cells for failing to follow orders.

The decision to enforce these new lighting restrictions on Islanders was made without any reference to their elected representatives in the States of Jersey. The same was true for the other regulations mentioned along with new ones that were despatched from the Home Office to the Lieutenant Governor with monotonous regularity. The States had no part to play in their implementation because that was the understanding reached with the British Government at the outset, albeit under some pressure. Changes to DORA and its regulations were simply registered in the Royal Court as they arrived and were to come into effect immediately. On a very few occasions only were there interruptions to the implementation of new legislation, principally as a result of administrative oversights or the need to clarify one or two points. The arrangement was clear: while the military authorities ensured the defence and security of the Island as part of the overall scheme for national defence, the States continued with the day-to-day running of the Island. On a few occasions only, would there be a need for the military authorities to directly involve the States in order to bring about a change. That is not to say, however, that the States of Jersey was not deeply involved in the war effort from the very start.

When war broke out, it was considered unnecessary to make any changes to the structure of the States or to its way of conducting business to allow for the new circumstances, and this would largely remain the case for the next four years. The States continued to function through a number of separate Committees with specific responsibilities. It was the role of these Committees to consider and propose new legislation to the assembly, and to oversee the execution of existing legislation in the Island – in other words to run the public services. The Committees encompassed a multitude of functions, including running the harbours, providing public assistance and administering the so-called lunatic asylum at St Saviour's Hospital. Throughout the war, the most prominent were the Island Defence Committee and the Finance Committee. Among the responsibilities of the Defence Committee was the organisation and running of the Militia, although direct control had diminished subsequent to the changes brought about by the 1905 Militia Law. The Finance Committee had the responsibility for the States revenues and expenditure. It was fortunate for Islanders that both Committees had a wealth of experience through years of political service, a fact that would undoubtedly help maintain stability throughout the four years of war.

The States had certainly come through the opening days of the war and the early weeks that followed outwardly displaying calmness and a business-like attitude to getting on with things, this despite the absence of the Bailiff's usual strong leadership at first. Yet behind the scenes, the first government crisis of the war had soon built up and needed urgent action to resolve. Within a few weeks of its mobilisation, the cost of calling up the Militia to defend the Island had threatened to bankrupt Jersey. Although service in the Militia was gratuitous in principle, the States had made a decision that from the very outset Militiamen should receive pay for the days that they spent on duty and voted £10,000 to cover the expense. Thus a major was paid sixteen shillings per day, for example, a sergeant three shillings per day and a private received one shilling and sixpence. In addition, there were field allowances for officers and separation allowances paid to all married Militiamen below the rank of sergeant, with four pence per day for a wife and two pence per day for each child. On top of this, there were the daily running costs incurred through the maintenance of Militia facilities. The average cost was soon running at between £1,100 and £1,500 per week, none of which had been in the Defence Committee budget for 1914. And there was little in reserve it seems. 'It is a matter of urgency that the States should be in a position almost immediately to raise part of the money required,' wrote the Bailiff on 18 August, 'as funds at their disposal towards the cost of mobilisation are practically exhausted.'[9]

The solution put forward by the Finance Committee was a loan. The States agreed to raise this through the issuing of government treasury bonds – an almost unprecedented move - to the value of £50,000. The term would be one year with an interest rate of 4 percent. Given the urgent requirement for Militia funding, the bonds would only be offered to local banks as opposed to a public issue that would have involved a far more lengthy process. When the banks had agreed to take up the offer, the only remaining hurdle was that the bond required a new Act by the States to authorise its creation – which was duly agreed on 11 August – and then for the Act to be sanctioned by Britain's Privy Council. But the Clerk of the Privy Council, a Mr Almeric Fitzroy, decided to refer the matter to HM Treasury for consideration, who responded by asking a series of questions on the matter. Although the Treasury had no direct responsibility for financial matters in Jersey, they were rightfully interested in ensuring that the Island's government was acting prudently. It all took time, and an exchange of several letters to progress. Clearly anxious to resolve the situation before the money ran out, the Bailiff bypassed the usual communication channel through the Lieutenant Governor by sending a telegram directly to the Home Office on 29 August. 'Funds now exhausted and absolutely necessary to raise money immediately by treasury bonds as suggested…'[10] The telegram worked as a letter sent that same day announced that the Privy Council would ensure the Act received Royal assent in the following week. The Finance Committee could proceed with arranging the bond.

There had been a suggestion that the States could pay for its new borrowing through the introduction of an additional Island-wide rate, or tax. The move was resisted, partly because there was hope that the Militia mobilisation would not continue for much longer and partly because of an apparent desire to minimise the impact of the war on Islanders. It was a commendable gesture, and indicative of the approach that the Bailiff and the States would maintain for as long as possible, even in the face of DORA and the wider war. In some respects, it is evident that there was some self-interest in this; no one wanted to see the advances and economic success that Jersey had made in the years leading up to 1914 destroyed by rash wartime changes. Like Alexander Coutanche who followed as Bailiff during the Second World War, Sir William Vernon appears to have chosen a position of safeguarding Islanders and their rights, while cooperating with the military authorities – albeit that the military authorities he was dealing with were British and benevolent rather than the enemy and occupying as was the situation between 1940 and 1945.

Nevertheless, neither the Bailiff nor the States could do much to mitigate the impact of DORA and its regulations on Islanders. For a small number of Islanders this was to become patently clear through the implementation of the most controversial and thoroughly oppressive regulations of them all.

7 THE ENEMY AMONG US

The treatment and fate of Jersey's 'Alien' community

At the beginning of November 1914, Mr Pitman had been on duty in the relay office of the General Post Office in St Helier's Broad Street. Among the Morse code messages passing through the equipment that evening had been one that happened to catch his attention. Pitman had detected the question being asked by an unknown source: 'Any naval news tonight?' Ordinarily, this innocuous request would have meant little. But this was wartime, and Pitman's suspicions were immediately aroused, particularly when his enquiry message requesting the person asking the question to identify themselves received no reply. He checked with the next 'sending station' on the line from London, which was in Exeter, but they were unable to say from where the message had originated. Aware of the possible implications of the question, Mr Pitman reported it to his superiors. It seemed that some person or persons unknown were interested in potentially sensitive military information concerning the Channel Islands.

Jersey's military authorities began an immediate investigation, which failed to pinpoint the transmitting source of the mysterious question, or to uncover any evidence as to who had asked the question and who was supposed to reply. But the fact that it had been sent was taken very seriously, not least because there was already a suspicion at Military Intelligence in London that there was 'some kind of leakage in Jersey'.[1] As a result, the investigation widened to consider possible sources for any type of security leaks. It did not take long to pinpoint a possible weakness that someone who wanted to could exploit. Could a spy be listening to potentially secret communications passing over the international telegraphy network that ran through the Island?

Jersey had possessed an electric telegraph connection with the British mainland via an undersea cable since 1858, the route running north from the small bay of Plemont in the north-west of the Island via Guernsey and Alderney to Portland in Dorset on the opposite side of the Channel. One year later another cable was installed between Fliquet Bay on Jersey's north-east coast and Pirou across the water in Normandy, which now provided the Island with a direct connection to Europe as well as providing a route for telegraph messages between Britain and France. The importance of these links was not lost on the military, particularly during the development of plans to send the British Expeditionary Force across the Channel in the event of war. Soon after that war broke out, there would be a decision to enhance Jersey's important undersea cable network links in order to improve the reliability of the connections. Britain had seized the opportunity to sever the German undersea cables travelling through the English Channel. One of these, which ran from Germany to New York via the Azores, was hauled up, cut and then diverted to create a second connection between Jersey and Britain, with the cable ends landed in the Island at Plemont once more and the other at Dartmouth in Devon. Furthermore, between the Island and France a new cable was laid, coming ashore at Grève D'Azette on the Island's south-east coast, and at Cancale near to Saint-Malo in Brittany.

In early September, the decision to invest time and effort into enhancing the network between Jersey, Britain and France must have seemed vindicated as the German advance into northern France threatened the more direct lines of communication between London and Paris. Yet with the extra reliance on Jersey as a point of interconnection between Britain and its army, and between the governments in London and Paris, there was also an increased need for extra security. It was recognised that an unauthorised interception of sensitive communications passing through the Island could have dire consequences, particularly if that information fell into the hands of enemy sympathisers. One way to make an interception was by tapping into the telegraphy network as it traversed the Island. Open overhead cables were found in various places between the landing points at Plemont, Grève D'Azette and Fliquet and the main telegraphy office in St Helier, which was located in Broad Street*. Local experts pointed out that where these open cables existed, someone with knowledge and appropriate equipment could easily intercept messages travelling over the wires. After Mr Pitman's report of a suspicious message in November, the military authorities urgently investigated possible locations for unlawful interception. Suspicions quickly focused on the cables running between the landing point at Fliquet and the harbour at Gorey from which point they continued to St Helier alongside the tracks of the Jersey Eastern Railway. Slung between wooden poles, the open cables ran through sparsely populated farmland and along quiet stretches of hillside. Moreover, as a report commissioned to investigate possible security risks pointed out, this was a part of the Island where 'suspects seem to be spread all along the line…'[2]

It was a remarkable claim because until the outbreak of hostilities a few months earlier, the suspects in question had been living quiet lives as part of the community. Yet by November 1914, fortunes of war had materially changed their status. Overnight, they and more than one hundred other Islanders had acquired the label and stigma of being classified as 'enemy aliens'.

The First World War would have an unfortunate impact on many different

---

* The building remains in use as the Island's main post office at the present time.

civilian groups during the course of its four years and in those years that followed. One of those most deeply affected were people who found themselves caught by the declaration of war living or working in a country now hostile to their nation. Declared 'enemy aliens', they would immediately come under suspicion as acting against the interests of Britain, regardless of how long they had actually lived there or what contribution they had previously made to its society. And while the civil liberties of all would be restricted as a result of the wartime Defence of the Realm (DORA) regulations, the rights of so-called enemy aliens would largely disappear. In their place were constraints, reservations, harassment and, ultimately in many cases, confinement or expulsion.

In one of its first steps after declaring war on Germany, the British Government rushed in a new Act to deal with foreign civilians living in Britain. The Aliens Restriction Act was passed on 5 August 1914. Under its strict terms, anyone designated an alien – that is to say anyone deemed not British by birth, parentage or nationalisation – had many of their liberties immediately suspended. They had to register with their local Police station, were to strictly limit their movement and needed to demonstrate a good character at all times along with a knowledge of English. Yet while all non-British nationals were considered aliens under the provisions of the act, its real target were those from countries Britain was then at war with. For the most part this meant Britain's German community, which numbered around sixty thousand people in 1914, and to lesser extent, the smaller number of Austro-Hungarian citizens living in the country. The new law would automatically extend to Jersey, under the arrangements made to implement the DORA regulations. As a result, there were immediate steps taken to deal with the threat believed to be posed by any enemy aliens living in the Island.

Until the war had started, few Islanders would have given much thought as to whether the Island's Germans and Austro-Hungarians represented any kind of threat. Indeed, it would have been far easier to overlook their existence alongside the mass of French 'aliens' visiting and living in Jersey. The one hundred or so members of the Island's German community (although community is probably too strong a word given they appeared to have had little in common save nationality), and far smaller Austro-Hungarian one, were mostly long-term residents who had come to Jersey for work, for leisure or in some cases through disillusionment with their own country. Among them were those who served in the Island's hotel and restaurant trade, including Gottlobb Nordbruch who had managed the Royal Hotel in St Helier's David Place for many years, and Ludovicus Frohmann, a well-known headwaiter at the nearby Hotel de l'Europe in Mulcaster Street. Others had jobs or businesses in banking, tailoring and other skilled professions. Most were married, almost all to wives of British, French or Jersey nationality, they were generally middle-aged or retired and possessed the means required to live a comfortable life in the Island. Until, that is, their world turned upside down with the Alien's Restriction Act coming into force.

The rupture of diplomatic relations between the warring nations left those foreign nationals who were living or working in an enemy country isolated from family, friends and dependents at home as transport and communication services were suddenly restricted or terminated. They were also left without political rights or representation, although the conventions of war did make some allowances for this. On 6 August 1914, the American Consular Agent in Jersey, Edward Renouf, assumed responsibility for the protection of the Island's German residents. As a neutral country at that time, the US Government had agreed to help safeguard German interests and subjects in countries that were now hostile to them. In compliance with the newly introduced Aliens Restriction Act, all enemy aliens in the Island had now to register with him. One of Renouf's first acts was to organise a meeting, which was attended by seventy-eight German nationals and five Austro-Hungarians, at the Town Hall on 20 August in order to ascertain whether any of them needed urgent financial assistance. The group – probably brought together for the first time – agreed that they would work to help any of their fellow countrymen suffering hardship as a result of the changed circumstances. Clearly anxious to impress a willingness to cooperate with their now hostile local government, they furthermore agreed to offer services as interpreters should Britain send prisoners of war to Jersey. In response, the local authorities asked for the group's pledge that their activities would not aid Germany or Austria-Hungary in any way, but be directed solely at assisting local members of their community. In the meantime, there was a move to put the necessary measures in place to monitor this newly defined group of potential security risks.

Under the powers conferred by the DORA, responsibility for all the Island's aliens – enemy as well as those deemed friendly - fell to the Lieutenant Governor. One of his first steps was to deal with those individuals considered to be the highest threat. Although a number of young men from Germany and Austria-Hungary had left the Island on or immediately before the outbreak of war, five at least remained including engineer Franz Linder and Anton Tauber, an Austrian waiter who had been overheard expressing pro-German views. Rochfort immediately ordered the arrest of this group and their despatch under military escort for internment in Britain. The British Government had established internment – that is the detention of people without trial – as a means to deal with enemy aliens deemed as being too dangerous to remain in the community, and a number of internment camps were established throughout the country. They were effectively prisoner of war facilities, complete with guards, fences and watchtowers. Some indeed were used to hold both enemy civilians and military personnel, although there was a clear distinction made between the two types of prisoner with generally better conditions for those incarcerated because they had had the simple misfortune to be living in Britain when war broke out. The largest was the huge Knockaloe Moar Camp built on the Isle of Man, which in 1916 would hold nearly twenty-five thousand internees. It took a while to fill, however, as there was generally more tolerance of enemy aliens staying in the community in the early days of the war, albeit under strict supervision.

After disposing of those men considered the highest risk, Rochfort's next step was to turn his attention to dealing with the enemy aliens that had been permitted to remain in the Island - for the time being at least. Recognising the importance of this task, and its potentially wide-ranging scope, he had soon sought to establish formal arrangements for its execution. On 9 September 1914, he informed the Bailiff that he was creating a new post, that of Aliens Officer, and that he had appointed Arthur Luxon to fill it. Pointing out the Island's proximity to France, Rochfort stated that there was the potential for aliens to land in Jersey with ease. Furthermore, he concluded, 'we have a good many aliens…resident here and it is a matter of importance all should be registered and suspicious cases be kept under surveillance…'[3] He was equally firm on where responsibility should lie for paying Luxon, who was a former honorary policeman. The costs associated with the new Aliens Officer would have to be met by the Island, the Lieutenant Governor announced, especially since the British Government had politely declined an invitation to pay for his salary and expenses.

Luxon had not hesitated to get on with his important new duties, even while waiting to hear who would eventually pay him. Despite the daunting and onerous nature of what needed doing, he set about his new role efficiently and zealously. As early as September 1914, he had started sending a stream of reports on alien activities to the Jersey District Office and the attention of Colonel J. Western, who was serving on the Lieutenant Governor's staff and operating in a delegated capacity for Rochfort. Western's role was monitor the reports for incidents and events requiring the attention of his superior. Considering the volume of reports Luxon generated, there was a substantial amount of information for him to sift through. Among the most important of Luxon's duties were the identification, registration and monitoring of all aliens in the Island. This included both those living there and those who were visitors, although measures adopted at the outbreak of war to prevent unnecessary people movement had reduced numbers of the latter. His remit included aliens regarded as both 'enemy' and 'friendly'. Those deemed friendly were people who came from countries allied to Britain, such as France and Belgium, and from neutral countries including Holland, Spain and Portugal. Yet even friendly aliens living in the Island had to give their details to the newly created Aliens Registration Office that had been established in less than adequate conditions at St Helier's Town Hall. 'The office is so situated that it is perforce a passageway to an inner office which is used for other business,' complained Luxon in a letter to the Attorney General. 'There is no counter or desk upon which to write; we only have a round table which is now not at all suitable, as the public who are continually calling at the office on business have our books and confidential papers spread out to their view.'[4] Despite the cramped workspace, Luxon seems to have managed to remain on top of his task however.

Keeping track of those aliens visiting the Island was achieved through the scrupulous inspection of the arriving passenger lists and by instructing hotel and guesthouse owners to report details of all foreign guests. On 2 October 1914, this diligence resulted in the first Royal Court case against someone who had failed to register. Irvingston Herbert Hakin was an American citizen, who claimed to be from New York. He had aroused suspicions, having paid his hotel bill with a cheque drawn on a Cologne bank and by the fact he could speak perfect German. Although the charge of non-registration would be dropped, Hakin was detained on suspicion of being a hostile enemy alien and he was duly sent to Britain for internment.

While most aliens complied with the new regulations, Luxon was kept busy trying to identify a small number of those living in Jersey who had decided to not register. For some, it may have been an oversight or misunderstanding, while others must have felt generally aggrieved at the need to do so. Rochfort's concern was that among these there might be some with more sinister motives for not coming forward. So Luxon made it a priority to find them, using a variety of detection methods. In the first place, there was the crude assumption that anyone with a foreign sounding surname could be an alien, especially if that name happened to sound German. While it was an approach that appeared to have yielded some results, it also led to considerable consternation and indignation among many summoned to the Town Hall in order to explain themselves. In December 1914, Luxon received a stinging letter from the grandmother of fourteen-year-old Ruth Muller after she had learned that the girl had been asked to attend the Aliens Registration Office and explain her background and that of her younger brothers and sisters. 'These children were born in British India of British parents and no stretch of the imagination would call them aliens,' objected their grandmother, who was the children's guardian while they were living in Jersey. 'They have a foreign name, and perhaps many generations ago their ancestors may have been foreigners, but as far as I know they have no relatives that are not British.'[5] In the face of such wrath, the investigation into the Muller children appears to have been quickly dropped.

Luxon could also rely on information passed to him by members of the public, some of whom were clearly inspired by the swirling spy stories and jingoistic writings in a number of the national newspapers on the subject of enemy aliens. Writing to the Lieutenant Governor in 1915, an anonymous individual expressed surprise to see one Henry de la Vaux at a concert. 'This [so] called gentleman besides spying our doings is corresponding with a German agency via Lyons and Geneva,' the letter claimed before adding an appeal. 'Is there no means to get rid of undesirable Frenchmen?'[6] For some of the aliens, the only way to bring a quick end to the suspicion and harassment was by changing their surname. Mrs Charlotte Möschke of St Helier, for example, went to great lengths to achieve this. Despite being British born, she was under strong suspicion due to intercepted letters from her German husband, Otto, which had contained vehemently anti-British views. He lived in South Africa, while Mrs Möschke and their three children had remained in Jersey. Given the separation, it took considerable effort on her behalf to convince the Jersey and British authorities to allow a name change. Others went further, deciding that the best course of action was to seek naturalisation as British subjects and to remove any taint of enemy alien identity permanently.

Luxon had another important though controversial method for monitoring any suspicious characters and registered aliens. From soon after the start of the war, Jersey had a censor who was reading their letters and telegrams. Censorship was widely used by all governments during the First World War as a means of controlling the flow of news and information. Press censorship was widely practiced. Postal censorship – that is the lawful interception and reading of private mail – was considered equally important. In Britain, a postal censorship system run by the General Post Office but controlled by British Military Intelligence was up and running within days of the outbreak of war. On 4 August 1914, the Lieutenant Governor received notification from the Home Office that a similar arrangement must be put in place for Jersey. 'I am directed by the Secretary of State to say that he had issued a warrant to the Postmaster General under which the Postmaster at Jersey will be authorised to submit to the Telegraphic Censors letters addressed to certain foreign residents in the Island.'[7] Recognising the serious and sensitive nature of such actions, the letter concluded by saying, 'the power this warrant gives you should be used with the greatest discretion; and any private matter not of a compromising nature…must on no account be seen by or disclosed to any person other than the Censors.'[8]

The man appointed as Jersey's Censor, and thus charged with exercising the greatest discretion in respect of private letters, was Edward Bishop, a seventy-year-old former colonel in the Indian Army. Like the Aliens Officer, with whom he would work very closely, his was an enormous undertaking, although two assistant censors joined Bishop's department to help along with two supporting clerks in due course. Colonel Bishop would also have a team of interpreters who laboured to translate the many languages used in the stream of correspondence under suspicion. During the first twelve months of the war alone, the translators examined thousands of letters regarded as suspicious, including all postal correspondence to and from France. Initially, they also reviewed telegrams coming to and being sent from the Island, although on the advice of the British Government, this was modified in September 1914 to address telegrams between Jersey and France only. Those going to the Britain were considered 'inland' and therefore not subject to censorship.

The process of censoring letters, and to a lesser extent telegrams, provided the perfect opportunity to monitor the activities of enemy aliens. Both inbound and outbound letters were opened and scrutinised for anything that could indicate pro-enemy activities. Anything suspicious that was noted in the correspondence was reported to the military authorities who in turn passed it on to the Aliens Officer to investigate further if it was considered necessary. As those under suspicion generally knew that their letters were being opened or at least monitored, there was a strong conviction that enemy aliens were using secret codes or other clandestine methods to evade the Censor. Any correspondence containing a random set of letters or numbers, for example, was sent for further analysis in an attempt to prove that it contained a hidden message. Other more elaborate methods of concealment were also suspected. The letter of one designated enemy alien, Albert Thielemann, was sent for analysis in June 1915 following a suspicion that it contained words written in invisible ink. The results were inconclusive, leading to a decision not to proceed with a planned prosecution.

When it came to monitoring alien correspondence, one of the biggest headaches for the Censor were the Island's Jesuit and other religious institutions. Among their students and staff there were a number of designated enemy aliens, although it was broadly accepted that given their vocation, the threat that they posed to security was a low one. Nevertheless, their letters were still subject to censorship, and there were some detected to be containing pro-German sentiments. With a reported five hundred letters per week emanating from these establishments, keeping on top of all correspondence proved a formidable challenge. In August 1915, the Censor suggested a compromise. All letters had to be signed by the writer in full – initials only were not permitted

- and the establishment's principal must inspect and counter-sign each letter before it was posted. And while there would be no restriction on the volume of letters sent, each should be limited to no more than two hundred words. The rules appear to have been only loosely followed, however, with the Lieutenant Governor having to write periodically and remind them to do better in order to avoid falling under suspicion of carrying out clandestine activities.

Part of the reason for trying to reduce the amount of time spent reading letters to and from those categorised as friendly aliens, was to allow the focus on those considered a high risk. From the start, there was a perceived threat to the Island's security, and there remained for most of the war a strong belief that some enemy aliens were up to no good in the Island, however fanciful the notion seemed. These beliefs had certainly strongly featured in Britain, where there was a growing sense of hostility towards enemy civilians living in the country, most notably directed at people of German origin. Years of pre-war military and colonial rivalry between the two countries had helped stir up tensions. Following the outbreak of hostilities, anti-German feelings soon increased. Agitated by newspaper reports of German atrocities against civilians in Belgium, the animosity grew into physical attacks on German civilians and the looting and burning of German shops and businesses in some of Britain's larger towns and cities. That level of disorder never spread to Jersey, perhaps due to a greater sense of tolerance towards foreign nationals and a greater respect for law and order. Yet there remained hostility directed towards anyone that was believed to be acting suspiciously, and that included most enemy aliens.

The spy fever that had gripped the Island during the early days of the war helped fuel suspicions that enemy agents and sympathisers were present and determined to act against British interests. Although the more fanciful spy stories soon waned, the relentless interest of the military authorities in enemy aliens helped maintain anti-German feelings against them. After spying, the widespread suspicion centred on a belief that people were signalling from the Island to enemy vessels lying offshore. German submarines had been increasingly active in the English Channel since the start of 1915, attacking and sinking vessels sailing to and from Britain. Despite the clampdown of DORA and the introduction of censorship, shipping timetables and destinations remained widely available in the Island and it led to a fear that enemy agents were signalling the information to prowling German vessels, or, as Mr Pitman heard on the telegram network, passing it on to others overseas. From all over the Island there came reports of mysterious lights shining out from the coast at night time. On 28 June 1915, for example, Private George Howard, a soldier serving in St Ouen's Bay claimed to have witnessed a clear exchange of signals between someone on the shore and a vessel said to be lying about a mile and half out to sea. After his attention was drawn to the vessel by strange lights, he claimed to have seen a flare go up that was answered by a similar flare launched from somewhere on the shore. 'The ship then signalled by means of a lamp,' Howard explained in a statement, 'and each signal was answered by a flare being dipped from the hillside.'[9] The alleged messaging went on for at least fifteen minutes and was also witnessed by local fisherman Albert Butel, who had lived in the area for twenty years and claimed to have never seen anything similar before.

In response, the Militia's West Battalion, which had responsibility for defending the area, sent out patrols at irregular hours in an attempt to discover whether or not something untoward was going on. Nothing was discovered, other than the usual lights present in the bay from uncovered farmhouse windows, while there was a suspicion that the lights out to sea may have come from a distant lighthouse. Nevertheless, the Lieutenant Governor took the matter seriously, expressing concern over why the Militia's strongpoints in the area had apparently not seen or reported the alleged signalling. 'Please warn the outposts in St Ouen's Bay that they have to very carefully watch should such signals be again displayed,' Rochfort instructed.[10] Although additional patrols went out for some time after the original report, no genuine evidence of signalling was ever discovered in St Ouen's Bay, or elsewhere for that matter.

The military authorities remained vigilant nonetheless, convinced there could be some in the Island determined find a way to assist the enemy. Heightening their determination was outside pressure from another source. The French admiral in command of the naval base at Cherbourg suspected that the Germans were secretly using the Channel Islands, and that enemy aliens living there were supporting clandestine activities. He petitioned the British Government to do something about it. 'I beg to request you to draw the attention of the Admiralty to the importance of the [Channel Islands] as a supply base for the German submarines and the absolute necessity to prevent that any information be furnished to our enemies by their compatriots who are still living there… It seems to me indispensable that greatest severity be adopted with regard to the measures taken as regards the residents of enemy nationality.'[11] The admiral's concerns were supported by *Monsieur* Jouve, the French Consul, who claimed that Jersey was suffering from the, 'very troublesome presence of numerous German subjects residing at large on the Island and who can perfectly well exercise espionage.'[12] In response, the Lieutenant Governor strongly refuted the claims. Rochfort had already established regular motor boat patrols around the Island and out to the offshore reefs of the Minquiers and Les Écréhous that lay between the Island and France to detect any possible clandestine activity, and introduced the monitoring of petrol imports to ensure that none was being passed on to the enemy. Moreover, he denied that any such spies existed in the Island, and strongly asserted that all enemy aliens present were under constant surveillance. Rather embarrassingly though, Rochfort did have to admit to one insinuation that involved him directly. 'It is true…that a German housemaid is in my employ,' he wrote to the Home Office in response to a query on the matter, 'she has been at Government House for five years without leaving the Island and is quite harmless.'[13]

The sense that Germans living in Jersey, both men and women, were harmless was not a view shared by all Islanders. In June 1915, suspicion fell on a Mrs Williams, or Emma Ramm-Thompson as she was also known, who lived in a house called Sans Souci located high up on a headland overlooking the Island's north-east coast. In a report received by Jersey District Headquarters in June 1915, a neighbour claimed to have seen signalling coming from Sans Souci, and that a corresponding signal had flashed back from the direction of the French coast opposite. Mrs Williams, the informant announced, 'was a German spy and a dangerous women.'[14] While this was one of many such denouncements, in the case of Mrs Williams the military authorities took the matter very seriously. She was not only a registered enemy alien and known to have German family connections, but also the overhead telegraph cable between Fliquet and Gorey that had been noted as a security risk ran past her property. The claims and circumstances were to lead to one of the most disturbing aspects of Jersey's First World War history.

Evidently, Mrs Williams' neighbours had had suspicions about what was going on at Sans Souci even before the war started. There had been rumours of strange equipment on the premises, and of meetings there with other known foreigners. It is also evident that after concerns had been raised about the security of the telegraph network, the military authorities took a closer interest in her activities. In common with other enemy aliens, however, after registration she had been permitted to remain in the community. When registering, she had given her name as Mrs Emma Ramm-Thompson, and claimed that she was the widow of Mr John Thompson, a British national, who had died in Essex some years earlier. The statement was to prove her undoing. In 1915, letters to Mrs Williams that were intercepted by the Censor revealed that in fact she was the wife of Karl Ramm, a German national who was still apparently living in Germany. Subsequent investigations revealed that some years earlier she had left Ramm, allegedly because of ill treatment by him, and begun a relationship with John Thompson, whom she never married. After his death, she had moved to Jersey with a Mr Williams, who had acquired Sans Souci as a home for them both. When Mr Williams subsequently died, Mrs Ramm had remained there, although under false pretences in eyes of the law.

Most damning of all, however, she had falsely declared such pretences on her alien registration form. It was the perfect excuse for the military authorities to remove the perceived threat to the telegraph cables posed by Mrs Ramm once and for all. On 29 April 1916, she appeared in the Royal Court, her identity now fully revealed, and charged with offences committed under the Aliens Restriction Act.

The Bailiff was in charge of the trial, and showed little sympathy towards her plea that she had not intended to do anything wrong or detrimental to the safety of the Island. Her advocate, who had only been appointed to the case a few minutes before her trial, did manage to offer an expression of deep regret on Mrs Ramm's behalf for giving the wrong name. Vernon accepted neither excuse nor apology. Noting where Mrs Ramm's property was situated, he was adamant that she posed a security risk and therefore should be removed from the Island. Moreover, under Jersey law she had not actually inherited the property, being the unmarried partner of Mr Williams, and therefore Sans Souci was forfeit to the Crown. He ordered Mrs Ramm's deportation and repatriation to Germany via England and Holland – which was the fate of those enemy alien women regarded as a security risk. But, prior to her removal from the Island, she would also have to serve a two-month prison sentence for making false statements on her registration papers.

Emma Ramm was not the only foreigner under suspicion of being up to no good in the Island. All enemy aliens were under scrutiny, with the military authorities prepared to seize upon any suspicion of wrongdoing. One of the most extraordinary and tragic episodes of Jersey's war focused the activities of two middle-aged German chemists and the alleged goings on in their homes. Edwin Kayser was a fifty-three-year-old German research chemist who had arrived in Jersey five years before the war started. He lived with his British born wife, Minnie, in a house in St Brelade's Bay, in which he had equipped a laboratory for carrying out scientific experiments. Prior to their arrival in Jersey, the Kaysers had resided in Britain and the US, and it was from the American company Proctor & Gamble that he received his work and a monthly salary.

Kayser was one of a number of German nationals living in St Brelade's Bay. From the war's outset, they were the subject of local rumours and gossip, with Kayser a focus of attention because of his laboratory, the presence of which had aroused lurid suspicions. A report from a Militia patrol that signalling lights has been observed coming from the area around Kayser's house simply fuelled matters. In September, the Police carried out a search of the house that confirmed the presence of the laboratory, but nothing to suggest that anything untoward was going on. Kayser insisted that his experiments were related to food production, and being undertaken for the benefit of a US company, not to anyone related to Germany. The explanation was accepted, although the Police did discover that Kayser, as a registered enemy alien, had contravened regulations by possessing a revolver and a car with petrol. For these offences, Kayser was tried and convicted under the Aliens Restriction Act at the end of October 1914. As well as a fine, his gun and car were confiscated and he had to report daily to the Police from that time on.

There the matter may have rested were it not for the determination of the Censor, Colonel Bishop, to prove popular suspicions that Kayser was acting on behalf of the enemy. His efforts appeared to come to fruition in a damning report submitted to the Lieutenant Governor in October 1915 that linked Kayser to another enemy alien in the Island. 'We are now almost able to confirm the suspicions that have long been entertained by us censors, and the general public, against two Germans – Kayser and Zimmerman,'[15] wrote Bishop. He went on to state there was strong evidence to suggest that far from conducting harmless experiments, Kayser was working on the production of dangerous explosives. Bishop had found witnesses who knew or had dealt with the German chemist and their evidence had suggested something sinister about his activities. Kayser had made certain casual comments in conversations that had aroused suspicions, and he had tried to order supplies and equipment that could have been used in the manufacture of explosives. In his report Bishop insinuated that Proctor & Gamble, while admittedly a US company, had some links to Germany. Furthermore, the Censor went on, there was another German chemist, fifty-two-year-old August Zimmerman, living a few miles away from Kayser. An intercepted telegram from Zimmerman had apparently been sent to a Swiss explosives company saying, 'Agree send proposals'. In the Censor's view, it was too much of a coincidence – both enemy aliens were clearly colluding and represented a threat to the Island's security.

The sensational claims led to a further search of Kayser's house and that of Zimmerman. In a surprise visit, the Police, accompanied by the Aliens Officer and the States' Official Analyst went through the properties, taking samples and looking for any sign of suspicious activities. Their subsequent report was conclusive: nothing was going on to suggest that either Kayser or Zimmerman were doing anything wrong. Moreover, Kayser had been in ill health for six months and had not worked, while Zimmerman did not have a laboratory. There was no evidence of collusion between the two chemists, who did not even appear to know each other. A further investigation by the Henry Le Vavasseur dit Durell, the Attorney General, found that the alleged witnesses were less than certain about their evidence and that the so-called Swiss explosives company actually dealt in medical dressings, the Censor having mistranslated the word 'sauter', which could mean both 'explosive' and 'wound covering'.

A report from the Attorney General suggested that Colonel Bishop had overstepped the bounds of his authority and had taken on what was clearly a Police matter. Rochfort agreed, and demanded an explanation from the Censor, who, in a series of letters and interviews, sought to justify his conclusions and demand recourse for what he felt were personal attacks on his integrity. Eventually, the row subsided, but the damage – as far as Kayser was concerned – was done. Local feelings against him had increased to the point where the Lieutenant Governor felt that the only option was to remove Kayser from this Island. In April 1916, Edwin Kasyer was interned in the Lofthouse Park camp in Yorkshire. His wife Minnie, being British born, was permitted to remain in Jersey. As for August Zimmerman, he too was allowed to remain in Jersey, but eventually sought voluntary repatriation in 1917, possibly because of the feelings of hostility against him.

Jersey may have got rid of Kayser, but it was not the last that the Island heard of him. Clearly feeling aggrieved, he soon began sending appeals to the Lieutenant Governor and the States. Minnie Kayser also wrote letters, on behalf of her husband. Could they be allowed to leave for some neutral country perhaps, or at least be interned in Jersey? Remarkably, even the Censor, perhaps feeling some remorse for his involvement in Kayser's arrest and incarceration, tried to intervene on the couple's behalf. In a letter to William Whitaker-Maitland, the Government Secretary, in August 1917, he noted the Mrs Kayser had recently had a serious accident to add to the anguish suffered as a result of her husband's internment. In Colonel Bishop's view, there would be no harm allowing Edwin Kayser to return home. But the Lieutenant Governor was unmoved. There were no facilities to intern Kayser in Jersey, it was announced, and it was considered to be too high a risk to allow him to return home. 'There is a popular prejudice against Mr Kayser's return to Jersey,' Whitaker Maitland wrote, 'and it is not considered that his return could be permitted, as it might lead to a disturbance in the neighbourhood of his residence.'[16] The letter concluded that this decision must be considered final, although this was certainly not accepted by the Kaysers.

The repatriation of Emma Ramm and the internment of Edwin Kayser took place at a time of increasing pressure to deal with anyone designated as being an enemy alien. While the initial focus had been against those individuals considered the most likely security threat, the net had been progressively widened to encompass all enemy aliens. Driving this was a growing, and officially sanctioned, anti-German feeling. The British Government seized upon the sinking of the liner RMS *Lusitania* by a German U-boat in May 1915, in which over one thousand civilians including women and children had lost their lives, as a graphic example of German barbarism. Subsequent official propaganda served to whip-up public outrage against Germany, with the obvious targets being those German civilians living in Britain. A spate of vicious riots directed against German homes, businesses and people followed in many cities. The rate of internment or repatriation of those enemy aliens still living in the community increased, partly to remove them from the community, partly to protect them from attacks.

Within months of the *Lusitania's* sinking, the Home Office wrote to Rochfort reiterating the official policy on enemy aliens. All men of military age should be interned forthwith. Any men that were above military age must be repatriated to Germany. All women should also be forcibly sent back to their home country, although, the letter admitted, this aspect of the policy was not being forcefully pursued in Britain. The only exemptions allowed were special cases, such as long-continued residence, inter-marriage or if the authorities were satisfied that the alien had 'become identified' with their adopted country. The final decision on this was in the Lieutenant Governor's hands, although an advisory committee in London would have to review and confirm the acceptability of any proposed exemptions. Anyone wishing to apply for exemption was required to complete a special form specifying the reasons why they should not be deported.

All except one of the Aliens in Jersey who were affected by the new conditions submitted a request to remain in the Island. Once their forms had been handed in, Rochfort considered these, along with a list of recommendations drawn up by the Attorney General in his role as Head of Police. The overall number of enemy aliens in the Island had decreased by then due to internments and voluntary departures that had already taken place. Excluding those in the Jesuit and other religious institutions, there were only fourteen men of military age present in the Island by August 1915, of whom nine were married to either British or French wives. Only one had a German wife. The recommendation of the Attorney General was that nine of these men should be interned, along with the one German wife. Of the remaining five, only two should definitely be permitted to remain in Jersey – there was doubt in the case of the other three. There were found to be nine men above military age, of whom all except one should be permitted to remain in Jersey. Of the eleven enemy alien women living in the Island, the Attorney General recommended eight exemptions from repatriation; the remaining three had either not appealed or were considered a threat. One of the latter cases, that of Mary Tischmeyer, it was noted that she should be allowed to sell her furniture before being forced to leave. The small number of enemy aliens still working or studying in the Island's Jesuit and other religious institutions remained a cause for special consideration. In line with British policy in such circumstances, they would be allowed to stay at liberty, but on the understanding that they remained confined to the premises of their institution and under the close supervision of their principal and only permitted outside if accompanied by a British subject.

Rochfort appears to have passed the Attorney General's recommendations straight on to the Home Office special advisory committee for endorsement. In a few cases they questioned the decisions, asking for more information on a number of individuals (including Emma Ramm who remained at liberty at that time), before acknowledging and accepting them in November 1915. Subsequent correspondence from the Home Office raised further questions, however. Was it strictly necessary to intern so many of the men of military age, for example; the Home Secretary had no real objections to letting at least six of those recommended for internment stay in the Island, subject to close monitoring of their activities. Such questions and options appear to have led to doubt in the Lieutenant Governor's mind over the wisdom of locking up or deporting a group of mostly middle-aged and patently harmless Islanders. Despite a letter from the Lieutenant Governor of Guernsey, General Sir Reginald Hart, in January that announced he had a 'batch of approximately twelve enemy aliens'[17] ready to send for internment and would Jersey like to send theirs along with this party, Rochfort back-tracked on his original recommendations. After further consultations with the Attorney General, he communicated to the Home Office that action would only be taken against four enemy alien women, who were now not resisting repatriation. Along with the child of one of them, they were sent from the Island to England in February 1916, and then on to Tilbury in Essex for transport to Flushing in neutral Holland. All other enemy aliens were now permitted to remain in Jersey, but conditionally. This meant that they could no longer work in hotels, the concern being they may overhear potentially sensitive conversations of visitors, and, as they were being frequently reminded, their continued liberty and presence in Jersey relied on them continuing to demonstrate exemplary behaviour. Any indication of malicious activity would result in arrest and internment or repatriation. For two enemy aliens, Arthur Madler and Charles Kroeggel, that appears to have been their undoing within weeks of the exemptions being granted. In February 1916, the Lieutenant Governor decided to intern both of them following a report from the Censor over the contents of their letters. They left the Island under escort for Alexandra Park internment camp in London. In April, Jacob Krudewig followed them, along with the unfortunate Edwin Kayser.

With the exception of Emma Ramm's deportation in June 1916, there appears to have been no further internments or forcible repatriations from the Island, although records are somewhat patchy. To Jersey's credit, both the governing authorities and the Islanders seem to have allowed some Germans to remain at liberty at a time when the national crusade against enemy aliens continued unabated. And to the credit of those German and Austro-Hungarians nationals who found themselves living in the Island during the war, there is no evidence to suggest that any were engaged in clandestine or hostile acts against Jersey or the British Empire. They had just happened to be in the wrong place at the wrong time, and all suffered to a greater or lesser extent as a result. They would continue to do so even after hostilities had ended in November 1918. After suffering the indignity of internment during the war, the fate of many enemy aliens was still to be repatriated even once the fighting was over. Britain was not ready to forgive or forget so soon after the horror of the trenches and the German U-boat campaign that saw the sinking of unarmed passenger liners.

Jersey too remained vindictive towards some of its former citizens after the fighting had ended. After spending nearly three years in an internment camp, Edwin Kayser was deported to Germany in February 1919. His wife joined him in January the following year, but unable to speak any German and unaccustomed to the culture, Minnie Kayser could not settle however. Between 1921 and 1924, Edwin Kayser would repeatedly petition the Jersey authorities, appealing for the chance to return to the Island in which he and his wife had evidently enjoyed living. Yet for each request he received a polite but firm 'No' in response. Clearly embittered, he asked for his confiscated revolver, car and petrol to be returned at least. The gun and the petrol, or at least the latter's value, were found and returned to him. The car, having languished outside the St Lawrence Arsenal for seven years, appears to have been beyond repair.

As for Emma Ramm, after the war she also wanted her confiscated goods back – in her case this being the house Sans Souci, its contents and some jewellery deposited with a local resident. In 1920, she received permission to return to Britain from Germany for three months only, from where she made her way to Jersey. But she was unable to persuade the person holding her jewellery to give it up, while as far as the local authorities were concerned, she had no right to her house or anything in it. Despite having clearly been party to the purchase of Sans Souci, she had done so in a false name, and, under the Jersey Law at the time, unmarried women could not inherit property from their partner. Furthermore, and most damningly, as an enemy alien she now could certainly not own property in Jersey. The house remained the property of the Crown, the Bailiff announced in a court case on the matter, and that Mrs Ramm had no right to remain in Britain more than the three months permitted. Without money or property, Emma Ramm was destitute. Vernon ordered her immediate deportation from the Island for a second time.

Emma Ramm was not a lady who was willing to give up on a cause, however, or to live with what she saw as a clear injustice. From her new home in Germany, she appealed at length to the British Government from 1921 onwards, and its officials entered into extensive correspondence with their counterparts in Jersey. Yet after much toing and froing, the matter was closed once more, with Britain accepting Jersey's case. In 1928, however, out of desperation, Mrs Ramm petitioned King George V to intervene on her behalf. 'I am now seventy-four and ailing…and have no relatives left either on my own or my late husband's side. I am thrown on poor relief, which at present amounts to sixty marks per month…From that abyss of pitiful destitution I raise my hands to Your Majesty for help.'[18] Her appeal had finally worked. Under pressure, the Island authorities accepted that, while the decision to seize Mrs Ramm's property was correct, it was perhaps overly harsh. They agreed to pay her an annual sum of £35, which represented the proceeds derived from the value of her estate in Jersey. The money would be sent if Mrs Ramm applied each year, but only on the condition that she proved to the British consulate in Germany that she was still actually alive. Sadly, for Mrs Ramm, it was all too little too late. In November 1928 she died, without ever having received a single penny.

If there was hostility towards Emma Ramm and her fellow enemy aliens during the war and afterwards, another and far larger group of Germans attracted the excitement, curiosity and even some jealously of Islanders. While the German military may not have succeeded in occupying Jersey during the First World War, German soldiers and sailors did arrive in the Island, albeit under very different circumstances than those of 1940 to 1945.

8 A CAMP BY THE SEA

German prisoners of war in Jersey

In the early hours of 20 March 1915, a crowd of curious Islanders had gathered near the entrance to St Helier Harbour's Albert Pier. Not deterred by the time or the cold layer of fog that was keeping the temperature below freezing that morning, this hardy group were determined to witness an event that had been long anticipated. They wanted to be the first in the Island to actually to catch a glimpse of the enemy against whom they had been fighting since August 1914. Rumours that a contingent of German prisoners of war would be arriving had stirred up considerable excitement, despite official attempts to keep the whole matter secret. 'The public have been on the "qui vive" to see something of the men against whom our troops and those of our allies are fighting,' declared the *Evening Post*, 'but despite the feverish anxiety…the military authorities took every care that the day and hour of the arrival of our German "visitors" would be kept as secret as possible…'[1] But the secret was out, as the presence of the curious spectators that morning demonstrated. And they got their reward not long after 6.00 am when a boat carrying the first batch of these so-called visitors passed through the harbour's pier heads and moored alongside the Albert Pier. Local curiosity as to who exactly were the Island's enemy was now to be satisfied.

The practice of capturing and imprisoning the enemy during wartime stretched back thousands of years. Once captured, however, the treatment received was something that had varied from army to army and from war to war. In 1907, in an attempt to civilise warfare and to spare soldiers and civilians from some of the worst excesses, an international peace conference held at the Hague in Holland had framed a series of rules to be followed by combatant nations. Among the articles of the Hague Convention there was a section that dealt with the treatment of prisoners of war. Both Germany and Britain were signatories to the 1907 Convention, and its predecessor that had been agreed in 1899. On the outbreak of war in 1914, therefore, people on all sides had waited anxiously for any news on whether or not the established conventions were being respected with soldiers and sailors now falling into enemy hands. Soon there was considerable consternation when early reports from Germany indicated that British prisoners of war were not receiving anything like the treatment expected.

News regarding the fate of early British prisoners of war came through both official and unofficial channels. They were mainly consistent in their conclusion that the Germans were not sticking to the rules. Critical accounts came from a small number of British prisoners who had managed to escape from Germany, while the reports of visitors from neutral countries to the camps revealed that squalid living conditions and ill-treatment were commonplace. Corroborating these accusations, albeit in a less sensational fashion, were formal reports arising from the offices of the United States Embassy in Germany, which was representing British interests following the declaration of war. Taking all of these sources into account, there seemed little doubt that the treatment being meted out to British prisoners of war in German hands fell far short of the requirements set out in the Hague Convention. Partly as a response, and partly due to its natural sense of humanity, Britain was determined to adopt a scrupulously correct attitude to German prisoners of war. The challenge – that in fairness was the one Germany was also struggling with – was the total lack of pre-prepared facilities for the processing, holding and sustenance of large numbers of captured men. This meant that in the early months of the conflict both sides were forced to improvise when it came to prisoner of war camps. At the very start of the war, the War Office decided that one of the places for just such an improvisation was Jersey. On 9 August 1914, just five days after Britain had declared war, the Lieutenant Governor received a telegram on the matter of prisoners of war. Clearly anticipating future military success, the War Office required Rochfort to make immediate preparations to receive captured enemy servicemen. Ominously, the telegram also stated that prisoners were going to be dispatched to Jersey that very day. Given this urgent need, temporary facilities would initially be acceptable, the communication went on to say, but the process of planning for a permanent camp should start as soon as practically possible. The locations chosen for both temporary and permanent facilities were at the Lieutenant Governor's discretion, but neither should be anywhere near fortifications or military facilities. It was not explained why the War Office regarded Jersey as a suitable location, but there was an intention to locate camps throughout the country, and with its surrounding waters, the Island would make for a secure choice. Just where the prisoners would be kept after their arrival was another matter. Nevertheless, mindful that the first batch was expected imminently, the military authorities in Jersey started looking for a temporary location in which to house them.

The Defence of the Realm (DORA) regulations gave Rochfort the authority to requisition buildings and land required for military purposes, so the scope was potentially wide, although in reality suitable sites were limited. One location with buildings and open space within a contained area was Springfield, the large agricultural showground located on the northern outskirts of the town. Hurried preparations were immediately made to convert this site. Sleeping accommodation was created inside the cattle sheds while latrines and wash houses were constructed in the grounds outside. To provide security, a 10 foot high perimeter fence was built along with a number of raised guard platforms. With the standard British practice being to confine captured officers separately from other ranks - ideally in more refined quarters wherever possible - St Helier's Brighton Road School was similarly taken over, and prepared to accommodate higher ranking prisoners. When they returned to school in September, the displaced children were to be located in alternative classrooms around St Helier.

These hurried preparations turned out to have been in vain, as no German prisoners of war arrived in August, or even September, by which time Springfield had been used to house men of the South Staffordshire Regiment. Brighton Road School was held in anticipation for a little longer, but then in October 1914 it too was handed over for use as a military hospital. The fighting retreat following the Battle of Mons back in August 1914 had meant that the British Expeditionary Force (BEF) had ended up with less German prisoners to cope with than was expected. And the small number who had been captured in the opening land battles of the war, along with batches of German sailors rescued from the sea after their warships had been sunk, were found accommodation in a temporary camp near Dorchester and at a number of other locations around the country. The situation was slowly changing however. Following the Battle of the Marne in September 1914, the renewed fighting until the end of the year had led to a steady increase in the number of captured German servicemen. By the start of 1915, Britain held around ten thousand prisoners of war distributed across a number of temporary and mainly rudimentary facilities, including prison ships moored on the Thames and elsewhere. With further numbers expected and no imminent sign of the war ending, there was a pressing need for more permanent arrangements. With this in mind, in December 1914 the War Office again wrote to the Lieutenant Governor with instructions to prepare appropriate facilities for holding prisoners in the Island.

In looking for a suitable site for a permanent camp in Jersey, two possible locations were soon identified. The War Office already owned some large tracts of open ground in the Island, at Les Landes where there was an area used as a firing range, and in St Ouen's Bay where there was an expanse of sand dunes acquired before the war for troop manoeuvres. An inspection of the former showed there would be problems with sourcing water, due to the underlying granite being so close to the surface and with only limited supplies available from existing wells in the area. The site at Les Blanches Banques, as the area of dunes was called, proved more promising. An extensive and relatively flat area existed at that time (as it does today) alongside the road called Le Chemin des Basse Mielles that leads inland from Le Braye Slip. It appeared to be ideal for a camp. Moreover, water could come from a reservoir situated on higher ground that overlooked the site and which would be fed from a well and small spring, while drainage could flow towards the bay and also make use of a large septic tank installed to serve St Peter's Barracks nearby. With this site now chosen, planning and design responsibilities were handed to Major Theodore Naish, the forty-six-year-old commanding officer of the detachment of Royal Engineers stationed in the Island.

Naish, who had also originally planned the proposed prisoner of war camp at Springfield, laid out a square area, roughly three hundred yards long and three hundred yards wide. This would mark the perimeter of the camp, with all of the buildings and recreation areas for the prisoners inside, and accommodation for their guards situated on the outside. Construction started in late December 1914, with ground works taking place to level the Les Blanches Banques site and the installation of water and drainage systems. Naish's plans allowed for forty-eight accommodation huts arranged in four parallel lines each with twelve huts. The lines were labelled 'A', 'B', 'C' and 'D', with 'A' line being closest to the public road that ran alongside the camp. For administration, 'A' and 'B' hut lines formed one 'wing' of the camp, 'C' and 'D' lines the other, with the two wings separated by the camp's main thoroughfare. Located alongside this were a number of the prisoners' communal facilities, with other buildings constructed in the middle of each wing. These consisted of two bath houses (one for each wing), each with ten shower cubicles with hot and cold running water, two latrine and ablution blocks, huts for washing and drying clothes and a cookhouse with storerooms attached. At the southern end of the camp stood a large fifty-bed hospital that included a small isolation ward for infectious patients. These buildings occupied about two thirds of the site, with the rest given over to a large grassy recreation area that doubled as a prisoner parade ground.

To secure the camp and its prisoners, a 10-foot high perimeter fence of wooden uprights and fixed barbed wire surrounded the whole site. To prevent prisoners approaching the fence, which was lit at night time, raised strands of barbed ran along the inside of the perimeter at ground level. To prevent curious locals approaching the camp, notices were places in the newspapers advising that people who got too close were liable to arrest. Watching over the fence and the camp were eight guard towers, one situated at each corner of the compound and one halfway along each side. These were connected back to the camp's guardhouse by telephone and there were push button alarms installed at intervals along the fence. The guardhouse, which included a small detention block with cells for holding prisoners undergoing punishment, stood outside of the perimeter fence at the northern end of the camp, along with accommodation and other facilities for the guards. The main entrance for the camp was also located there.

Orders to fabricate the wooden camp buildings went to British companies experienced in constructing army huts, from which Naish had derived his designs. They were then shipped to the Island for assembly by local building companies that had responded to notices placed in the Island's newspapers to tender for the work. Local contractors also constructed the perimeter fence and built the brick and concrete bathhouses and ablution blocks. The prisoner accommodation huts were all of a uniform size, sixty feet long by fifteen feet wide, with twelve windows and a door at each end. Each stood on raised brick piles, both to keep the wooden structure out of contact with the potentially damp soil below and to make it difficult for the prisoners to dig escape tunnels from beneath the hut. Each hut had a stove for heating and was lit by electric lights, as was the perimeter fence at night. News that electricity was being installed caused quite a stir among Islanders, who were generally curious to know what was going on at the camp. Given the novelty of this form of power and that its use had been largely limited to St Helier, there was a certain amount of surprise that the prisoners would have use of a modern service not then available to the majority of Islanders.

When it came to guarding the camp at Les Blanches Banques, the British Army would initially provide a complement of soldiers from a force called the National Reserve. This had been organised before the war from officers and other ranks who had completed their active military service and had fulfilled any subsequent army reserve obligations, yet were willing to remain liable for recall in the event of war. The age limit for being eligible for the National Reserve was fifty-five-years-old for officers and sergeants and fifty for corporals and below. Those found to be either young or fit enough when recalled to service could be sent to serve with an active unit. Most were posted to home defence units, however, in order to release younger men for overseas service, or were allocated home service roles such as prisoner of war camp guards. In terms of a regimental affiliation, the home defence units of the National Reserve were attached to Territorial Force battalions as 'supernumerary' companies. Thus, the one sent to the Island to guard its prisoner of war camp had the grand title of 10th Supernumerary Company of the 5th Battalion, Hampshire Regiment. Its commander and the first camp commandant was Lieutenant Colonel Gregory Haines who had formerly served in the Royal Warwickshire Regiment and who had reached the age of sixty-two by 1915. Considering that his advanced years easily breached the upper age limit for members of the National Reserve, it is clear that there was some leeway in who exactly was allowed to serve in wartime.

Haines' command, which arrived in Jersey at the same time as the prisoners, initially numbered one hundred men, although it later increased to one hundred and thirty, excluding officers and clerical staff. This increase would be partially filled by local recruits responding to notices placed in the newspapers asking for volunteers aged between forty-one and fifty-five. It would also later change its name when along with other supernumerary companies it became part of the newly formed Royal Defence Corps (RDC). From 1916, therefore, the camp garrison became the 351st (Protection) Company, RDC. Haines also had a number of officers within his establishment, included an adjutant, a medical officer and two lieutenants attached as interpreters.

As the camp neared completion, the preparations for it to receive its first inmates intensified. On 18 March 1915, the Lieutenant Governor's office wrote to the Attorney General, Henry Le Vavasseur dit Durell, advising that a ship bearing the first batch would arrive in St Helier Harbour in two days' time. While the army would deal with the prisoners' security, he requested a Police presence to ensure that civilians were kept at a safe distance. There was also a request to keep the information confidential from the public and to prohibit photographers and cinematographers from approaching the quayside. There had already been rumours sweeping the Island that the prisoners' arrival was imminent, stirring up a wave of eager anticipation. 'The community has been prisoner-mad during the past few days,' exclaimed one local newspaper, 'and while the responsible military officials kept quite cool, the public were making half hourly pilgrimages to the quays and helping to disseminate some of the "authentic" information flying around.'[2] Clear evidence that contractors at the camp were making their final preparations to leave along with the leaked news that the Militia's Medical Company had been placed on standby to deal with any wounded prisoners seemed to confirm that something was imminent. Yet there had been so many false alarms prior to 20 March that in the end only a modest crowd would turn up to witness the prisoners' disembarkation. Unfortunately for this crowd, impromptu barriers diligently manned by members of the paid Police kept the public well away from the harbour. But contrary to the original orders, members of the press were allowed to pass, however, with arrangements made for them to report on and photograph the disembarkation.

The reporters found the Albert Pier, alongside which the prisoners' ship had tied up, surprisingly busy and full of dignitaries to witness what was widely regarded as an important event in the Island's history. Among those present were the Bailiff and the Attorney General, both seemingly intent on facing the enemy for the first time. At 6.30 am, they got the chance as the SS *Lydia*, a London and South Western ship well known to Islanders but which had been taken over for naval service discharged her human cargo. She carried 596 German prisoners of war and sixty to seventy British Army guards who were accompanying them. A strong detachment of the South Staffordshire Regiment awaited their arrival on shore and were there to provide additional security on the pier and along the road leading to St Helier's Western Railway terminus, the immediate destination for the prisoners.

Once formed up on the quayside with the help of accompanying military interpreters, the Germans were then marched off the pier and into sight of the curious crowd of civilian onlookers. Quite what those Islanders had expected is unknown, but it appears that there was disappointment that the enemy were not quite as menacing as they had been portrayed. 'It must be confessed that none of them looked very bloodthirsty,' commented the *Morning News*. 'There were men whose physiognomy seemed to indicate a low mentality, and a number of them were obviously rude uncultured peasants, but all appeared light-hearted and cheerful enough.'[3] Perhaps as a show of bravado, the prisoners broke into song and waved to the bemused spectators as they passed by, singling out some young women in the crowd for special attention. A number of them reciprocated with the waving of handkerchiefs – much to the consternation of other onlookers - as the three trains carrying the prisoners departed St Helier for Don Bridge Station in St Brelade. From there, they were marched to the camp at Les Blanches Banques to begin their time in Jersey.

The group of prisoners who had arrived on 20 March were joined two days later by a further batch of 399, raising the overall total in the Island to 995, of which 645 were from the German Army and 350 from the German Navy. They were all men who had served as 'other ranks', such as privates, corporals or sergeants, rather than officers. Although no specific records appear to exist today as to individual prisoner details,[*] certain information indicates the origins of at least some of the newly arrived men. From their cap bands, it was clear that most of the German Navy men came from ships sunk by the British in the early months of the war. There was a large group from the light cruiser SMS *Mainz*, sunk in the Battle of Heligoland Bight on 28 August 1914, and a smaller number reportedly from the SMS *Nürnberg*, which had been lost during the Battle of the Falklands in December 1914. There were also sailors from armed liner *Kaiser Wilhelm Der Grosse*, which had been scuttled after a fierce battle off the African coast in August 1914 and from the armoured cruiser SMS *Blücher*, lost at the Battle of Dogger Bank in January 1915. Those who had served in the German Army were mainly infantrymen from Saxon and

---

[*] German prisoner of war records were destroyed in a Second World War bombing raid.

Bavarian regiments, along with a scattering of cavalrymen, known as Uhlans. There were also reportedly members of the Prussian Guard present, although these may have been identified through the wishful thinking of reporters and onlookers, anxious to catch sight of men from this elite corps.

Prior to their arrival in Jersey, most of the prisoners had been held on a prison ship, the converted ex-Allan Line liner SS *Scotian*, moored off Ryde on the Isle of Wight. By contrast, their new camp and its location must have represented a considerable improvement. 'No camp could be more pleasantly situated than Jersey,' wrote one neutral observer who visited Les Blanches Banques, 'which is on the sea-shore at a distance of seven and half miles from St Helier.'[4] As well as choosing a site with a pleasing outlook, it seems that the planners and contractors had carried out their work with great thoroughness and attention to detail when building and fitting out the camp. The accommodation huts were roomy, with each prisoner having a mattress, pillows, sheets and three blankets for his bed. Communal dining rooms were equipped with tables and benches as well as a piano for accompanying music. The hospital was said to be fully equipped, with a well-stocked medicine dispensary. In time, the prisoners would also organise a barbershop, tailor's shop, boot repair shop, library and post office. There was a certain sense of incongruity for some Islanders in this apparent comfort, who clearly felt envious of the conditions enjoyed by their erstwhile enemies. 'Well built, commodious and elaborately equipped quarters, with ample space in both the living and sleeping rooms, the latest culinary appliances, electric light everywhere, hot water pipes to warm even the cells and hot and cold baths,' was how the editor of the *Morning News* described the camp. The huts at Les Blanches Banques, he went on to say, 'are a good deal ahead of the average Jersey working-man's home, and a palace as compared with the Militia barracks at Grève d'Azette.'[5]

While the reports of luxury may have been somewhat overstated, it is clear that, from the outset, the British authorities were determined to build a first class prisoner of war camp on the dunes in St Ouen's Bay. Their motive for so doing was probably twofold. Firstly, that given the opportunity, resources and materials, the British Army will always aim for high specifications – regardless of the ultimate use of the facility. Secondly, in response to the reports emanating from Germany, Britain was determined to demonstrate a strict observance of the Hague Convention's agreed treatment of enemy prisoners of war. Regardless of the actions of their enemy, there would be no stain on Britain's reputation as far as the Les Blanches Banques camp was concerned. A report provided by the United States Embassy, whose representatives had inspected the camp in April 1916 in their then role as neutral observers, confirmed that this was indeed the case. Among the comments that were made was a statement that, 'this camp seemed almost to be a model of its kind, and the men appeared to be in extraordinarily good physical condition.'[6]

The prisoners' health and well-being was supported by a regime that clearly complied with aims laid down in the British Prisoner of War Bureau rules that stated, 'everything possible is done to provide the prisoners with recreation - mental and bodily...'[7] As mentioned earlier, from the outset one third of the camp's area had been set aside for sporting activities. There was a football pitch and volleyball court laid out, along with a tennis court created initially from gravel but later given a concrete surface. For further exercise, the prisoners were taken in groups on five- to six-mile route marches two or three times per of week and permitted onto the nearby beach for bathing during the summer months in groups of four hundred men at a time. Inside the compound, there were also plenty of activities arranged to keep the prisoners occupied. Hobbies such as model boat building, painting and fretwork carving were encouraged. The prisoners arranged lectures, study and educational classes along with music and theatre performances, with the camp reportedly having a fine brass band with twenty-three instruments, a fifty-voice choir and a stage for improvised repertoire performances. The latter was located in a YMCA hut donated to the camp by the American branch of that organisation in September 1916, before that country entered the war on the Allied side.

The canteen in the prisoners' YMCA hut was permitted to stock certain luxury goods for the prisoners, including imported cigars, as well as extra rations. Food does seem to have been in plentiful supply and it was cooked and served up by a team of eleven prisoners under the watchful eye of a German sergeant major who in his former career had been a master cook. The daily diet for each prisoner consisted of one and half pounds of bread, half a pound of meat – either fresh or cured such as bacon – eight ounces of vegetables, a tin of condensed milk, butter, cheese, jam and the occasional cake. In the early days of the camp, meals were eaten in a number of spare accommodation huts that had been converted into dining halls. This practice would stop following the arrival of a further batch of 240 prisoners in October 1915 and another 450 in July 1916 that took numbers present at Les Blanches Banques camp up to over 1,500. As a result, there was a need to use all of the existing spare accommodation huts and even to build three more, much to the annoyance of the prisoners who felt that their camp was becoming too cramped. Complaints were dismissed, however, because the space per inmate remained well within the regulations laid down, a fact confirmed by a further visit from American Embassy representatives in September 1916.

As well as physical and mental stimulation, the spiritual needs of the prisoners were met through visits to the camp by local church ministers. A chaplain from St Helier's Jesuit community at Notre Dame du Bon Secours regularly visited to hold Catholic services, while members of the local Protestant clergy attended to the needs of those of the Lutheran faith. Although the camp lay within the boundaries of the parish of St Brelade, it appears to have first fallen under the responsibility of the adjoining parish of St Peter. Following the first death of an inmate, a sailor named Karl Brundig who died in August 1915 after an epileptic fit, the funeral service took place at St Peter's parish church with Brundig buried in the churchyard there. It was a grand affair, with hundreds of his comrades accompanying the coffin from the camp to the church and present at the interment. Perhaps such a display prompted the Rector of St Brelade to check again on where exactly the camp had been built. Discovering that it actually lay in his parish led him to insist that any further burials must take place in his church, with the associated funeral fees paid into his coffers. Thereafter, the camp's inmates were under the care of the Rector of St Brelade, who would bury seven more deceased prisoners before the end of the war, one who died of cancer, one who drowned while bathing in the sea, one from dysentery, one from gastritis and three who succumbed during the 1918 flu epidemic. He would also bury one of the camp guards, Private George Hanlon, who died from pneumonia in November 1916.

George Hanlon was typical of the guards stationed at the Les Blanches Banques camp. He was an old soldier who before the war had served in the Lancashire Fusiliers and the Royal Garrison Artillery. Although he had been born in Manchester, by August 1914 he was living with his wife and family in Sandown on the Isle of Wight and worked as a labourer. Almost immediately on the outbreak war, he rejoined the army aged forty-three, but this meant that he was not suitable for active service. As a result, Hanlon was posted to a reserve artillery unit stationed on the Isle of Wight, but was discharged from the army in December 1914 on the grounds of being medically unfit. Yet even that was not the end of Hanlon's military career. He subsequently re-enlisted in the Hampshire Regiment, which accepted him, despite his age and health, for a unit formed to guard prisoners of war on the ships off the town of Ryde. When some of those prisoners were sent to Jersey in 1915, George Hanlon came with them.

While serving in the Island, Private Hanlon and his fellow guards lived in the purpose built accommodation constructed next to the camp outside the perimeter fence. In common with their charges, these huts were heated and lit with electricity provided by a specially installed generator that also drove the pump used to provide running water to the camp. From the summer of 1916 onwards, they also enjoyed access to their own YMCA hut and canteen, provided and staffed by the Jersey branch of that organisation. This hut had been moved from its original location at the Militia summer training camp nearby, which was no longer being used as a result of the outbreak of war. The guards' role was of course to ensure the security of the camp and its inmates, although in normal circumstances they did not enter the compound. By agreement with the camp commandant, it was the responsibility of the prisoners to manage their own internal discipline, with designated leaders overseeing the activities inside the compound. The British guards only became directly involved if the rules, as laid down in camp's regulations, were broken.

Among the most serious breaches of the rules was attempting to escape from the camp, although this did not prevent a number of prisoners doing just that. Considering its location on an island off the French coast, the motivation for these activities may have been less about getting home and more about breaking the monotony and frustrating the guards. One man who was found to be missing from the compound, for example, returned of his own free will a few days later. Another – reportedly mad – escapee made it as far as St Helier where he approached a British soldier with a request for directions to Government House because he had something important to tell the Lieutenant Governor. These single escapes were made by cutting through the wire or by slipping out unnoticed by the guards. There were two more sophisticated escape attempts by groups of prisoners, both of which involved tunnelling under the camp's perimeter fence.

The first, ultimately unsuccessful, plan involved digging a tunnel from a small summerhouse constructed by the prisoners attached to one of the huts in 'A' line, which was closest to the road running alongside the camp's perimeter. A diagonal shaft dug from underneath the floor of this summerhouse went down deep enough to reach a layer of solid sand. From there, an unlined tunnel just big enough for a man to crawl through ran horizontally below the fence and under the road. Air was provided through a series of small holes pushed up to the surface using stolen drainage rods. Light came from a lamp fashioned from a biscuit tin filled with beef fat. The excavated sand was disposed of at night, using the wind to gradually blow it from under the raised floor of the hut. Despite the ingenuity used in its building, the tunnel was located when a camp guard walking outside the perimeter fence discovered one of the ventilation holes after his walking stick disappeared into the ground. The second attempt, which took place in July 1917, was more successful in that the prisoners managed to complete the construction of another tunnel without being detected and actually escaped from the camp. The tunnel, which led under the adjacent road once again, originated from below the floor of a nearby accommodation hut with access through the wooden boards courtesy of a carefully sawn trapdoor. Nine prisoners used the tunnel to escape from the camp taking tins of food and blankets with them. Their taste of freedom was short lived however. After roaming around for a few days, and being spotted by a number of people, the escapees were finally cornered in a small wood close to St Brelade's Bay and 'arrested', before being handed back to the camp guards.

Apart from these unauthorised exits from the camp, prisoners also left its confines for exercise as mentioned, and to undertake work. The first prisoners to arrive in March 1915 had worked inside the camp helping to complete its construction. Although the civilian contractors had finished the buildings and perimeter fence, prisoners undertook the construction of roads and pathways within the camp, with material collected by working parties from a nearby quarry. Once work on the camp was complete, small working parties of prisoners also went out to undertake other similar tasks for the military authorities. At St Peter's Barracks nearby, for example, gangs of prisoners were used to construct and widen roads there and worked on laying out a recreation area. Yet the availability of such work was quite limited, and so the majority of inmates remained inside the camp filling their time with sport, hobbies and educational activities. But as time went on, British thoughts turned to how to make better use of the ready and growing pool of labour that was idling away in the country's prisoner of war camps.

At the end of December 1916, there were fifty thousand German prisoners held in camps across Britain, including those at Les Blanches Banques in Jersey. With more and more of the nation's men joining the armed forces or becoming involved in other essential war related activities, attention focused upon using this large and captive labour source to fill some of the gaps in the national workforce. Using prisoners of war for work was permitted under the Hague Convention, which had clearly set out the terms for doing so. The work given must not be excessive and should have nothing to do with assisting the country's military operations, for example. It also stipulated that prisoners must be paid for any work at a rate comparable to that which would have been paid to serving soldiers if they were asked to do the same task, with any monies earned going towards improving the lives of prisoners or given to them on their release from captivity. When it came to who could be made to work, the Hague Convention allowed discretion based upon rank and aptitude. Britain decided that it would exempt all officers and non-commissioned officers, unless they volunteered, but include all men of private rank or equivalent. With those rules in place, Britain set about employing prisoners in a wide range of duties, with many being allocated to the country's farmers to help the agricultural industry.

In August 1916, the Lieutenant Governor had formally raised the question of using Jersey's German prisoners for work in the Island. Given the shortages of labour following the departure of the French reservists and the subsequent loss of men volunteering for the British Army, Rochfort reasoned that there seemed a perfect opportunity to employ prisoners on local farms. Such an action could also free up other Islanders to join the army, a cause that was dear to his heart. The States' Defence Committee's response was less enthusiastic however. It believed that local farmers would be very reluctant to pay the going rate to enemy prisoners working on their land - it would simply be very unpatriotic to do so. If a lower rate could be negotiated, then it might be possible to come to an arrangement. But the Lieutenant Governor's hands were tied by the conditions set down by the War Office. Writing in response to a question about locally negotiated pay rates, its answer stated that, 'I am sure you will appreciate how difficult it would be for us to justify lending prisoners to private persons in Jersey on more favourable terms than we allow to private employers in this country.'[8] Rochfort was clearly undeterred and still keen to find a use for the Island's prisoners. In October he proposed they be used to build a new road in St Ouen's Bay, not far from the Les Blanches Banques camp. The answer from the civilian authorities was yet another polite but firm no. Citing a lack of money and the fact that it would potentially take away work that could be undertaken by local men after the war, the Defence Committee President, Jurat Walter Aubin, declined the request even if lower wages for the work could be agreed. 'Do not feel inclined to undertake work however low the rate of wage is presented,' he firmly noted following a meeting with the Lieutenant Governor.[9]

Clearly exasperated by the responses received, Rochfort advised the War Office that despite his efforts, the local civilian authorities had no interest in using the prisoners. In January 1917, the decision was therefore made to remove all prisoners from the Island and to send them to camps in Britain where they would be employed on work. 'If farm labour is so plentiful in Jersey that farmers will not take them at the price,' the War Office tersely informed the Lieutenant Governor, 'there seems no more to be said under this heading.'[10] Yet even as preparations began for the prisoners' transfer to Britain, he received a conflicting enquiry from the States' Food Production Committee asking whether prisoners would be available to work at the harbour helping to load potatoes during the forthcoming export season. They would apparently be an enormous help in making up for the 'great labour shortage'.[11] In a flurry of negotiations between the Lieutenant Governor, Deputy Bois who was president of the States' Food Production Committee, and the War Office it was agreed that six hundred prisoners could be used for work on the quays, at the standard rate of pay. The rest of the prisoners would return to Britain.

On 15 February 1917, the first batch of five hundred prisoners to depart travelled by train from St Brelade to St Helier and marched under military escort to the Albert Pier where a ship waited to transport them back across the Channel. A second batch of five hundred more departed the next day. Escorting them were the men of the 351st (Protection) Company RDC, whose ranks included a number of the Islanders who had joined while the unit was stationed at Les Blanches Banques. The destination for the prisoners – and possibly the guards as well – was a camp located at Frongoch in northern Wales, although this may have been a short lived home because it was subsequently used to hold Irish republican prisoners rounded up after the unsuccessful Easter Uprising.

Their six hundred former comrades who were left behind in far more pleasant conditions at Les Blanches Banques had new guards and a new camp commandant. Lieutenant Colonel Walter Stocker had left the Island in March 1915 as commanding officer of the Jersey Company, and served throughout its training in Ireland and later at Aldershot. The forty-eight-year-old former Militia officer had also gone to France and into the trenches with the volunteers from the start of 1916. Yet he struggled with the arduous conditions of life at the front, and after a period of illness in May that year, Stocker had returned to active service only to suffer a serious collapse in July. For a number of weeks subsequently, his condition was life threatening before it gradually improved. On recovery, it was obvious that he could not return to the Jersey Company at the front, much to Stocker's dismay. He was able to continue serving as an officer in the Jersey Militia, however, and was offered and accepted the post of commandant at the Les Blanches Banques camp in charge of those prisoners who remained to work in St Helier.

Negotiations between the Lieutenant Governor, the States' Defence Committee and the various companies whose ships needed loading settled the details of the work that the prisoners would undertake. Their day would start with a train journey to St Helier, with the first shift beginning work at 7.00 am and continuing until 1.00 pm. After a one-hour lunch break, the second shift started at 2.00 pm and worked through until finishing at 8.00 pm. The rate of pay for the work, which went on for seven days a week, although with a half day on Sunday, was eight pence per hour. The army would provide the necessary security for the prisoners while travelling and when working, and, as an extra precaution, women were prohibited from going onto the pier while the Germans were present. The intention had been for the prisoners to start work in early May, although they were not actually needed until the beginning of June and then continued through until August when work came to an end. With that, transport was arranged for the prisoners to be sent back to Britain, and this took place on 29 August, while the camp at Les Blanches Banques could finally close.

Yet this wasn't quite the last that Jersey saw of German prisoners of war. The British Army had not yet relinquished its interest in the 'model' camp at Les Blanches Banques. During 1917, the number of enemy prisoners in British hands steadily increased as Allied offensives ground slowly forward in

France and Belgium. While most could be put to work in Britain, the rules on exempting any soldier above the rank of private meant that camps there held a growing number of non-commissioned officers who, under the agreed rules, had no obligation to undertake work. A camp was required to house a large group of those who were not engaged in any meaningful role in Britain. The solution was to send them to Jersey. On 12 April 1918, a ship arrived in St Helier's Harbour bearing the first batch of eleven hundred prisoners of war being sent to the Island, the vast majority of whom were from the German Army. In charge of this new complement and its guards was a Major Allpress, who had previously served as a captain in the Bedfordshire Regiment.

News of their impending arrival had prompted the States' Food Production Committee to enquire whether any of them would be available for work on the harbour quays once again. The Lieutenant Governor could not say so with any certainty, given that the new batch of prisoners were not obliged to undertake work, but a visit to the camp after their arrival eased concerns. Despite there being no obligation for the prisoners to work, a representative for the men gave assurances that they would willing to do so at a rate of pay comparable to that given to local labour. Two hundred and eighty volunteered, and were duly sent to the harbour each day to work until 7.00 pm. Given the shortages of labour in the Island at that time, their presence was gratefully welcomed. As for their comrades, they settled down in the same routine of sports, leisure and recreational activities that had been enjoyed by their predecessors, including the regular walks and swims.

This would continue until October 1919, nearly one year after the war ended. On Sunday, 5 October, the German ship SS *Melillia* would arrive in St Helier Harbour to take the first batch of prisoners home. As with the time of the original arrival of prisoners of war in March 1915, there would be a large crowd of Islanders present to watch the departing Germans who numbered 860. Brought to the quayside by military escort, once the prisoners stepped on board they became free men once more and were warmly welcomed as such by the ship's crew. With luggage loaded, the ship left its berth and departed Jersey, the prisoners reportedly singing lustily the hymn 'Comrades Farewell' as they left. A second ship, the SS *Villareal* would take the remaining batch of three hundred men a few days later.

Once empty, the Les Blanches Banques camp was dismantled with its equipment and huts disposed of in a public sale. After this, all that remained to remind Islanders of their wartime 'visitors' were the graves of those comrades, one in St Peter's Churchyard and seven in St Brelade's. They too were destined to leave the Island eventually, but it would take another war and a lot more German burials in the cemetery before that took place.

JERSEY'S GREAT WAR

Major General Sir Alexander Rochfort, KCB, CMG, who was the Island's Lieutenant Governor and its military commander-in-chief from 1910 to October 1916

Major General Alexander Wilson, KCB, who became Jersey's Lieutenant Governor in October 1916

JERSEY'S GREAT WAR

The Dean of Jersey, the Very Reverend Samuel Falle (seated in the centre) with members of the Jersey Contingent prior to their departure from the Island

Cheery members of the Jersey Contingent on their departure from Jersey in March 1915

One of the military ambulances purchased from funds raised in Jersey and sent to the front

Militant Suffragettes' Miss Lall Forsyth and Miss Agnes Buckton in Jersey before the war trying to raise local support for the campaign to win greater rights for women

JERSEY'S GREAT WAR

Preparing 'comfort' parcels to send to the troops was a popular and well supported civilian activity

Fund raising campaigns were a way for Jersey's civilians to show their support for the war effort

Société Jersiaise

The Jersey Branch of the British Red Cross Society established a number of Voluntary Aid Detachments (VADs) soon after the outbreak of war with their members serving as nurses both in the Island and overseas

JERSEY'S GREAT WAR

The 'enemy' in the Island – German prisoners of war march to attend the funeral of one of their own at St Peter's Parish Church watched by curious Islanders

The Prisoner of War camp at Les Blanches Banques was home to nearly two thousand German soldiers and sailors at one point

Société Jersiaise

A shortage of men led to openings for women in the Island, including its first female 'posties'

9 ENGLAND EXPECTS

National Registration and adopting compulsory military service in Jersey

Along with thousands of other British soldiers, Private Howard Leopold Davis, the youngest son of Jersey-born businessman, yachtsman and philanthropist Thomas Benjamin Davis, waited nervously for the order to begin the advance on 1 July 1916. For six days beforehand, British artillery had been pounding the German defences on top of the prominent Thiepval Ridge, which Davis' unit, the 17th Battalion, Highland Light Infantry, was due to attack. The unprecedented weight of shelling should make the task an easy one was the assurance given by their commanding officers. Surely, no one could survive such a bombardment. The enemy's barbed wire defences, which lay in wide belts on the slopes of the ridge, should be cut to pieces, their machine guns and artillery smashed or buried under the chalky Picardy soil. Given this, Davis' battalion, along with more than one hundred others stretching out for miles on either side, was almost certain of a walkover on that first day of the Battle of the Somme. It was not to be, for 1 July 1916 proved to be a devastating day for the British Army. The preliminary bombardment had failed to destroy the enemy defences, cut the barbed wire or kill enough German soldiers to permit the promised walkover. Far from it. Most British troops, including Private Howard Davis, who emerged from their trenches faced heavy and accurate rifle, machine gun and artillery fire. Many never made it across no-man's land; before nightfall, sixty thousand British soldiers had been killed or wounded, among them Private Davis who would succumb to the injuries he received that day two months later. Grief stricken, his father would later create a magnificent park to the memory of his son and give it to the people of Jersey for their enjoyment to the present day.*

Thomas Davis would not be the only Jersey parent grieving after the Battle of the Somme. On its first day alone, at least nine Jersey soldiers lost their lives while serving in the British Army, while another died fighting alongside them in the army of France. By the time of the battle's unsatisfactory conclusion in November of that year, the fighting on the Somme had claimed the lives of many more Islanders, among them twenty members of the Jersey Company, killed in just three days of intense battles between 6 and 9 September for the villages

---

* T.B. Davis also gave an experimental farm at Trinity in memory of his son and built a hall at Victoria College to bear Howard's name.

of Guillemont and Ginchy. As with many of the Kitchener volunteers, the Battle of the Somme was the Jersey Company's baptism of fire. After spending months serving on a quiet sector of the front, it was their first time to leave the trenches and cross no-man's land to attack the enemy. The same was true for most of the Pals Battalions, many of which incurred heavy losses in the fighting. The Battle of the Somme also tragically exposed the folly of placing men from the same community into a single unit and then sending them together into such costly actions. As a result, the days of the Pals Battalions were numbered; the British Army would learn that lesson at least from the battle.

The Battle of the Somme would also spell the end for Kitchener's New Army of volunteers. Too many would lose their lives in the fighting, or be sent home wounded. To continue the war – and the war did continue of course - Britain needed more men. Finding them would place a further strain on communities throughout Britain, including Jersey where the question of compulsory military service was an issue that would challenge the Island more than any other to arise since the start of the war.

The question of compulsory military service in Britain had first come up long before the Battle of the Somme started. There had been a growing awareness from mid-1915 that despite the early recruitment success, Britain required further men if the country was to win what was increasingly becoming obvious would be a long and costly war. There had also been a drawback soon apparent with the Kitchener campaign. In the haste to enrol volunteers, too little screening had taken place as to who was actually joining up. It was soon discovered that among the eager volunteers there were lots of skilled workers. As British industry expanded to meet the demands of wartime production, many of these men would have been far more useful to the nation's war effort working at home. Although some men were subsequently released from the army and sent back to their civilian workplace, the oversight had fuelled a growing argument that a more selective system of recruitment was needed. It came at a time when the number of volunteers coming forward was also in decline. With the army needing one hundred and forty thousand new men per month just to sustain its hugely expanded size, actual recruiting figures in the summer of 1915 were falling far short of these requirements. A case began to be made for a new law to ensure that those who were reluctant to come forward could now be compelled to do so. Conscription – that is the compulsory enlistment of men into military service - began to be seriously discussed by the British Government in the spring of 1915, although politicians and the military remained divided over the prospect of abandoning the country's long held tradition of voluntary military service. Nevertheless, it was agreed that as a first step it would be advantageous to assess Britain's potential manpower to meet military and industrial needs, and to identify those men who could be called-up for military service if it was required. On 15 July 1915, the British Parliament passed the National Registration Act to fulfil this purpose.

The new Act empowered the government to compile a register of all persons in the country between the ages of fifteen and sixty-five. Everyone within this category had to complete a form giving his or her personal details and circumstances. National Registration Day was set for 15 August 1915. The new law only applied to Britain and did not extend automatically to the Crown Dependencies, although it was expected that Jersey, Guernsey and the Isle of Man would follow Britain's lead. With that clearly in mind, the Home Office had sent an advance copy of the Act to the Lieutenant Governor on 2 July 1915, requesting that, 'you will take into consideration the question of the application of the National Registration Act, when passed, to Jersey.'[1] It was another of those polite wartime requests that while tacitly acknowledging the rights of Islanders to set their own laws, it left little doubt over what Jersey was expected to do. Rochfort consulted the Crown Officers on the best approach to adopt and their advice was clear. This was not just another DORA regulation; the implications of National Registration were more wide reaching. The States must have the opportunity to debate the matter, and on 31 July, its Members met in session to consider the application of National Registration in Jersey. As expected, there were no dissenting voices against the proposal, only questions about exactly how and when registration would take place.

The newly agreed law mirrored that of Britain, while the process of registration was also virtually identical. National Registration Day would also take place on 15 August in Jersey, with the Constables of each parish given responsibility for the organisation of it, then for subsequently maintaining the registers, which were to be kept up to date as people's circumstances changed. As in Britain, every person between the ages of fifteen and sixty-five who were living or staying in the Island on 15 August had to register, including, as the law rather bluntly stated, 'prisoners in prison, persons interned in an internment camp, certified lunatics or defectives, and inmates of hospitals or similar institutions…'[2] The only Islanders excluded were members of the Active Militia, who were already considered to be serving soldiers, although rather confusingly members of the Militia Reserve had to register their details. The forms used, which were different for men and women, collected each individual's name, age, place of residence, marital status, the number of family members dependent on them, their profession or occupation, the name and occupation of their employer, and their nationality if this was not British. There was also a requirement for the individual to state if he or she was employed by a States' Committee and to provide details of any other work or profession that the person was capable of undertaking if required. During the week preceding Registration Day, parish officials, with the help of volunteers, distributed forms to each household. Every eligible person had to complete and sign their form by midnight on 15 August, after which time the forms would be collected within six days. Once each person's details were checked and verified as being correct, they received a 'Certificate of Registration', which had to be kept up to date. The obligations under the law did not end there however. Islanders were subsequently required to notify any change of residence within twenty-eight days of moving, with anyone going between two parishes requiring a cancellation on one parish register and then an entry in that of the new one. Failure to do so could result in a prosecution and a fine of five pounds, while anyone falsely claiming to have registered was liable to imprisonment, with or without hard labour, for up to three months and a possible fine of £20.

Despite the short time allowed to get everything into place, National Registration Day came and went without too much fuss in the Island. 'When all's said and done, the registration in Jersey appears to have been carried out very satisfactorily,' commented the *Morning News*, adding wryly, 'Everybody seems to have endeavoured to fill up the forms to the best of his, or her, ability, and to give the enumerators as little trouble as possible.'[3] With the information now gathered, compiled and analysed, it revealed a number of interesting facts and figures. The most important was that between the ages of fifteen and sixty-five, there were 3,297 unmarried men and 6,657 men who were either married or widowed. Of these, 3,900 were aged between eighteen and forty-one, which was the age range for compulsory military service. These numbers excluded the 1,800 men already serving in the Active Militia.[4] All the information that was obtained was entered into a central indexing system, with the main, secondary and potential occupations of men particularly noted. Any man on the register who worked in a job that was considered essential for the war effort had their entry marked with a black star. Importantly, men of military age were grouped according to their age, marital status and occupation, and had their details entered onto separate pink forms. In the event that compulsory military service became necessary at some point in the future, these forms would provide the information on the order in which men should be selected.

The results of Britain's National Registration Day revealed that just over five million men of military age were not serving in the armed forces at that time. Of this number, around one and half million were both unmarried and not working in roles considered essential for the war effort. They were ideal candidates for the army. The question was how to persuade them to join up.

The results of National Registration intensified debate in Britain on the possible introduction of compulsory military service, particularly given that the rate of volunteering was showing clear signs of diminishing. Before taking any final decision, however, there was an agreement by the government that one last drive to attract volunteers should take place. The job of organising it was handed to Edward Stanley, 17th Earl of Derby, the Director-General of Recruiting, with his subsequent efforts known as the Derby Scheme. It focused on those men that National Registration had shown were between eighteen and forty-one and neither in the armed forces nor working in an essential occupation. Each man was asked to either enlist straight away, or to indicate their willingness to do so if required. Those in the latter category would be grouped according to their marital status and age, with the youngest, single men being the first to receive a call-up into the armed forces as and when they would be required. There were assurances given that married men would not have to join up until all categories of single men had been exhausted.

While the Derby Scheme recruitment campaign did not directly encompass Jersey, Islanders were permitted to sign up to its terms by indicating their willingness to enlist if required. The Island's authorities were determined that as many as possible did so. On 5 October 1915, a campaign of directly appealing to serving Militiamen began at St Peter's Barracks where the men of the West Battalion and A (West) Battery were paraded. The Lieutenant Governor was the first to address them. 'During the first twelve months of war the voluntary system had been equal to the occasion,' Rochfort told the men. 'But that was not the point. At such a crisis as the present, it was not a matter of what we had done, but what we could do to finish the war…and he had no hesitation in saying that any eligible man who held back without good reason was evading his duty to the country.'[5] The Bailiff followed this with a speech of his own. After emphasising the points already made by the Lieutenant Governor, Vernon warned that if men failed to respond to this campaign by volunteering, then compulsory military service was inevitable and would come into place very soon.

Similar appeals to the other Militia units followed and the results indicate that they had a positive effect. Throughout October and into November, more than two hundred men came forward to enlist at the Jersey District Office, a considerable increase on the numbers seen in the preceding months. Furthermore, forty-nine others attested under the terms of the Derby Scheme, agreeing to join the army when they were required. Yet despite this success, it was still a relatively small number when compared to all those men whom National Registration indicated were eligible. Pointing out that the Town Battalion was 1,430 strong, and that National Registration had shown that there were a further 1,500 men in St Helier between the ages of sixteen and forty-five not serving in the Militia or the armed forces, the *Morning News* questioned how effective the recent recruitment campaign had really been.

'The three Militia parades held ostensibly for the purpose of rousing military ardour to the pitch necessary to cause a large percentage to volunteer are now chapters of history,' it noted, 'and if one judges by general indication, there has been no great rousing of patriotic fervour.'[6]

While this was no doubt irritating, the Island's civilian and military authorities could dismiss local newspapers bemoaning the lack of patriotic fervour in Jersey while considering their next steps. A more serious challenge appeared in the final months of 1915 however. On 20 October, a letter on the subject of the Channel Islands' contribution to the war effort appeared among the columns of the *Bystander*, a popular British tabloid publication. 'Is it not a fact that the Channel Islands' Militia has been standing by for twelve months at the expense of the taxpayer?'[7] wrote Major George W. Redway (retired) of South Kensington, before going on to claim that both Jersey and Guernsey were holding back their militias – whom he recognised as excellent troops – from overseas service. A few days later, on 31 October, a similar charge from the same person appeared in the *Sunday Times*. 'From the only part of the British Isles where compulsory gratuitous military service is the established law, the army has received no assistance whatever; we refer of course to the Channel Islands.'[8]

Whatever Major Redway's credentials as a commentator on such matters, the articles provoked a storm of protest in Jersey. Both the *Evening Post* and *Morning News* quickly put aside their own views and publically leapt to defend the Island's reputation. Challenging Major Redway to justify his accusations, they pointedly claimed that he was not only wrong factually – the Channel Islands had already sent several thousand men to serve in the British Army – but that he was overlooking the service that had been done by the Militia, and which, 'involved night after night exposed to the winter winds and rains while patrolling our coasts...'[9] Behind closed doors, the accusations had also stirred up a great deal of annoyance and activity in the States. Whatever the validity of Major Redway's claims, Jersey's commitment to the war effort had been a sensitive subject since the troublesome campaign in December 1914 to raise a contingent for overseas service. So there was a concerted effort not only to refute the assertions, but also to demonstrate categorically that Jersey was doing its bit. A report on the recruitment statistics in the Island up until that time was requested. On 29 November 1915, the Attorney General, Henry Le Vavasseur dit Durell, was able to report his findings to the States. He told the assembly that since the start of the war:

- There had been 829 volunteers for the British Army, including those who had joined the Jersey Company, and eighty-seven more for the Royal Navy;

- To this must be added ninety-eight other men who had volunteered to leave the Island and work in Britain's munitions industry;
- There were believed to have been 1,490 Jerseymen already serving in the armed forces when the war broke out;
- An estimated 500 men who had been born in Jersey were believed to be serving in the military contingents of Australia, Canada, New Zealand and South Africa.

This all made a grand total, the Attorney General announced, of just over three thousand men. And this took no account of the more than two thousand French reservists who had rejoined their regiments at the start of the war, or the huge contribution made by thousands of Militiamen in the defence of their Island. Thanking the Attorney General for his comprehensive figures, the Bailiff proposed that they should be brought up to date, printed, and forwarded onto the Lieutenant Governor for submission to the British Prime Minister. The Island of Jersey, Vernon was sure, had every reason to be proud of its contribution to the war thus far.

Rochfort did indeed pass the figures on. 'Owing to numerous paragraphs which have appeared in the London Press reflecting upon the lack of support given by the inhabitants of this Island to His Majesty's Government in the present emergency, I would urgently request you to bring these facts to the notice of the proper authority in order that due publicity may be given,' he wrote in his covering letter to the Home Secretary. Adding also that another 272 Islanders had volunteered for military service but had been found medically unfit, and that over four hundred Old Victorians were also serving, he concluded by saying that, 'I am further requested by the States to express to His Majesty's Government the unswerving devotion and loyalty of the inhabitants of Jersey to His Majesty.'[10] It is not clear what the response of the Home Secretary was to the figures, or indeed whether the Prime Minister ever saw them. Yet it would have been understandable if he had not. At the end of 1915, Herbert Asquith, the British Prime Minister, had other more pressing matters on his mind.

The Derby Scheme had succeeded in encouraging thousands more volunteers to enlist and in persuading over two million men to attest their willingness to join-up when they were required. Despite this, the judgement was that the campaign had overall been a failure. Analysis showed that many thousands of single men who were working in non-essential occupations had not responded. With the government having given assurances that married men would only be called-up after those who were unmarried, one way out of the dilemma remained. There would have to be a new Act of Parliament enabling the compulsory call-up of single men into the armed forces. On 27

January 1916, the British Parliament passed the Military Service Act 1916. This was just a first step however. Four months later, on 25 May, the Act was extended to include those who were married.

The new Act effectively enlisted all men between the ages of eighteen and forty-one into the armed forces, making them liable for military service as they were required. The only part of Britain that was excluded from the Act was Ireland because of political concerns that such legislation would stir up nationalist unrest there. Using the information obtained through National Registration, the selection of who would be called-up took place according to age and marital status, with the youngest, unmarried groups being called up first. There were certain automatic exemptions, given to church ministers for example, and for men working in occupations already considered essential to the war effort, and therefore 'starred' on the National Register. Anyone else who believed that they should be exempt from military service had to make an appeal to one of the Military Service Tribunals that were established throughout the country. The principal grounds for a man, or his employer, to appeal under was to prove that his work was essential for the war effort. Anyone who failed to persuade a Military Service Tribunal that their request for exemption was valid could appeal to a Central Tribunal. Anyone found trying to cheat the system faced tough legal penalties as well as the likelihood of public condemnation.

Britain's Military Service Act did not automatically apply to the Crown Dependencies, all of which were self-governing territories of course. Yet there was a strong presumption that all three would introduce a similar law and so extend the principle. The question was not about if it would happen, it was about the how and the when. In Jersey, the Bailiff was also anxious to ensure that for the Channel Islands at least, there would be a coordinated approach to the matter. Writing to his Guernsey counterpart shortly after Britain had enacted its first Military Service Act, Vernon expressed a view that Jersey would, 'particularly appreciate the desirability and the advantage of both islands finding common ground, and following the same line of action…' He also noted that when it came to introducing compulsory military service, there was little appetite to avoid or delay moral obligations by attempting to invoke longstanding privileges. 'We do not want to incur and to have perhaps deserved, in the after-war period, the reproaches of our English and Scotch fellow counterparts nor the undisguised contempt of our French population.' An inter-island conference was planned for March 1916 in order to discuss the matter in detail.

But within days of Vernon's letter, news reached Jersey that at least one Crown Dependency was prepared to demonstrate its commitment to Britain's cause without further deliberation on the matter. At the start of February 1916, the Isle of Man Government announced its intention to adopt the British legislation virtually as written. On 3 March 1916, the Military Service (Isle of Man) Act came into effect and placed all of that Island's male population between the ages of eighteen and forty-one under liability for military service in Britain's armed forces. The move was certainly in keeping with the spirit shown by that Island during the period of voluntary military service. A comparative report produced by the Attorney General for the States showed that since the start of the war, 3,712 men had enlisted voluntarily from a Manx population of just over fifty-two thousand.[11] Jersey, by comparison, had seen less than half that number of volunteers during the same period from a similar size of population. While there may have been mitigating factors behind the disparity, the Isle of Man's recruitment record and willingness to embrace compulsory military service underlined how important it was for Jersey to avoid being seen to procrastinate over the matter of conscription. 'We submit that the Island should follow the noble example of the Isle of Man,' challenged the *Morning News* in anticipation of a forthcoming States debate on the matter. 'Does Jersey wish to be bracketed with Ireland? Do Jerseymen wish to take part in the defence of the Empire or do they not? Let Jersey live up to her reputation, and without being asked to, voluntarily place her sons at the disposal of their King and Country.'[12]

On the afternoon of Saturday, 3 June 1916, the States of Jersey assembled in special session. The preamble stated, with all due pomp and ceremony, that their purpose was to 'deliberate on the measures it would be proper to take in order to place at the disposition of His Majesty for service outside the Island the resources in men of military age which may be found available in the Island in the course of the present war.'[13] The matter of compulsory military service had understandably attracted considerable attention among Islanders. As a result, the public galleries that looked down on the States' Chamber were packed that day, with those who were unable to gain access crowding the staircase leading up and hallways below. Among those in the private gallery were a number of uniformed staff officers from the Jersey District Office, along with the French Consul, *Monsieur* Jouve, who perhaps felt the need to remind the States Members of the sacrifices already being made by the Island's French community. Mindful of the occasion, the Bailiff wore his formal robes. With the Lieutenant Governor sitting solemnly beside him, Vernon had risen to give the opening address.

> I should be failing in my duty as His Majesty's deputy in the Island if I had not taken the opportunity of convening the States and in using the prerogative of the Crown in this case,

after consultation with the Lieutenant Governor, in order that you might be given the chance of doing what I know you are determined to do – to take once more and more fully your share in this great struggle. It was to give you the opportunity of exercising your chartered rights and privileges that I call you together today…you value highly, as you should, those advantages and privileges; you value even more highly your right to initiate your own legislation.

You have sent to the front a large number of volunteers, but, like England, so long as you can do more, you may consider that you have not done enough, and you should be given an opportunity…We and our great allies are fighting for those great ideas of civilisation which to our way of thinking make life worth living. More than that, we have to win the war. Men are wanted. We must avenge the fallen and fill the gaps.

I must, however, perhaps remove misapprehensions. No country would be properly fulfilling its patriotic duty if it sent every man into the field. Such a policy is out of the question. Only such men as can be properly spared from the indispensable avocations can be disposed of; that is every man of fighting age owes service, but you must enable agriculture, munitions work, shipping, indispensable trades and commerce to be carried on for the very sake of the war you have to wage.

Such an opportunity only occurs once in a generation and it is now to you to take such measure as you may consider necessary to meet the situation.[14]

As well as emphasising his skill as an orator, Vernon's slow and very deliberately spoken speech set the scene for the historic and unprecedented decision facing the Island. It was unthinkable for Jersey not to follow to Britain's lead to introduce compulsory military service, particularly in light of the Isle of Man's swift move. Yet it was also imperative not to undermine the Island's longstanding rights to make its own laws. Moreover, while there was no doubting Britain's need for soldiers if the country was going to continue and eventually win the war, the Bailiff was right to remind the assembly that they needed to consider the future well-being and security of Islanders as well. The challenge that had dogged Jersey since the start of the war was now on the table: what came first, the needs of Britain or the needs of Jersey?

It seems that such a profound question could not be resolved in just one afternoon's States' session. Despite a plea from the Attorney General for Members to act as the Isle of Man Government had and to adopt the principle of compulsory military service without any delay, there was agreement among Members to defer the final decision for a few more weeks. In that time, the Defence Committee was given the task of drawing up a full Military Service Act for the Island, which was to be debated in a fortnight. It turned out that these timescales proved too brief for the Committee to complete the necessary work, however, and so the debate was again deferred, for a further two weeks. In the meantime, the Island received the surprising news that Guernsey had agreed to introduce compulsory military – independently of Jersey despite an apparent agreement to cooperate on the matter.

Anxious to seen as making a proper contribution to the war effort, Guernsey's States had agreed to a radical proposal put forward by that Island's Lieutenant Governor. Accepting Britain's Military Service Act largely as written, General Sir Reginald Hart VC, GCB, KCVO, proposed the suspension of the Island's Militia Law, and the disbandment of the Guernsey Militia for the duration of the war. In its place, a new British Army regiment would be formed, the Royal Guernsey Light Infantry (RGLI). All men in that island between the ages of eighteen and forty-one would be compulsorily enrolled into the new regiment, for either overseas service with its 1st (Service) Battalion or to remain in Guernsey on home defence duties with its 2nd (Reserve) Battalion. The 2nd Battalion would also be responsible for training drafts of replacements for its overseas service counterpart.

It was a decision that now placed further pressure on Jersey to resolve its position on conscription and move forward by putting an appropriate law in place. There was a widespread expectation that this would happen on 8 July 1916, when another special States' session was convened to review the Defence Committee's plans for compulsory military service. But this turned out to be just a provisional review of the proposals; there was a further States' session planned for 24 July to debate, and hopefully approve them. On that day, it fell to one of the Defence Committee members, Deputy Francis Bois of St Saviour, to present the proposals for consideration. Bois had taken on the job of drawing up the new Act on behalf of the Defence Committee, working with the Attorney General and Solicitor General on the detail. He started by reminding the assembly and the audience watching from the packed galleries that the question of compulsory military service was, 'the most important the States had ever been asked to consider. Up until the present it had been understood that the Militia was to be kept for home defence only,' Bois elaborated. 'They were now proposing that Jersey should depart from that principle and should send men compulsorily to serve in the Imperial forces abroad.'[15] Duly advised, the States began working their way through the new Act, article by article.

For the most part, the Military Service Act drawn up by the Defence

Committee was similar to that of Britain. Mindful of the Island's independent legislative powers, Bois had chosen to extensively reword the majority of its clauses to give them a distinct local flavour however. He had also needed to incorporate the Island's Militia Law into the clauses, something that Britain did not have to do when designing its Act. In contrast to Guernsey, the Defence Committee planned to retain the Militia for home defence duties after the introduction of compulsory military service. There were also other, more subtle, variations from Britain's Military Service Act. They were additions that caused particular concern to the Lieutenant Governor, who was the first to respond to Bois and his proposals. Although such an intervention was permitted because Lieutenant Governors had the right to address the States Assembly it was not normal procedure. Rochfort's early intervention indicated how strongly he objected to the proposed Act. Without attempting to disguise his disappointment at what had been brought forward, he challenged what he saw was an approach that was more about retaining men in Island than about sparing them for the army.

'The first object of the Bill was to provide for men for service overseas,' Rochfort reminded the assembly, 'the second to provide men for the defence of the Island.' The proposals presented had these priorities the wrong way round he contended, before outlining his primary points of objection. First, Rochfort claimed that the proposed Act would result in virtually no men being made available for overseas service. The 1905 Militia Law, which would still be in place after the introduction of conscription, required that a minimum of 1,800 men remain in the Island for home defence. Added to this number would be those men who were granted exemptions under the new law and those who were likely to be found unfit for military service. Second, Rochfort continued, it handed too much authority to the States, or rather the Defence Committee acting on behalf of the States, to exempt men, or whole groups of men, from military service. Under the proposed Act, these men would not have to submit their claim for an exemption to a Military Service Tribunal if the Defence Committee decided they were working in an occupation considered as essential for the Island. While accepting that a similar arrangement did exist under the British Military Service Act, Rochfort pointed out that its purpose was to ensure the continuity of vital war industries, none of which could be said to exist in Jersey. Finally, Rochfort concluded, the Act's proposed tribunal arrangements were insufficiently impartial. The parish Constables would select members for the Island's Military Service Tribunals, while the Defence Committee would choose those to sit on the Central Tribunal, to deal with appeals. This was all considered too insular and too close to local politicians who may have a conflict of interest. It would be far better for the Privy Council in Britain to appoint the members of the Central Tribunal, to ensure distance and impartiality.

Endorsing the Lieutenant Governor's views were the opinions of the Crown Officers. The Solicitor General, Charles Malet De Carteret, felt strongly enough on the matter to make his first ever speech to the States. Referring to a number of suggested amendments put forward by the Lieutenant Governor, he stated that, 'if they were adopted, all difficulties would be obviated.'[16] The States Members were not to be persuaded however. Expressing general satisfaction that the Defence Committee's proposed Act met the needs of Britain, while protecting the needs of Jersey, they passed the new '*Loi sur le Service Militaire*' that afternoon, with minor amendments, none of which addressed the concerns of the Lieutenant Governor or the Crown Officers.

The matter was far from closed however. The new Act still needed approval from the War Office, the Home Office and the Privy Council before coming into force, and the Lieutenant Governor and the Crown Officers were determined to change it. Despite the concerns of the Jersey officials, the War Office appears to have been reasonably relaxed about the States' proposals however. Commenting in a letter sent to the Home Office and the Privy Council, who were still considering the matter, the War Office said there were certain concerns over allowing States' Committees to grant wholesale exemptions, and some suggested additional wording for three articles, but there was only a need to consider changes if the new Act was still under discussion. Rochfort was determined that the matter should remain under discussion. In late August, he travelled to London to meet representatives of the Home Office, the War Office and the Privy Council. While the detail of the discussions is unrecorded, they resulted in a letter being sent on 14 September from the Privy Council to Jersey's Bailiff. Although the style and words were mollifying and conciliatory, the message was plain: the British Government was not prepared to accept Jersey's Military Service Act as it had been proposed. Changes were required, to deal with the concerns that had been raised by the Lieutenant Governor and the Crown Officers during the States' session on 24 July.

First, the letter proposed that it would be better to remove certain clauses relating to the need to retain men for the defence of the Island. Responsibilities for its defence rested with the British Army, not with the States of Jersey. And the British Army would ensure that an adequate number of soldiers remained in the Island, drawn from those men found unfit to serve overseas or those exempt from military service on the grounds of an occupation that was considered essential. Together with men aged below eighteen and above forty-one, they would now constitute the ongoing Jersey Militia, and remain bound to serve under the terms of the Militia Law. Moreover, if there were not enough men left in the Island, reinforcements would be sent from Britain. Second, while it was accepted that States' Committees could exempt men that they employed directly, they could only do so in consultation with the Lieutenant Governor. Third, the clause allowing the Defence Committee to grant wholesale exemptions to classes of men that it believed to be engaged in work of national importance should be completely removed, with such decisions left in the hands of a Military Service Tribunal. Finally, it should not be for the Defence Committee to decide who sits on the Central Tribunal to hear appeals, but representatives chosen by the Privy Council. In general, the letter concluded, it would have been better had Jersey's Military Service Act had more closely followed that of Britain.

The letter was read out at the start of another specially convened States' session on 27 September 1916. Perhaps because of the grave implications of letter – the British Government was effectively overruling Jersey's elected representatives - Rochfort took the time to assure the Defence Committee there was no slight intended towards its members or their intentions. Speaking on its behalf, Deputy Bois reciprocated by assuring all that the Defence Committee was fully aware that the Lieutenant Governor was acting in good faith. Nevertheless, no decision on what to do was taken that day; the matter was deferred yet again, this time to another States' session to take place in the following month.

On Thursday, 24 October the States met once more to discuss Jersey's proposed Military Service Act. Given the issues and the principles at stake it was to be a memorable sitting, and one that was held under the gaze of those in the packed public and private galleries once again. The session began with a speech from the Defence Committee's President, Jurat Walter Aubin, in which he set out the findings of its review of the Privy Council's recommendations. Reminding the assembly that while the States were anxious to provide as many men as possible for military service, it was the duty of the Island's elected representatives, not the British Army, to decide how many could be spared. It was also the responsibility of the States and its Committees to decide how many were required for the defence of the Island and for its well-being. And when it came to well-being, Jurat Aubin elaborated, the most important consideration was ensuring the continuation of the agricultural industry. 'Their lordships will thus see that in all cases where agricultural labour is concerned and upon which industry the existence of the Island practically depends, no other portion of the Empire has been so greatly tried as has the Island of Jersey…'[17] It was a fact, he went on, that at the start of the war, Jersey had lost over two thousand of its French citizens, almost all of whom had been employed as agricultural labourers. Furthermore, since the start of the war, the availability of seasonal labour from France had practically dried up. Consequently, the States and its Committees must be able to exempt men not only from overseas military service but from Militia service also in order to ensure that sufficient numbers of experienced agricultural workers remained in the Island. 'The States should recognise that it will be more economical to have the Militia duties fulfilled by men possessed of leisure time, or who are engaged in work of secondary importance that often demands little special knowledge, and which can be done by either women or children.'[18]

In conclusion, the Defence Committee did not accept the amendments requested by the Privy Council, Aubin announced, but stuck by its proposed law as the most expedient way to introduce compulsory military service. However, mindful of the delicate situation, he proposed that a delegation of States Members, led by the Bailiff, should to travel to London to make the case to the Privy Council in person.

Jurat Aubin's speech had introduced a new dimension to the question as to whether the needs of Britain or Jersey came first. In the Defence Committee's view, the needs of Jersey were intrinsically bound to the needs of the agricultural industry, which had to function even in wartime. Moreover, to ensure that it could, it was necessary not only to exempt certain classes of men from military service overseas, but to release them from their local Militia obligations also. It was a claim that immediately exposed a rift that had simmered since the early days of the war. Amid considerable uproar, a number of Members rose to speak against the Defence Committee's position. Jurat Philip Aubin challenged the claim that French seasonal labourers had been unavailable since the start of the war. The truth was that they were still coming to Jersey, he asserted, albeit in admittedly smaller numbers. He also challenged the statement that Jersey's agricultural industry had been hardest hit in the conflict. The truth was, he declared, that in no other place in the Empire had farmers enjoyed more prosperity, on a per acre basis, than in Jersey. Jurat Giffard was more scathing. 'The Committee seemed to forget the times in which we lived,' he claimed. 'With them it seemed to be business as usual and yet we were in the midst of a stupendous war. The King was calling on all his children to rally round him. Were we going to be ranked with those who opposed everything?'[19] The Rector of Trinity, while pointing out that the agriculturist community was strongly represented in the States Assembly, believed that in its report, 'the Committee had put the interests of the Island before those of the Mother Country.'[20]

There was further opposition to the Defence Committee's position from the Lieutenant Governor once more, as well as a thinly veiled threat that the Island was adopting a risky stance by continuing to oppose Britain's views on the matter. 'We are living in serious times,' he reminded the assembly. 'Is it right in these serious times to raise questions and cause delay...? It would be, would it not, a graceful and patriotic act if the States acceded to the wishes of His Majesty's Privy Council. The Prime Minister has intimated, as you all doubtless know, that at the end of the war all the constitutions of the Empire should be put into the melting pot and recast on geographical and racial lines. It is my ardent desire that the British Government will then be in a position to say that Jersey has given loyal support to the Mother Country throughout the war, and therefore deserved to retain its privileges.'[21]

The States was still not persuaded by such claims or threats however. The proposition of the Defence Committee to reject the Privy Council's amendments and to send a delegation to explain their reasons why was approved by a large majority. The question of compulsory military service in Jersey was again put off until another day. For the Lieutenant Governor, both the solution and the overall situation continued to be unacceptable. Immediately following the States debate he took steps to counter the Defence Committee's position. The Crown Officers were requested to draw up a report on the matter, and this would be placed alongside any representation made to the Privy Council by the Defence Committee. Two days later, on 26 October, the Crown Officers presented their findings.

The thrust was simple: the Defence Committee wanted to exempt Jersey's agricultural workforce from military service, both overseas and in the Island, in order to protect the agricultural industry. The net result would be that comparatively few men actually left the Island for overseas military service. Furthermore, it would place the major burden of recruitment on the town population, which had already contributed more volunteers than the country parishes. The Crown Officers' report also questioned the Defence Committee's assertion that the loss of French agricultural labour at the start of the war and its continued unavailability since meant that retaining local skilled labour was imperative if Jersey was to meet food production demands. Admittedly, some two thousand French workers had left at the start of the war, but others, including the medically unfit and those men with six children or more, had remained. Furthermore, the number of French workers available had increased as they returned from active service for various reasons. Turning to the availability of seasonal labourers, those available had certainly declined from the 2,281 that came to the Island in 1914, yet five hundred had still arrived to work in 1916. Moreover, most French women who resided in the Island were employed on the land, along with women and children from the town. All this meant that while potato production was down, with 43,522 tons exported in 1916 compared to the pre-war average of 55,322 tons, in financial terms farmers were doing considerably better. The value of potato exports in 1916 stood at £572,306, which was more than £200,000 higher that the pre-war average. In conclusion, the report stated, it would be fair to say that 'Jersey farmers have undoubtedly been inconvenienced by the war, but not more so than the agricultural districts of the United Kingdom.'[22]

With the Crown Officers' report to hand, the Privy Council met on 7 November, and considered the States application for a meeting. In the politest possible terms, the request was denied. Subject to certain small concessions and clarifications, they announced, the proposed Jersey Military Service Act should be amended along the lines already indicated and without further discussion. In Britain's great struggle, the Privy Council concluded, the Island must of necessity fall under the arrangements for the defence of the nation as a whole, and not be treated as an isolated or a local matter. The Privy Council letter was read out to a dejected States on 21 November 1916. While some Members bemoaned the fact that their deputation had been declined, others adopted an 'I told you so' tone in their statements during the debate. Most just wanted the matter settled once and for all. It fell to the Attorney General to remind them that the question of compulsory military service had been ongoing since the start of June, at which time the States had determined to act 'as a matter of urgency'. Since then, Le Vavasseur dit Durell revealed, the States and the Defence Committee had considered Jersey's compulsory military service commitment no less than sixteen times, and yet, five months later, the final decision was still outstanding. 'May His Majesty the King be able to say of Jersey, as he will certainly be able to say of Guernsey, "Well done, thou good and faithful servant"?'[23] he questioned.

The matter of Guernsey's approach to compulsory military service was a subject returned to time and time again during the debate that followed. It was pointed out that Guernsey had decided on a simple principle: that every man between the ages of eighteen and forty-one was considered to have enlisted in the British Army and would be liable for active service if needed. Requests for exemption were dealt with initially by a District Military Service Tribunal, with the Island's Royal Court acting as the Central Tribunal. The Guernsey Militia was disbanded for the duration of the war, with responsibilities for the Island's defence placed in the hands of the Lieutenant Governor and the British Army. There was a general conclusion that it would be sensible and the most expedient approach for Jersey to adopt a similar position. The Defence Committee was given two days to draft the necessary law, which they duly did. On 23 November 1916, the States were presented with a Military Service Act that to all intents and purposes was that already in place in Britain, the Isle of Man and Guernsey. Even the wording was modified to remove the distinct Jersey flavour. Amid fractious recriminations over whose system was best, that of Jersey or that of Guernsey, the new law was passed unanimously. It was left to the Bailiff to conclude. Congratulating the Defence Committee on its good work, Vernon told Members that it was no fault of theirs that the original law has not been passed months ago. 'If the bill had been carried on without outside influence,' he remarked wistfully, 'it would have been on the statute book long ago.'[24]

There had been one final twist in Jersey's difficult path towards introducing compulsory military service. Under the terms of Britain's Military Service Act, a man could claim exemption 'on the grounds of a conscientious objection to the undertaking of combatant service.' This highly controversial option had been included in recognition of those who because of a strong religious or moral belief felt that the taking of human life was unjustified in any circumstances. Conscientious objection had been included as grounds for exemption under the terms of Jersey's originally proposed Military Service Act, which had been passed by the States but rejected by the Privy Council. The subject had come up on occasions during the debates, with brief, usually contemptuous and inconclusive discussion on the matter. While the focus had been on more fundamental issues, the matter of conscientious objection had been left to the end. On 23 November 1916, when the States were reluctantly agreeing to accept the law insisted upon by the Privy Council, the proposed exemption from military service on the grounds of conscientious objection was raised by the Rector of St Peter, the Reverend Francis De Gruchy. He spoke strongly against the principle and moved that the clause allowing it be removed. 'This was a time of national crisis,' he reminded Members, 'and there should be no conscientious objectors.'[25] A number of others spoke up with the same views, one claiming that by having the clause in its law Britain had actually created conscientious objectors. Only one, Jurat Philip Aubin, spoke up in favour of retaining the clause, although four others joined him in opposing its removal when the clause was put to a vote. The remainder agreed to remove conscientious objection as a reason for exemption from military service, thus making Jersey the only place in Britain where it did not apply. This despite the fact that the Militia Law it had replaced had allowed exemptions for Quakers on religious grounds. Ironically, the States of Guernsey had attempted to do the same when passing its Military Service Act, but it had been firmly told by Britain that the clause must remain. For reasons unknown, Britain subsequently accepted Jersey's decision. Perhaps wearied by then over the lengthy arguments that had preceded the law's passing, there was simply not the energy for another round of debate.

The whole matter of bringing in compulsory military service had been a bruising encounter, and one that Jersey had ultimately lost. Although there had clearly never been any intention to avoid introducing a Military Service Act that permitted conscription in the Island, it was also clear that the majority of States Members had also wanted to mitigate its worst effects on the population. The fact that doing so would have helped secure Jersey's agricultural industry was certainly a motivating factor, although it is impossible to say how many Members were interested in short term profits rather than the long term interests of the Island. The question of town versus country had also come into focus once again, with claims that an unfair burden of the war effort was being placed on the former. There was still much to be more said on this matter as the war progressed. Passing the Military Service Act was just the start for the Island. Implementing conscription was going to disrupt the lives of thousands of men and their families as never before.

10 KING OR COUNTRYSIDE

Dealing with the conflicting needs of military service and agricultural production

In the one hundred years since its construction at the height of the Napoleonic Wars, St Helier's dominating Fort Regent had seen thousands of soldiers pass through its gates. Yet on 27 March 1917, the group who had approached the old fortress represented a first. Unlike those who had gone before them, the twenty-nine nervous looking individuals reporting for duty on that day were their Island's first conscripts. Under the terms of Jersey's new Military Service Act, they had no choice but to join the British Army. Their presence meant that the time of the volunteer was over; from that day forward, Jerseymen were now liable for compulsory military service outside of their Island.

In the weeks before, volunteering in Jersey had enjoyed a final flourish. There had been a period of thirty days between the Royal Court approving the new Military Service Act on 23 February and the law actually coming into force. Now faced with the inevitable, 232 Islanders had decided to come forward and volunteer for military service before their call-up papers arrived. No doubt some of them had one eye on posterity, deciding it would be better to avoid the post-war stigma of being labelled as a conscript rather than as a volunteer. Others may have only felt free to volunteer for the British Army now that their own local regiment had been disbanded – in far from auspicious circumstances.

The passing of Jersey's Military Service Act had meant an end to the Royal Militia of the Island of Jersey, for the remaining duration of the war at least. After seven hundred years of proud tradition, and two and a half years of loyally guarding their Island, the Militia was disbanded. There was very little ceremony involved in its demise. Uniforms and equipment were hastily handed back, outstanding accounts settled for provisions bought, buildings and facilities emptied and mess furniture sold off to the highest bidder. For the Militiamen, it was a decidedly unsatisfactory end to what for many had been years of unstinting service. The end meant that after 23 February, the now redundant Militiamen had been faced with two options: either to wait for the inevitable call-up or to volunteer immediately for overseas service. Those choosing the latter option had just thirty days to do so.

The late rush to avoid conscription meant a welcome boost to the Island's overall number of volunteers. Statistics compiled by the States showed that between the start of the war and compulsory military service coming into force,

1,833 Islanders had enlisted in Jersey. While the majority had chosen to join the British Army, included in this number were 167 men who had opted for the Royal Navy.[1] The total figure indicated that around 8 percent of the Island's pre-war male population had joined up as volunteers. This was slightly lower than in Britain, however, where around 11.5 percent of its male population had volunteered for military service before the implementation of conscription in that country. Jersey's number was also lower than that of Guernsey, which had a volunteering rate similar to Britain, and considerably less than the comparable figure for the Isle of Man. In that island, figures indicated that around 15 percent of its male population had volunteered for military service.[2] The Jersey authorities were at pains to point out mitigating factors that could explain the disappointing variances. First, and most significant, was the sudden loss of so many French reservists at the start of the war, and the subsequent need to replace them with local labour. This had meant fewer men free to consider volunteering. While Guernsey admittedly had a French population of its own, the immigrant community in that island was smaller than that found in Jersey and therefore the loss was less widely felt. The Isle of Man did not have an equivalent population group present there at the start of the war, and so was not similarly affected, thus leaving more men free to volunteer for military service. Furthermore, the Isle of Man had no compulsory Militia service, just a local volunteer company of soldiers. This meant that from the very start of the war Manxmen had less restrictions imposed on volunteering. Nonetheless, the figures were a source of some concern to the Island's authorities who had already endured the scrutiny of the local newspapers from time to time and specific criticism from the likes of Major Redway in the national press. Yet with compulsory military service now in place, the expectation was that the Island would put aside any reservations over its volunteering record and look forward to making a full contribution to Britain's war effort.

Notices placed in Jersey's newspapers at the beginning of March had explained the process by which men would be called-up. Using the information that had been obtained from National Registration and kept up to date subsequently, the military authorities possessed a complete picture of the Island's male population between the ages of fifteen and sixty-five. Crucially, it showed those men of military age, who now had been grouped into twenty-three separate 'classes', beginning with eighteen-year-olds and ending with those who were forty-one. There was no difference between married and single men; that distinction had been dropped by Britain in May 1916, and therefore was not included in Jersey's Military Service Act. From 25 March 1917, all men in these twenty-three classes were considered to have been enrolled into Britain's armed forces for the duration of the war. They were now regarded as a member of the Army Reserve, awaiting their call-up. The initial groups of men to receive theirs were those in the First and Second Classes, who were aged eighteen and nineteen respectively. Each individual received an official notification by post, stating the date that he had to report for duty and where he should go. For men living in St Helier this was Fort Regent, for those in the eastern parishes it was Grouville Arsenal and for those living in the west of the Island, it was St Peter's Barracks. From 27 March, the first recruits had begun arriving for duty.

After reporting as instructed, the new recruits received a medical examination that if they passed meant that their military service began with immediate effect, either in the Island or overseas on active service. But in contrast with their Guernsey counterparts, the new conscripts would not join a Jersey regiment. For them there was no equivalent of the Royal Guernsey Light Infantry (RGLI). Instead, within a few days of reporting for duty the majority of Jersey conscripts found themselves on a boat bound for Southampton or Weymouth and then on to the Hampshire Regiment Depot in Winchester or that of the Dorsetshire Regiment in Dorchester. Others who followed would find themselves serving in a wide variety of different British Army regiments and corps. The reason was because Jersey had decided to send its conscripted men straight to the British Army, which would determine the unit in which those men would serve. It meant that the Jersey Company, which had left in March 1915, remained the only formed unit that the Island sent for overseas military service during the First World War.

The reason for Jersey's different approach to that of Guernsey was largely one of timing. The proposal by General Hart, the Lieutenant Governor of Guernsey, to create a new regiment for that Island came before 1 July 1916. The disastrous first day of the Battle of the Somme had graphically served to demonstrate the tragic consequences of grouping men from the same community into one military unit and then sending them into battle together. The Accrington Pals, for example, lost 80 percent of its 720 men killed, wounded or missing on 1 July 1916, while the 1st Battalion of the Newfoundland Regiment, which was itself from another Island community, suffered nearly 90 percent casualties among its 780 men ordered to attack enemy positions. Jersey's much delayed Military Service Act appears to have given time for the full realisation of what such collective losses as these meant for communities where, overnight, hundreds of families had lost a relative in action. While Jersey's Lieutenant Governor had offered to form a Jersey regiment for overseas service from the Island's conscripts, the War Office declined to accept it. This proved to be a sensible decision. Although Jersey would miss the prestige of having contributed a regiment of its own at the front, Islanders were subsequently spared from

JERSEY'S GREAT WAR

the tragedy of losing hundreds of men in a single day's action. Guernsey, by contrast, would experience just such an episode in November 1917 when the RGLI suffered heavy losses at Masnières in its first major battle, and then again at Le Doulieu in April 1918 in what turned out be its last.

Timing also played a part in the second factor behind the decision not to form a Jersey regiment, along with the personalities involved. Guernsey's General Hart had been the driving force behind the formation of the RGLI. Influential, energetic and zealously patriotic, Hart was a man half way through his tenure as Guernsey's Lieutenant Governor and was determined to leave his mark on that Island's contribution to the war. In the second half of 1916, Rochfort, by contrast, was coming to the end of his six-year term as Lieutenant Governor of Jersey. In view of his declining health, the British Government appears have taken a decision in the autumn of that year to recall Rochfort and replace him in Jersey. Knowing that he was due to leave, Rochfort was less inclined to press too hard for a legacy in the form of a Jersey regiment. On 6 October, he made a low-key departure, leaving with the Island's thanks and best wishes. Two months later, Jersey's former Lieutenant Governor would be found dead at his London apartment. The sixty-six-year-old had suffered an angina attack.

Rochfort's replacement arrived in the Island on 7 October, immediately following his predecessor's departure. Major General Alexander Wilson, KCB, who was fifty-seven at the time, was another experienced army officer who had seen service in India, Australia and South Africa before the First World War. Prior to his appointment in Jersey, he had served in Egypt with responsibility for the defence of the Suez Canal against the Ottoman Turks, a role for which he received a mention in despatches. In contrast to his predecessor, there would be little time for Wilson to settle into the role of Lieutenant Governor however. His immediate pressing task after arrival had been to gain agreement on the still unresolved and fractious subject of Jersey's Military Service Act, which he achieved on 23 November 1916. His second important task was to oversee the implementation of conscription in the Island, while at the same time disbanding the Militia and forming a new military unit to take over its defence responsibilities.

Under Jersey's originally proposed Military Service Act, the Militia would have remained in existence to provide a defence force for the Island, with some of the conscripted men retained at home to fulfil this purpose. Following the decision to disband the Militia entirely, there was a need for some form of alternative arrangement. During the debate on the matter, there had been a suggestion from the Lieutenant Governor that soldiers could be sent from Britain if required. This was not an idea welcomed by the States however. The defence of Jersey was a responsibility that Islanders had proudly taken upon themselves to provide for generations, and, despite the end of Militia service, the belief was that the responsibility should remain in the hands of Jerseymen.

The new unit that would assume the duties of the Militia was titled the Royal Jersey Garrison Battalion (RJGB), which was quickly brought into existence in February 1917. Despite the new name, it was clearly a derivative of its long serving predecessor. The RJGB's insignia and symbols were those previously associated with the Militia while its first and only wartime commanding officer was sixty-six-year-old Lieutenant Colonel Ludlow Bowles, who had previously been in command of the Militia's West Battalion. It acquired the buildings and facilities formerly used by the Militia, although given that it would have a smaller establishment, the military authorities did not need all of them. The army retained Grouville and St Helier arsenals in use, along with Fort Regent and St Peter's Barracks, but vacated the arsenals at St Peter, St Lawrence, St Martin and St Mary leaving only the caretakers and their families in place. There was a suggestion made that the States take over these now unused facilities to house the families of married soldiers serving in Jersey and use their extensive grounds to grow crops.

The men who served in the RJGB during the First World War had a wide variety of backgrounds, professions and ages. The majority had at least one thing in common however. They were considered as being unsuitable for active service at the front. Following medical examination, the newly conscripted recruits were categorised as being either 'A', which meant that they were fit for active service overseas, or 'B', which meant that they were capable of serving overseas or at home but only on second line duties, or 'C', who were those men considered only suitable for duty at home. Within each of these categories, there were a number of sub-categories to grade a man further and to help place him in a role for which he was considered suitable. Most of the men who joined the RJGB had been medically assessed as being in the lower sub-categories of 'B' or as category 'C'. The majority of its men joined the unit straight after their call-up for military service and subsequent medical examination. As time went on, joining this group were others who had previously served overseas, but through wounds or illness had now been re-categorised as no longer suitable for active service. Lance Corporal Frederick Gibbons, for example, had served in France before returning home to join the RJGB. Gibbons had won the Military Medal in March 1916 at Loos as a member of the Jersey Company, but being wounded meant that he was re-categorised as suitable for home service duties only.

The majority of men who joined the RJGB when called-up in Jersey had previously served in the Militia. Logically, therefore, they would retain their rank and take up duties similar to those that they had been undertaking previously. In contrast to their time in the Militia, however, they were now full-time soldiers as opposed to serving on a part-time basis. Having this permanent complement meant that the RJGB could fulfil its duties with fewer men than the Militia had required. Thus, the Battalion's establishment was set as fifteen officers and 464 other ranks allocated between a headquarters unit, A Company and B Company. Throughout the spring and early summer of 1917, recruitment took place to achieve this number from among those Jersey conscripts found to be suitable for home service only. Yet even after reaching its target, the process of recruitment into the RJGB would steadily continue. Although it required just fewer than five hundred men to be at full strength, nearly eleven hundred men would actually serve with the battalion at one time or another. The reason for this turnover of personnel was that as the health or fitness improved of men initially judged unsuitable for active service, they could be re-categorised and sent for service overseas. After departing, their position was filled by either a new recruit or a man no longer fit for active service at the front. As well as former serving soldiers from Jersey, this latter group also included men who had no affiliation with the Island but arrived from a number of British Army regiments to serve with the RJGB later in the war. Around one hundred men in this category were present in 1918, the majority from the Leicester Regiment, the Northumberland Fusiliers and the York and Lancaster Regiment

While the RJGB formed the infantry component of Jersey's defences from 1917, the Island also continued to possess the reassuring presence of artillery. Although the Royal Jersey Artillery (RJA) had been disbanded together with the other Militia units, following the introduction of the Military Service Act in February 1917, there was a new unit formed to take its place. The 110th Company, Royal Garrison Artillery (RGA), operated the South Hill Battery's two fixed 6-inch harbour defence guns and provided mobile artillery support using a number of the Militia's horse-drawn 4.7-inch QF weapons. With an establishment of around 250 men, its commanding officer was Major Herbert Sorel Le Rossignol, who had formerly been in command of the RJA. Later in the war, the unit would undergo a change in identity, becoming A (Administrative) Battery, 36th Fire Command, this newly titled unit having its headquarters in Guernsey while being responsible for controlling all of the artillery in the Channel Islands.

Together, the RJGB and 110th Company, RGA formed the principal units of the Island's permanent garrison. By the time they came into existence, most other British Army units had departed. Since August 1914, the South Staffordshire Regiment had been the largest present, mostly to train recruits for active service at the front but also to provide the reassuring presence of full-time military forces in Jersey. During their stay, the soldiers of the 4th Battalion and 11th Battalion of the South Staffordshire Regiment had been a very familiar sight in the Island. In common with earlier garrison units, they had mixed with and gained many friends among Islanders, becoming very much part of the community. Yet they were only transitory visitors. Changing priorities led to the British Army requiring the presence of these two units elsewhere. The 11th Battalion had left in May 1915, therefore, moving to Harrogate in the north of England. Thereafter, the 4th Battalion remained in Jersey for another sixteen months, but then it too had departed in September 1916, first to Marske in North Yorkshire, and then to go on active service with the British Expeditionary Force (BEF) on the Western Front from October 1917.

There was one other military unit, or semi-military at least, formed in the Island in the aftermath of disbanding the Militia. This one was strongly supported by the new Lieutenant Governor who was eager to ensure that at least some of the Militia's traditions would continue. Prior to February 1917, Jersey's Militia Law had required the call-up of young men from the age of sixteen for military training. With such obligations no longer included in the Military Service Act, Wilson had encouraged the formation of a new unit that would continue with these earlier principles.

In March 1917, the Island's newspapers announced plans to form a local Scouts Defence Corps. Something very similar had already existed in Britain since the start of the war, created and championed by the irrepressible scout leader Lord Baden-Powell. With his encouragement, local Scout organisations had organised their members into small units that received basic military training which included rifle practice. Their role was to provide support to the army if the country was invaded, carrying messages or guarding facilities for example. Given that Jersey's Militia Law was in place at the time, which meant that local young men already began military training at the age of sixteen, a similar arrangement was not considered necessary or practical for the Island. Following the disbandment of the Militia, that situation had changed however. Led by their District Commander, George Le Cocq, who had founded the Boy Scout movement in Jersey, local Scout leaders had raised the possibility of forming a Scout Defence Corps drawn from young men aged fifteen to eighteen. Following Wilson's strong endorsement, there was an appeal made for volunteers to come forward for the new unit. The response was immediate and substantial, with over sixty-five scouts signing-up within just a few days. It was decided that these volunteers would form the 1st Troop of the Scout Defence Corps, with others allowed to join once the troop's initial period of training was complete.

The role of the Scout Defence Corps was, 'to have a trained force of young men who would be immediately available for the defence of the country should their services be required during the war.[3] To fulfil this, the scouts received military training that included signalling, camp cooking, first aid, trench building and rifle shooting. They also took part in physical training, athletics and cycling. Wherever possible, training and duty took place at times that minimised the disruption to daily life, which was important given that most of the corps' members would have then been in full-time employment.

As well as supporting the principle of training young men for military service, the Lieutenant Governor had another motive for establishing this supplementary unit for the Island's defence. From the very start of his tenure in Jersey, Wilson was on a mission to ensure that the Island released as many men as possible for military service overseas. Any measure that would help fulfil this purpose was welcome. While accepting the need to retain some soldiers in the Island for its defence and that others were required to remain behind to ensure Jersey could continue to function, he clearly believed that the purpose of the new Military Service Act was to provide the men Britain needed to continue with the war. Wilson was determined to send as many as could be spared.

In common with those already passed in Britain, the Isle of Man and Guernsey, Jersey's Military Service Law permitted the exemption of men from military service on certain grounds. These included anybody who had been 'starred' during National Registration as being in an occupation that was considered essential to the war effort. In Britain, some categories of 'starred' men, such as those working in the munitions industry, received wholesale exemptions from military service. The case for such automatic group exemptions in Jersey was much less obvious however. In the end, it was limited to just a select number of States' employees whose roles were considered essential to the running of the Island. They included harbour engineers, lighthouse keepers, Police officers and specialist sanitary workers. Anyone else who believed that their job was sufficiently essential to keep them at home had to apply for an exemption, and prove that their case to avoid military service was a valid one.

The first opportunity to apply for an exemption followed the enactment of the Military Service Act on 23 February 1917. With the law not actually coming into force for a further thirty days, men or their employees had this period to complete and lodge an application for exemption. Some men also decided to undertake a voluntary preliminary medical examination in order to determine their army fitness category, with men judged 'B' or 'C' by army doctors thought likely to be more successful in their appeal against compulsory military service. These medicals took place at the Brighton Road Military Hospital in St Helier. It was soon obvious from the number of men who were hoping to be examined that the volume of applications for exemption was likely to be considerable. 'It should be known that the number of names already on the list for voluntary medical examination is rather more that the medical staff at Brighton Road can deal with all this week,' the *Morning News* had noted. 'It is therefore useless and only a waste of time for any more men now to proceed to the District Office with the idea of getting medically examined before the 25th [of March 1917].'[4] By that deadline day, the number of applications for exemption was revealed to be 2,850. It was evident that the tribunals established to consider applications were going to have a busy time. The newspapers also noted satirically that it was going to be a busy time for the lawyers as well, who were expecting a bumper summer making exemption claims on behalf of their clients.

Just who would sit on Jersey's Military Service Tribunals was being finalised at the same time as the preliminary medical examinations were taking place. There would be three tribunals organised along parochial lines in the same fashion as with the previous Militia arrangements. The Western District Tribunal would deal with applications for exemption arising from St Brelade, St Peter, St Ouen, St Mary, St John and St Lawrence, while the Eastern District Tribunal considered those from Trinity, St Martin, Grouville, St Clement and St Saviour. The Southern District Tribunal would be exclusively for those applications submitted by men living in St Helier. In accordance with the Military Service Act, and very much in line with local wisdom, the parish Constables would appoint the members of their District Tribunal, with every parish involved having at least one representative among them. To be considered for inclusion, all potential tribunal members had to be vouched for as men (there were no women chosen) of honour and good integrity. The minimum number needed for a District Tribunal to be quorate was three, which included the chairman who had the casting vote in the event of a tied decision. Importantly, all District Tribunal members were expected to declare an interest in and step down from taking part in any individual appeals with which they had a personal involvement. It was a rule that was certainly sensible in theory but actually very difficult to achieve in practice in a small island such as Jersey.

Each of the Island's District Tribunals was effectively a court, with the chairman and its members having the roles of judge and jury. Making the case for the 'prosecution' were representatives from the military, whose role was to persuade the tribunal that a man should be released for military service. Those appointed for this task were Captain Hugh Tennant for the Western District Tribunal, Captain John Nugent for the Eastern District Tribunal and Captain Léonce L'H Ogier for the Southern District Tribunal. All were experienced former Militia officers of good standing who now had been found senior commissions in the new RJGB, Ogier was the unit's Adjutant, while Nugent commanded A Company and Tennant commanded B Company. Making the case for the 'defence' could be the man who was applying for an exemption or more often his employer who had to submit reasons why their employee should be considered as essential for the war effort. The help of lawyers was also sought if a man, his employer or his family could afford to pay the fees. As in a court of law, both the military representatives and those claiming exemption could summon witnesses to support their arguments if they were able to add something for or against the case for military service.

The Island's new Military Service Act set out three reasons for which a man could claim an exemption:

1. On the grounds that it is expedient in the national interests that he should, instead of being employed in military service, be engaged in other work in which he is habitually engaged or in which he wishes to be engaged in this Island or, if he is being educated or trained for any work, that he should continue to be so educated or trained;
2. On the grounds that an injustice would ensue, if the man were enlisted for army service owing to his exceptional financial or business obligations or domestic position;
3. On the grounds of ill health or infirmity, in which case the tribunal may ask for a medical report.[5]

In other words, a man could claim that his occupation or the work that he was then training for was essential to the nation's war effort; or that him joining the armed forces would result in serious hardship to his family or an important business he was running; or that his heath left him unable to undertake military service. As previously noted, there was no option to claim an exemption on the grounds of conscientious objection.

If the District Tribunal accepted any of the three permitted reasons, it would award the man an Exemption Certificate, which he had to retain at all times to prove his status. Exemptions could be 'absolute', 'conditional' or 'temporary', the decision as to which was granted being at the tribunal's discretion, but it must clearly state which type it was on the Exemption Certificate. Conditional or temporary usually meant the certificate was valid until a prescribed date, at which time men could reapply to a District Tribunal for a further exemption from military service and prove once again the reasons for doing so. Anyone who had his application for exemption refused by a District Tribunal had an opportunity to appeal against the decision, although he had to give notice of his intention to do so within three days. Any such appeals were heard by the Central Tribunal, which in Jersey's case was established as being the full Royal Court, which was convened as necessary to review applications. By the same measure, the military representatives too could make an appeal to the Royal Court if they considered that the District Tribunal's decision was incorrect.

With the structure in place and the applications for exemption received, Islanders had eagerly awaited the first District Tribunal to take place. 'Local interest will for a week or two to come to be centred in the happenings before the military tribunals of the Island,' commented the *Morning News* at the start of April, with the public, 'keen to know the results of the cases heard.'[6] The public did not have long to wait. On 13 April 1917, Jersey's first District Tribunal held under the terms of the Island's Military Service Act sat in session at St Saviour's Parish Hall. A small crowd of interested spectators were present, grateful for the warming presence of gas heaters on what was a chilly spring morning. Before the tribunal were fourteen applications, all from men who were aged between eighteen and twenty-one following a decision to hear the cases of the youngest age groups first.

There were two absolute exemptions granted at the outset of the day, for applicants on the grounds of ill health, with both men having failed their army medical examination. The tribunal dealt with remaining twelve applications, which in all cases came from men who were working in the Island's farming industry, individually. The first to come before them was that of Walter Le Boutillier, a farmer from a property called Highbury in the parish of St Saviour. He was applying on behalf of his eighteen-year-old son, who was also called Walter. The boy not only suffered from ill health, his father claimed, but was indispensable to the efficient working of his farm. Furthermore, elaborated Le Boutillier, his farm was already very short of labourers and with him suffering from chronic rheumatism, there was no one else to call upon. After listening to the statement, the tribunal chairman had reminded Le Boutillier that these were far from normal times and those who were already working hard must work harder still. Nevertheless, young Walter received a conditional exemption, valid until the end of August after which time that year's harvest should be complete. At the end of this application, the chairman had also reminded those present that at times such as these, people needed to consider employing women to supplement the workforce. The next applicant claimed that he had tried doing just that, but said Mr Cook, a farmer from Bagot in St Saviour, spraying crops was skilled work that women simply couldn't manage. For that reason, he needed his employee, eighteen-year-old Auguste Le Boutillier, to remain on the grounds that his agricultural business was work of national importance. The tribunal accepted the argument. Auguste also received a conditional exemption until the end of August.

Similar claims for exemption were given in the majority of the subsequent applications that day. Farmers needed their young farm labourers, which in many cases were their sons, to remain in the Island in order to keep their farms running. In the majority of cases, the applications were accepted and a conditional exemption from military service granted. In total, ten exemptions were handed out, with only four applications being refused. George Godfray of Hue Farm, St Saviour, had applied for an absolute exemption for his twenty-one-year-old son Stanley on the grounds that his work was of national importance, that by Stanley leaving it would result in personal hardship, and because his son was in ill health. It appears that not being specific enough was Godfray's downfall however. The District Tribunal refused to grant Stanley any exemption and he had to join the army forthwith. Eighteen-year-old Alfred Goupy was another who was refused because, the tribunal pointed out, his father would still have another son, who was sixteen-years-old, to work on his farm. It was the same for twenty-one-year-olds Walter Mourant and Clarence Amy, both of whom failed to convince the tribunal members that their cases were sufficiently strong. They would have to join up and serve their country on the battlefield rather than on a field in Jersey.

The Southern District Tribunal, which sat in St Helier's Town Hall, followed three days later on 16 April with seventeen applications under consideration. In contrast with the Eastern District Tribunal that had preceded it, the applicants in St Helier came from variety of professions and backgrounds. The balance of exemptions to rejections was also different, with nine applications granted - almost all conditionally - while eight others were turned down. The most poignant application had come from Victorie Bitot, a French immigrant's widow who worked a farm in St Helier's Vallée Des Vaux with the help of her two sons, Albert aged twenty-six and Alfred, who was twenty-one-years-old. With two other sons already serving in the armed forces, one with the RJGB and one in the Canadian Army, she claimed to have already suffered greatly as a result of the war. The tribunal's chairman was unmoved however. While accepting her hardship as 'quite possible,' he told Mme Bitot that it was the same for many others. Moreover, he said, 'if you were living in France, all your sons would be serving in the army.'[7] The judgement was that one son, Albert, would have to join up, while Alfred could remain in Jersey – until the end of August that year at least.

On that same day, the first Western Tribunal was held in St Peter's Parish Hall to hear applications from ten men, almost exclusively from the farming industry and applying for exemption on the grounds that their work was of national importance. In eight cases, the applications were granted, though conditionally until the end of August once more. Of the two who were refused, Samuel Le Brocq seems to have been somewhat unlucky given that the majority of other agricultural workers had received exemptions that day. It was pointed out that he had only recently taken up farming, however, and, as the tribunal chairman firmly stated, it looked like he had only done so to avoid military duties. Despite Le Brocq's protestations to the contrary, he was sent to join the army.

And so it went on. The tribunals typically sat for three days each week, and continued week after week. By the end of 1917, official figures would show there had been 2,296 individual applications, from which 1,557 men were granted an exemption from military service. The breakdown of applications between the three District Tribunals were as follows:

District Tribunal	Number of applications	Number of exemptions	*Percentage exempted*
Western	762	625	*82%*
Eastern	623	498	*80%*
Southern	911	434	*48%*

Given the agricultural nature of the country parishes, it was always going to be more likely that the Western and Eastern Districts would grant a greater number of exemptions than the Southern District. Yet to some of those living in St Helier, the disparity between town and countryside highlighted a clear injustice. An anonymous letter writer commenting on the situation in November 1917 complained to the *Morning News* that if people, 'take a bike and ride round the country, you will never credit that Jersey has conscription. Any Sunday afternoon you will meet dozens of young men in civilian clothes airing themselves…The farming community is highly organised for protection, and unless the town folks begin to act they will bear the brunt of the Military Service Act and the farmer's son will get off with a whole skin.'[8] The *Evening Post* considered the matter in its editorial column with a more measured tone, but it still pointed to the apparent unfairness of what was going on. 'It is quite clear that in the opinion of the tribunals we cannot spare more men from the land…Rightly or wrongly, the needs of agriculture and other industries have been made paramount to everything else – even the need for men in the army. One result has been keeping at home young unmarried men who were classed as 'A' category by the army, and the sending to the trenches of men nearly twice their age, many of them with young families.'[9]

The number of men being granted exemptions by the country tribunals was also a matter causing concern to the Lieutenant Governor. Writing to the Home Office in June 1917, Wilson stated that some four thousand men between the ages of eighteen and forty-one had been medically examined by that time, but of these, only 1,500 men had actually been enlisted for military service, of which the larger percentage came from town. 'It will be seen that the tribunals have not been hard on the land,' he observed bluntly, 'and that the whole question resolves itself into the desire to keep the present labour in the Island.'[10] Matters came to a head when Wilson raised the issue of what appeared to be over-generous granting of exemptions by the District Tribunals with the Royal Court, which was sitting in session as the Central Tribunal for appeals. Speaking on the Lieutenant Governor's behalf, Captain Ogier handed a breakdown of exemption figures to the Central Tribunal's members, claiming that, 'this return clearly shows the inequality of sacrifice which exists in the Island.' There were, he stated, young and fit 'A' category men being exempted in the country parishes, whereas the town was sending men to the army from 'B' and even 'C' categories. This should be rectified by revoking all exemptions given to 'A' category men, thus releasing them for military service. In their place, the Lieutenant Governor would arrange for an Agricultural Company to serve in Jersey, drawn from men unsuitable for active military service. They could be men from Jersey or Britain. Furthermore, Captain Ogier pressed, more use of women should be made on the Island's farms, allowing men to leave for military service. 'In almost every part of England and Wales, there are now some two hundred thousand women who are doing real national work on the land,' he stated. 'They are carrying on to the farms the same patriotic enthusiasm which inspires their menfolk by land and sea.'[11]

The Central Tribunal members, under the leadership of the Bailiff, were dismissive of the claims however. In response, Vernon observed that the inequality that appeared to exist in the Island was because the country parishes needed to provide the food for the people of the town. Quite rightly, therefore, the tribunals were very reluctant to exempt 'A' category men but had to do so due to the shortage of experienced agricultural labourers. 'It would have been better,' Vernon concluded tersely, 'if the Lieutenant Governor had forwarded a memorandum of his statement, so that it might be transmitted to the tribunal.'[12] There was also a heated response from Jurat Edward Le Boutillier, who was sitting with the Bailiff, to the claim that local women could do more. 'Jersey country women had done as much as they possibly could,' he declared, 'it was not fair to make statements as had been made.'[13]

Yet the statements had been made, and the message back was clear. The civilian authorities would oppose attempts by the military authorities to enlist as many young men as possible if doing so jeopardised the well-being of the Island. And the well-being of the Island depended on an agricultural industry that could continue to function. Wilson knew that in order to gain the release of more men for military service, and particularly the young men being retained on the farms, he needed to find a way around this impasse.

Aware that many of the initial exemptions had been conditional, and permitted men only to remain in the Island until after the harvest in August 1917, Wilson set about locating an alternative source of agricultural labour. His concern was that after August 1917, the District Tribunals would simply renew the conditional exemptions, extending them to cover the planting season in the following year. One option considered was periodically releasing members of the RJGB from military service for agricultural work. Britain had adopted such a solution, although there had been considerable annoyance in the Island at the thought that newly conscripted Jerseymen were working on British farms rather than those at home. Wilson had been forced to respond with clear statements that Jersey's soldiers had gone for military training in Britain, not to work on the land. He also responded to questions asked by the civilian authorities over the availability of local soldiers saying that the men conscripted into the RJGB were also fully engaged in training during the summer of 1917, and therefore not available as labourers.

An alternative to employing British soldiers was to use those of the enemy instead. In Britain, there was a growing employment of German prisoners of war as farm labourers. In Jersey, Wilson's predecessor, Rochfort, had already tried and failed to have this solution adopted in 1916, at a time when there were more than 1,500 German prisoners of war in the Island. In the summer of 1917, the six hundred prisoners who remained at the Les Blanches Banques camp were working solely at the harbour, and they would only remain in the Island until the export season had ended. Yet if German prisoners of war were not considered appropriate as labourers in the Island, there was an alternative scheme running in Britain that might prove more acceptable. While the Island's civilian authorities may have baulked at the prospect of paying enemy soldiers and sailors for their work, perhaps they would accept the option of paying enemy civilians instead. Wilson was determined to find out.

By the start of 1917, Britain had a ready source of potential civilian labour available for use in agricultural and other work. More than thirty thousand male enemy aliens of military age had been interned since the start of the war, with many of them languishing in camps on the Isle of Man. Some of these men had recently accepted a release on parole in order to undertake supervised civilian work, either for the government or for private employers. By the middle of 1917, there were eight hundred such men who were working as agricultural labourers in Britain. The reports on their performance and reliability had been satisfactory, and the British Government was willing to expand the scheme. At the start of June 1917, Wilson enquired about the availability of any internee labourers for work in Jersey. 'There is a manifest desire to retain men who should certainly be liberated for military duty when the period of temporary exemption granted them expires,' he asserted, 'and the offer of alien labour now available would efficiently meet the situation.'[14] Perhaps mindful of the previous experience with attempts to use enemy prisoners of war in the Island, the Home Office agreed to provide some men on the understanding that farmers in Jersey would definitely use them. To help gain acceptance, it was agreed to offer only Austro-Hungarian internees and possibly those of Turkish nationality, but not Germans nationals. Wilson proposed the idea to the States' Defence Committee.

Despite the concession on nationality, the Defence Committee hesitated to accept the offer. There remained a reluctance to pay the enemy, whether military or civilians, to work in Jersey and concerns over having these internee labourers at large in the community. Perhaps mindful that as recently as 23 May that year, the States had announced that the shortage of labour in the Island was becoming an urgent situation, the Committee nevertheless agreed to gauge the interest of farmers in the scheme. On 9 June 1917, Island newspapers had carried a small notice asking for anyone interested in the 'employment of interned alien enemies in agriculture' to make an application. They had three days to do so. The response was strictly limited. By the closing date on 12 June, only twelve applications had been forthcoming, although the number crept up to twenty over the days that followed. Yet regardless of the farmers' response, Wilson was determined to push forward with the scheme. His intention was to set an example by meeting whatever demand for internee labourers existed, in the expectation it would encourage further applications. On 15 June, therefore, he wired the Home Office asking for the twenty internees requested to be sent immediately. Travelling under military escort, the men arrived in Jersey on the following day. After a medical examination at the Brighton Road Military Hospital, they were assigned to their new employers.

In order to save on the time and expense involved in creating and staffing a guarded camp, the internee labourers were to be housed and fed on the farms to which they were sent. The scheme allowed the farmers to deduct the cost of lodgings from the wages of their allocated internees, which had been set at the same rate as those of an equivalent civilian agricultural labourer. These accommodation arrangements also meant that there was no need for the men to visit local shops to buy food, or to travel back and forth between a camp and their place of work. While on the farms, the men were not treated as prisoners. They had the liberty to leave when not working, although they could travel no further than two miles from their farm unless special permission had been granted. This agreement would allow them to visit church on a Sunday, for example, but not to roam around the Island. The internee labourers also had to obey a curfew that meant being back on the farm by eight o'clock each evening. The Constable of each parish in which the men worked was given the responsibility of ensuring that the internee labourers stuck to these rules. Responsibility for the overall scheme rested with Major George Le Maistre Gruchy, who ran the National Service Bureau from an office at 10 Hill Street in St Helier.

The twenty men who arrived in June 1917 were all Austro-Hungarians who previously had been held either in an internment camp at Feltham in Middlesex, or at one located at Alexandra Park in London. The majority had worked in Britain's hospitality industry prior to the war, mostly as restaurant waiters or in similar roles. Quite what they thought of being sent to Jersey for work on a farm is unknown, but for the most part they seem to have settled down and got on with their allotted duties. From the start it was clear that some of the farmers who employed the men did not think too much of their new workers however. The first complaint about an internee labourer arrived at Major Le Maiste Gruchy's office less than two weeks after the men's arrival. A farmer who had taken one of the men, an Austro-Hungarian called Josef Lojos, reported him as unfit for duty. Lojos was allegedly suffering from 'mental depression', although a doctor at the Brighton Road Military Hospital had diagnosed 'premature aging and poor physique' as the reason he was unable to undertake the assigned agricultural work. Lojos was sent back to the camp at Alexandra Park. During the next few weeks, he was followed by Martinn Burgera, who was said to be ill tempered and addicted to drink, Samuel Carace, who was found to be absent from his farm without leave on two occasions and Ignatz Alfera who was also found to be unfit for manual labour.

Yet while these men were going back, coming in the opposite direction were seventy-one further internee labourers. The Lieutenant Governor's suspicion that more farmers would take advantage of the scheme once it was established proved to be right. The demand for men increased steadily after the arrival of the first group. The second group, all of whom were Austro-Hungarians except for one man who was Turkish, came from the huge internment camp on the Isle of Man, travelling via the camp at Alexandra Park in London to reach Jersey on 7 July. In common with those who had arrived in June, these men were distributed throughout the Island according to demand. The take-up showed that farmers in certain parishes were more willing to accept the scheme than those in others. Trinity, for example, had the largest number of internee labourers, with twenty-one men, while St Saviour was second highest with sixteen. St Ouen and St Lawrence by contrast, two of the largest parishes and both predominantly rural, took only one man apiece, while St Peter and St Martin had three and four each respectively.

Wilson was determined to ensure farmers were not holding back from taking on internee labourers in order to gain exemptions for their sons in August. He was aware that since the arrival of the Austro-Hungarians, the option of using them instead of local labour had come up as a question in many of the District Tribunal hearings. The response given by the majority of applicants seeking an exemption from military service was that the internee labourers were simply not an effective substitute for experienced agriculturalists. Anxious to better understand the situation, Wilson had written to all parish Constables requesting that they give their views on the performance of the Austro-Hungarians. He received a mixed response back. While there were no complaints from some Constables, others held views that were less encouraging. The Constable of St Brelade, for example, believed the use of internee labourers was only partially successful. Of the eight men employed in his parish, just one was said to have given entire satisfaction. The Constable of St Clement concurred. In response to the Lieutenant Governor's query, he observed that it would be fair to say that, 'The farmers put up with these men, for want of anything better…'[15] Only one of the Austro-Hungarians in St Clement, a man who had previous agricultural experience, was reported to be performing acceptably. That was the crux of the issue as far as most Constables were concerned: the fact these men had little or no experience in, and little stamina for, the work for which they had been brought to Jersey meant that they could never really replace experienced local labour.

Wilson was determined to retain the Austro-Hungarians in the Island nonetheless. While freely sending back men genuinely unsuitable for the work through ill health or because of their blatant transgressions, he instructed Major Le Maisha Gruchy to try relocating men classed as unsatisfactory by their initial employer. This would become more challenging as the harvest had ended in August, when a flow of dismissal requests followed, the farmers being understandably reluctant to continue paying for labour that they no longer needed. Wilson remained resolute however. He was not going to follow the same path taken previously with the Island's prisoners of war; the internee labourers were going to stay in Jersey so they would be available in 1918. It was a way to keep the pressure on the civilian authorities to permit more young Islanders to leave for military service. Wilson had set about finding expedient solutions to the situation. He offered to use the now empty Les Blanches Banques POW camp to house unemployed Austro-Hungarians. It would be better still to encourage the farmers to allow the men to remain on their premises until further work became available. The drawback of this latter approach was that the internee labourers were left with more free time, much to the disquiet of the farmers and the parish Constables.

In September 1917, the Attorney General, Henry Le Vavasseur dit Durell, had written to the Lieutenant Governor about the activities of one Austro-Hungarian. Franz Hodina, who was working in St Clement but now said to be 'roaming around the said parish all day long,'[16] much to the annoyance of several parishioners who demanded that steps be taken to remove him immediately. Another, Max Horkey, was arrested in St Helier for being drunk and disorderly in October 1917. The magistrate listened to Horkey's indignant claims that the treatment he was receiving in the Island was more fitting for a pig than for the man he was. Such claims clearly made little difference however. The Austro-Hungarian was jailed and then deported from the Island back to Alexandra Park.

There was an issue arousing greater concern than just internee labourers who were roaming around their parish or getting drunk however. The real worry was in whose company they were spending their spare time. Writing to the Lieutenant Governor again in September 1917, the Attorney General warned that, 'it will be difficult to keep these enemy aliens from keeping company with women, and of course disorder may follow.'[17] While the Austro-Hungarians may have been accepted as necessary for the Island's economy, morality insisted that there could be no question of any romantic liaison between the men and local women. In spite of the restrictions on how far the internee labourers could travel from their farms and a limit on the time to which they could stay out, reports indicated that a number of the men were attending local band performances in the evenings. More worrying still was that some had been seen in the company of girls. In August, the Constable of Grouville had reported that one of the internee labourers in his parish, Carl Schönbauer, was in a relationship with a French woman, although the Constable insisted that blame lay with the woman, who was said to have encouraged Schönbauer. The Censor had also intercepted a letter from one Austro-Hungarian based in St John to a local girl that clearly suggested a relationship between them existed. Another Austro-Hungarian, Ernest Fuchs, had begun a relationship with his employer's daughter that had had resulted in her becoming pregnant. After this was found out, Fuchs was sent back to Britain immediately.

In response to such occurrences, the parish Constables were reminded of their responsibility to enforce the curfew. That did not prevent the most scandalous relationship of all from starting in September 1917. It was between Austro-Hungarian Wenzel Wagner and a local woman. Making matters worse was the fact that both Wagner and the woman were already married, the latter to a soldier in the British Army who was stationed at Fort Regent. When her husband discovered his wife's affair, it led to a public altercation between him and Wagner, much to the dismay of the authorities. After spending time in detention, the Austro-Hungarian was released and allowed to remain in the Island on the understanding that he would end the relationship. Letters intercepted in January 1918 implied the relationship was continuing, however. This time there would be no forgiving; Wagner was promptly returned to Britain.

Despite the complaints of some employers and the outrage of the authorities at times, the majority of internee labourers would remain in the Island into 1918. When the war ended in November that year, just under half of the ninety-one men who had been sent to Jersey were still present. By that time, some of the farmers had clearly become attached to their foreign labourers and would be sorry to see them leave. Writing to the Home Office just after the war, one asked to retain the services of Henry Ceselin a little longer. 'I must say that when the war was on he has always shown that his sympathies were for the British,' Philip Le Feuvre explained, 'I would be very grateful sir, if you would allow me to retain the man till a further date as it would allow me to get on at this busy time…'[18] The war was over, however; the internee labourers had to leave. Despite the requests of Le Feuvre and other farmers, in March 1919, the Island lost its temporary wartime workforce.

Given their small number, the Austro-Hungarian internee labourers were never more than a token workforce in an island that required far more that ninety-one men to operate its agricultural industry. For the Lieutenant Governor, they were an important token nonetheless. In his campaign to release as many of the Island's men as possible for military service, the imported labourers represented a means to counter claims that Islanders could not be spared. Wilson also urged that more use should be made of a far larger group of potential employees who were to be found already in the Island in 1917. The pre-war population of Jersey had included 27,884 women. By 1917, the war had already begun to change the lives of many of them, and would continue to do in the future.

11 | A WOMAN'S WORK

Wartime options and opportunities for the Island's women

'There was a time when the opinion was generally held that women were unreliable and subject to great variableness. But the war had changed all this. It had shown that when put to the test, women were possessed of as much strength of character and as much determination to do and dare as were men.'[1]

Although these words hardly seem out of place today, prior to August 1914 and the start of the First World War, many people – both men and women - would have dismissed the sentiments they expressed as being mere fanciful thinking. Yet the fact that they were spoken publically in October 1917 to a packed Assembly Room in St Helier's Town Hall reveals how far the outlook for women had changed in just three years. Moreover, the fact that the speaker was a woman who was there in an official capacity, and that she was responding to a demand from local women for more opportunities to take up wartime roles, would indicate that this change was unlikely to be a short lived one.

While it is easy today to think of the First World War just in terms of trenches, barbed wire and mud-filled battlefields, it is also important to recall the impact that it had on civilian lives and society in general. This was the first mass conflict of the modern industrial age in which nations pitted their entire strength against each other rather than just their armies and navies. In such a war, it had soon become impossible for the combatant nations to overlook the potential contribution from all sections of society. As a result, the conflict would become the first in which significant numbers of women played an organised and vital role in its outcome. If the First World War irrevocably changed the lives of millions of men, it also did the same for those of millions of women, including many from Jersey. By the war's end, they would find nursing and administrative roles in support of Britain's armed forces at home and abroad. They would take over men's jobs, gain new responsibilities and assist in Britain's war effort towards ultimate victory. And they would even find themselves in uniform as members of the army, the navy and the air force.

Yet all of this was almost unthinkable in 1914, when the role and status of women in society remained very different from that found at the present time. Traditional family and professional values had firmly placed most women in the home or into jobs that were very different to those undertaken by men at the time. This division of roles between the sexes was clearly evident in Jersey just prior to the First World War. In Aquila Road, for example, which was a typical working class street in St Helier, the 1911 Census* reveals that there were 344 residents living in its sixty-four dwellings, of which just over half were women. When it came to the number employed in work, the situation was markedly different. Out of those residents who were aged between fourteen and seventy-years-old, statistics show that 93 percent of Aquila Road's men had jobs compared to 46 percent of women. Men were also employed in a wider variety of occupations, including tradesmen, such as builders, painters, blacksmiths and plasterers, as butchers, bakers and retailers and in more specialised roles including photographers and as a general practitioner. A smaller number worked in unskilled roles, such as labourers and dockworkers. Among Aquila Road's women residents, the situation was significantly different. Their variety of occupations was considerably reduced, with over three quarters of the women who worked employed in three distinct job roles: as dressmakers, as launderers and ironers or as domestic servants. Just six of the road's women worked in retail, while one other was a clerk and one was employed as a printer.

Turning to the Island's countryside, the contrast between the number of men and women who worked in 1911 and the roles they were employed in was equally pronounced. Taking a similar sized sample of residents in the rural parish of Trinity, for example, it reveals that whereas 89 percent of men had a job, only 34 percent of women were employed. The majority of those male workers understandably had roles that were associated with agriculture, as farmers, farmhands, herdsmen and so forth, while around one fifth worked in other occupations, including tradesmen and quarrymen. While some of the area's women had farm-related occupations, most had to accept similar roles to those of their town counterparts, principally in dressmaking, laundry or as a domestic servant. Only one among the women residents, twenty-nine-year-old Agnes Newbegin, worked in what might be described as a professional role, which in her case was as an assistant schoolteacher.

While traditionally held values may have restricted employment opportunities for women in pre-war societies, their rights were also limited under the law. None of the European great powers that went to war in 1914 had permitted their women citizens to vote in major elections or to stand as members of their respective parliaments. The progress towards changing this situation had been slow, even in relatively enlightened countries such as Britain. The last major reform of the electoral system in that country, entitled the Representation of the People Act of 1884 (the Third Reform Act), had enfranchised 60 percent of the male population, but still excluded all women from the right to vote. There was also little prospect of women receiving the right to become a Member of Parliament in Britain as the law limited that

---

* The last Census taken before the First World War.

position to men only. A similar situation existed in Jersey at the time, with little prospect of any change in the foreseeable future.

There were some people in the pre-war years that were determined not to accept this situation. They wanted to bring about meaningful change in women's rights, by whatever means they considered necessary at times. The women's suffrage movement had emerged in Britain during the closing years of the nineteenth century as a force that was championing the cause for that change. In the years leading up to the First World War, it developed into a number of different Suffragette societies, led by prominent reformers such as Emmeline Pankhurst and Millicent Fawcett. A lack of progress, or even recognition of their cause by the British Government, had led to some of these societies adopting increasingly militant actions in order to bring attention to their cause. Suffragettes had openly broke the law, by smashing windows in London, for example, or by setting fire to buildings in some extreme cases. Other campaigners had taken more direct personal action, such as chaining themselves to railings or by going on hunger strike after they had been imprisoned for their offences. The most high profile of these instances occurred in 1913 when campaigner Emily Davison had walked in front of the King's race horse at Epsom and had died as a result of the subsequent collision. Whether she had meant to kill herself remains uncertain to this day, yet Davison's death had helped to raise more awareness of the Suffragettes and their cause by demonstrating the lengths to which some women were prepared to go to in order to achieve equality. Frustratingly for the campaigners, there remained little sign of the British Government's intention to change things despite such actions. It was going to take the war for the situation to begin changing.

Women in Jersey appear to have toyed with the suffrage movement before the war, rather than openly embrace it. Speakers from Suffragette societies had been invited to the Island, addressing freethinking organisations such as the Jersey Centre for Theological Society in August 1913. That month had also seen two members of the Women's Social and Political Union, which was a prominent Suffragette society in Britain, distributing protest leaflets in St Helier. Their motive appears to have been to encourage greater support for their cause among the Island's women, with their presence causing considerable interest. Labelled as 'Militant Suffragettes' by the local newspapers, Miss Lall Forsyth and Miss Agnes Buckton were both veterans of window smashing campaigns in London, and both had spent time in Holloway Prison as a result of their actions. There was a mixed response to their presence in the Island. While some passers-by were openly hostile to them, others were interested in what the women had to say. A number did express general support for the principle of women having the right to the vote, but deplored the militant methods then being employed to achieve it. The reported response from Miss Forsyth was prosaic and unrepentant. 'Christ, you will remember, broke the laws, because they were wrong, because they were unjust,' she told one newspaper reporter, 'We are in the same position.'[2]

The outbreak of war in August 1914 presented the Suffragette leaders with a dilemma. While a small number had argued for continuing their protests, the majority quickly agreed that the appropriate response was to suspend campaigning and cease militant activities for the duration of the conflict. There was a widespread recognition that German victory in the war would pose an even greater threat to everyone's liberties, so it was regarded as more preferable to support Britain's war effort. There was also a realisation that the war presented an opportunity for women to demonstrate their worth in society, and to achieve political concessions as a result. It had also been reasoned that as more of the country's male population left to fight, there would need to be an increasing reliance upon women to fill the jobs that the men had left behind. And the more the nation relied on women, the greater the chance to gain support and recognition for women's rights. It was a political risk for the Suffragette movement, but with most women in Britain soon rallying behind the war effort from the beginning of the conflict, it was one that most Suffragettes had believed that they had little choice but to take.

As noted in an earlier chapter, the first real wartime role for women in Jersey had been to organise and participate in campaigns aimed at supporting the war effort. They had come together in groups to sew, knit, collect, package and fund-raise for both local and overseas good causes. Most prominent in these efforts were women from the Island's upper classes who had assumed leadership roles in charge of the various committees, leagues and societies. Their backgrounds had given them pre-war experience as patrons, presidents and coordinators in many of the Island's charitable organisations, while their established network of contacts, either directly or often through their husbands, also lent them access to key government, religious and military figures. Louisa Stocker, the wife of the Jersey Company's commanding officer, was prominent in a number of campaigns, for example, including the *Morning News* Xmas Gifts Campaign that ran from 1914 to 1916, and which saw the dispatch of more than a thousand seasonal parcels to soldiers and sailors serving overseas.

One of the most important of Jersey's wartime charitable organisations was formed on 10 August 1914, under one of the Island's most prominent women. Lady Julia Vernon, wife of the Island's Bailiff, had been made president of the newly established Jersey Branch of the British Red Cross Society (BRCS). It was going to provide Jersey women with their first real opportunity to do something more for the war effort than just knitting or collecting. Its members would have the chance to undertake nursing and other roles supporting the military by serving in one of the Island's Voluntary Aid Detachments (VADs).

Female nurses had been part of the British Army since the Crimean War in the 1850s, when Florence Nightingale had assumed the role of improving hospital conditions for sick and wounded soldiers. The Army Nursing Service (ANS) had continued this tradition in the years that followed with small numbers of female nurses working in British Army hospitals at home and serving abroad in support of military campaigns. Following experiences in the Boer War, a new organisation was formed in 1902 to expand and improve army nursing. The Queen Alexandra's Imperial Military Nursing Service (QAIMNS), named after the wife of King Edward VII, provided female nurses for the large military hospitals to be found in Britain prior to the First World War. Following recognition that an expanded nursing service would be required in the event of war, Britain had also created the Territorial Force Nursing Service (TFNS) in 1908 to recruit and train part-time military nurses and which could mobilise in the event of war to support the British Army's Territorial Force of part-time soldiers. One year later, the army had also begun a 'Scheme for the Organisation of Voluntary Aid in England and Wales'. Under its remit, the BRCS and the St John's Ambulance would train volunteers who could undertake supplementary nursing roles in wartime. Its members – who were either men or women – were formed into Voluntary Aid Detachments (VADs) led by a commandant and organised along military lines. Women VAD members, were issued with uniforms consisting of mid-blue coloured dresses, white aprons with a prominent red cross and white nursing caps.

Jersey was not included in the 1908 pre-war VAD scheme, even though the St John's Ambulance had been present in the Island since 1884. In 1914, under the direction of Lady Vernon, it had not taken long for the new organisation to become established. The Jersey Branch of the BRCS, which would operate from No. 1 Beresford Street in St Helier, had divided the Island into three districts for administrative purposes. In common with the system already used by the Militia, these were the West District, the East District and the Town District, each of which was led by one of the organisation's vice presidents. Before the end of 1914, a fourth St Clement's District was also established. The role of these districts was to arrange and oversee branch activities across the Island, with their funding coming from membership fees, collections and donations. The branch's principal operational units were three VADs, which were designated VAD Jersey 2, VAD Jersey 4 and VAD Jersey 6. Each VAD had quickly reached and exceeded its full complement of volunteers, which had been established as twenty-four BRCS members. In charge of each VAD was a commandant and a lady superintendent, who was expected to be a trained nurse, and they had the support of an appointed medical officer and a quartermaster. To become a full VAD member, volunteers were required to train for and pass examinations in both nursing and first aid. By the end of 1914, 148 women had done so. Later in the war, as further volunteers completed their training, there would be an expansion that included a VAD Jersey 8 and a Jersey Reserve VAD.

During 1914, the activities of these VADs were very much focused on Jersey, reflecting the general situation at that time. When the German advance in the opening weeks of the war had threatened to bring the fighting either near to or even within the Island, preparations had focused on this meeting the needs of this eventuality. VAD members were placed on standby to assist the military and civilian medical services as needed. There were 106 ambulance carts organised for use transporting the wounded, and prepared for mobilisation to six medical centres organised throughout the Island. Volunteers had also worked to prepare a ready supply of bandages, surgical dressings and splints at a 'hospital stores' department established at 41 New Street in St Helier. When the direct threat of an enemy attack decreased later that year, this effort was switched to making medical supplies to be dispatched to the central store of the BRCS in London. This work of producing medical supplies would continue in the Island for the remainder of the war, and include a team of both men and women that would construct larger items such wooden crutches, bed tables and bed rests.

In November 1914, the decreasing invasion threat now allowed the Jersey Branch of the BRCS, which in November 1915 would combine with the local St John's Ambulance to form the Jersey Joint War Committee, to begin focusing its attention and efforts on overseas activities. Hospitals staffed by VAD personnel had already opened in Britain to supplement and support the efforts of the established military hospitals. Within twelve months of the war starting, there were over eight hundred in existence, and operating from requisitioned public and private buildings throughout the country. The majority of VAD hospitals provided convalescent facilities for wounded men who had undergone medical treatment at a military hospital. A growing number of VADs had also begun to serve in France, Belgium and elsewhere overseas, despite some initial resistance from members of the existing army nursing services. To serve outside Britain, VAD volunteers had to agree to become 'mobile', which was something that a considerable number of those who had joined in Jersey were prepared to do. They were paid while away and could be asked to undertake a range of administrative duties as well as nursing.

Among the first VAD volunteers to serve outside the Island there were three probationer nurses who left early in 1915. Their placement was not working with British wounded, however, but instead as members of a BRCS unit based in Saint-Malo that was helping attend to the large number of French Army casualties being treated there. Hundreds more would follow them on 'mobile' service overseas. By 1917, there were 157 VAD volunteers on 'active' service, which represented nearly half of the Island's 354 women VAD members at that time. Eight of these volunteers had remained in the Island, attached to the Brighton Road Military Hospital to assist the army medical staff working there treating Jersey-based soldiers who had fallen ill or those men sent to the hospital for convalescence from wounds or illness incurred on overseas service. The majority of volunteers had gone to Britain, to work in facilities throughout the country, from Brighton to Inverness and from Chatham to Llandudno, with some serving in VAD hospitals while others worked in those that were operated by the army. A lesser number travelled to France for service there in some of the many British military hospitals located behind the front line, at Rouen for example, or near to the ports along the Channel coast. In theory, these locations were many miles from the actual fighting and therefore any personal danger should have been minimal. In reality, bombing raids by German aircraft on camps and facilities in the areas well to the rear of the battlefields became increasingly commonplace as the war went on, and this would lead to a number of deaths among VAD volunteers, although none from Jersey. A few women were happy to undertake assignments that were even more adventurous, travelling to distant theatres of war. In 1917, three of them, Ellen Ereaut, Florence Gladstone and Alice Le Brocq, served in a BRCS Hospital in Malta, while Eileen Lindsell went to Salonica to work with the British forces fighting in the Balkans. But the VAD volunteer who achieved the greatest distance from home was Alys Buck, a twenty-two-year-old single woman from St Helier, who reached Egypt for service in a military hospital there.

The BRCS and its VAD volunteers would continue to provide their valuable services in the Island and overseas throughout the war. While some of the more traditionally minded members of Island society might have taken issue with the idea of young, single women going overseas to work, they must have at least had comfort in the fact that these volunteers were undertaking nursing duties, a role which was widely held to be a suitable for ladies. The same could not be said of the second group of women who had left the Island to work. The 'munitionettes', as they would become known, took on jobs that before the war were almost exclusively the preserve of men, much to the initial disapproval of many of those who felt it was not a woman's place to be taking on such work.

On 17 March 1915, Britain's Board of Trade issued an appeal for women to come forward and register their willingness to undertake 'war service' work. They had to report to their local labour exchange for paid employment, which could be in one of a number of jobs that included industrial, agricultural and clerical work. Significantly, among the opportunities were positions in the munitions industry. The decision to ask women to take on work manufacturing munitions was a reflection of the growing crisis in the nation's war effort. Britain had entered the conflict in 1914 with a small, all professional army and a munitions industry that was capable of producing this army's weapons and ammunitions. As trench warfare gained its grip on the battlefields in France and Belgium, and the British Army had expanded, the demand for munitions, and in particular heavy guns and artillery shells, had increased. The daily expenditure of shells, which had become the principal means of taking the war to the enemy, had grown enormously as artillery became more dominant. Any major offensive actions served to increase the shell usage rate, which soon highlighted the limitations of Britain's munitions industry. In May 1915, the situation had become known as the 'Shell Crisis' with newspapers taking up the story and firmly laying the reason for recent British battlefield failures on the shortage of shells. While there were other factors that contributed to these battlefield failures, the situation with munitions production could not continue. Britain needed to reorganise and greatly expand its munitions industry. And that would mean opening new factories and employing thousands of new workers at a time when increasing numbers of men were also required for the armed forces. There had been no option but to ask women to undertake work that was formerly almost the exclusive preserve of men.

In Jersey, there had been a first appeal in July 1915 for Islanders to work in Britain's munitions industry. Newspaper notices had requested volunteers who were skilled in 'engineering, shipbuilding and kindred trades' to report to St Helier's Town Hall. The appeal was solely directed at men however. Some fifty had responded and were interviewed by a representative of Britain's newly formed Ministry of Munitions, which had been established to galvanise the nation's production efforts. It would not be until the end of that year, and an intervention by Jersey's Dean, that efforts to recruit women from the Island had really started. The Very Reverend Samuel Falle had already been at the forefront of efforts in 1914 that were aimed at getting Island men to volunteer for the Jersey Contingent. In 1915, he had turned his attention to supporting the nation's munitions industry. Falle, who was then sixty-one-years-old, had been Jersey's Dean since 1906. His position had given him both considerable influence in the Island and a wide circle of contacts in Britain as well. Through one such contact with the owners of a munitions manufacturer in Barrow-in-Furness, he began arranging employment with that company for a number of Island men and women. Once this became widely known, other Jersey women approached the Dean with requests for work in Britain. Seeing the opportunity for Jersey to further aid the war effort, Falle entered into negotiations with the Labour Exchange in Birmingham, which had a number of munitions manufacturers operating in and around the city. After lengthy discussions, there was an agreement for the Island to send a number of its women to the Midlands.

In Jersey, Falle had approached the Constable of St Helier, John Pinel, for assistance in the development of a formal scheme to recruit Island women for work in Britain's munitions industry. Pinel agreed to act as the local assessor for candidates, establishing an application process that included the production of suitable references, an interview and a medical examination at the Town Hall for all candidates. The first batch of twenty-five who were accepted left the Island on 8 February 1916. The Dean accompanied them to Weymouth where that town's Mayor greeted the Jersey party with a reception. He had also helped with arrangements for the Island's workers to sign-up for war work at the town's Labour Exchange. With that process completed, the women boarded a train for Birmingham where a number of volunteers from its city council waited to collect and escort them to accommodation arranged by the local housing committee.

This first batch of Jersey's women workers were employed at Kynoch Ltd, a long-established munitions manufacturer operating from a large factory complex located in Witton on the northern outskirts of the city. Production there had progressively expanded since the start of the war in response to the growing demands of the military. A typical week's output at Kynoch had included twenty-five million rounds of rifle ammunition, seven hundred thousand rounds for revolvers and over one hundred thousand artillery shell cases. At the peak of the war, eighteen thousand people would work at the factory, typically on twelve-hour shifts with production running twenty-four hours a day. Many of the workers were women, who would acquire the nickname 'munitionettes'. The majority were from lower class backgrounds, where their education and status would have limited their pre-war employment opportunities. While this background may have precluded them taking on wartime roles such as nursing, which usually required its volunteers to have some form of qualification and be of good 'social standing', it had not prevented them from taking up jobs in the munitions industry. They had to be prepared to work long hours in mostly repetitive roles, accept a lower wage than the men who often worked alongside them and understand that the job was only open to them for the duration of the war.

Despite these conditions, and the physically demanding nature of the work itself, many of those who did take the opportunity discovered that it was a liberating experience for them. This would have been especially true for those women who had travelled from places such as Jersey to work, and who now had to live independently away from their families and homes. Despite the disparity with men, their wages were typically higher than those that could be earned at home, and they were often living in large cities with plenty of opportunity to socialise with their fellow workers. It was clearly a popular choice for Jersey women. By 1918, there were over five hundred of them working in Britain's munitions industry, in places such as Barrow-in-Furness, Birmingham, Coventry and other locations across Britain, and in roles manufacturing not just ammunition but also weapons, tanks and even ships. The work, while liberating in some ways, could also be unhealthy and at times highly dangerous. Over-exposure to the chemicals used to manufacture explosives slowly poisoned many women workers, for example, turning their hair orange and their skin yellow. This would lead to munitionettes acquiring another nickname of 'canaries', with the effects on a woman's health potentially serious in some extreme cases. More serious still was the threat of explosion. Many munitionettes worked with the high explosives used to fill the shells, which could be extremely volatile. There were a number of explosions caused by accidents, some of which were minor, some catastrophic. One of the worst came on 5 December 1916 at the Barnbow munitions factory situated near Leeds. Several hundred munitionettes had just started their shift filling shells when a massive blast occurred that killed thirty-five women instantly, and wounded many more.

For Jersey women not prepared to leave the island for work in the munitions industry, the First World War would still present the chance for them to experience new roles and occupations at home. The steady departure of men for military service overseas would create a growing range of opportunities for them, although most were on the understanding that the job was only there for the duration of the conflict. Many employers had offered to guarantee that men who joined up would be able to return to their old roles when they came back from war. Nevertheless, the condition was one that many women were prepared to accept. Some of those that did created a stir in the Island. There was widespread publicity given to the first women to take over postal deliveries, for example, with Miss Lillian Smith gaining a brief fame when she started work as a 'letter carrier' in June 1916. Miss Smith, whose parents had been employed by the local Post Office for many years, took over a delivery round in the St Luke's and Havre Des Pas districts of St Helier. There was the novelty of Sarah McQueen taking over as the stationmaster from her husband at Pontac on the Jersey Eastern Railway in 1914, and remaining in the role for the duration of the war. There was also some bemusement as women began taking over transport jobs, becoming drivers for delivery companies and even working as bus drivers. Despite most having to give these jobs up at the end of the war, this necessity would help bring about a longer term change in the island. To make driving easier for their new women employees, local transport companies would have to invest in additional motor vehicles, a move that hastened the end of horse-drawn transport on the Island's roads.

Given its predominance in the Island, the agricultural industry should have presented the greatest opportunity for women in Jersey to find wartime work. The departure of thousands of military reservists at the very start of the war and the subsequent loss of volunteers and then conscripts for military service would progressively strip the countryside of its men. From early on in the war, the Constable of St Helier had tried to establish a 'labour exchange' that would find farming work for those people in the town whose jobs had practically disappeared when tourists had stopped coming to the Island after August 1914. Yet despite the apparent shortage of labour on the Island's farms, the scheme was not a great success with many farmers contemptuous of the efforts made by inexperienced town dwellers on their land and others unwilling to accept women workers.

Pinel nevertheless remained determined to find ways of encouraging more of the Island's farmers to accept a greater use of female labour. He was mindful of efforts made by the British Government to formalise the employment of women on the land through the creation of a number of labour organisations. These included the Women's Forage Corps, the Women's Forestry Corps and the Women's National Land Service Corps. All three were merged in 1917 to form the Women's Land Army (WLA). In 1918, Pinel was instrumental in establishing a Jersey branch of the WLA, under the presidency of his wife Anna. By June of that year, it would have one hundred volunteer members, all of whom had been placed to work at various farms throughout the Island. The women wore khaki uniforms, and received one pound per week along with their food and accommodation if they were employed full-time on a farm, or five shillings a day for those who chose to work on a part-time basis. The local WLA members, or land girls, also received training at the States' Experimental Farm, a facility established before the war to support the Island's agricultural industry. The only restriction placed on them was that they could not work at farms that were employing any of the Austro-Hungarian internee labourers.

The local committee, by their own admission, had found it challenging to get farmers to accept the principle of a Jersey branch of the WLA. Most of those who did so were very satisfied with the work done by their land girls however. The Moor's farm in St Ouen, for example, which was said to have been a pioneer when it came to women labour, were complementary about the six land girls working there. François Houillebecq who farmed in St Clement stated that he was highly pleased with those who worked for him and could not have wished for better. Yet not all were quite so supportive towards the scheme. One young woman complained that a Clarence Le Brun who farmed in St Lawrence had badly mistreated her and two fellow land girls. She claimed that Le Brun had made them start work at half past five in the morning, and then continue until ten o'clock at night on some occasions, with only brief time allowed for their breaks. Moreover, he had refused to pay them the agreed overtime rate, a situation that Constable Pinel pronounced had resulted in conditions that, 'not been work but slavery.'[3] Nevertheless, the young woman said that she still enjoyed the work and was willing to continue if she was treated fairly. But at Pinel's insistence, she and her colleagues were found work on another farm.

For some women, it was not sufficient to be simply working in support the war effort. They had sought a more direct involvement with the nation's armed forces. At the start of the war, the opportunities for women in the British Army and Royal Navy were mainly limited to nursing roles. A number of enterprising and determined organisers had soon begun finding other ways of showing their support however. Some of the pre-war Suffragette leaders had decided to turn their attention towards supporting the war effort directly, founding the Women's Emergency Corps (WEC) in August 1914. In a short time, it would have thousands of members. Although this organisation's principal focus was to provide charitable support for underprivileged communities in Britain and to French and Belgian refugees now in the country, some of its members began to support the military. Those with the skills and means volunteered to become army drivers or despatch riders, while others assisted by providing educational classes for soldiers in training.

Following this early work of the WEC, there had emerged a new women's organisation in 1915, which was one organised in a more military fashion. The Women's Legion (WL) was founded in Londonderry in 1915 to help deal with a growing shortage of men available to undertake the army's administrative and catering roles. Although its members were not formally members of the armed forces, the WL volunteers had worn army-style uniforms, complete with caps and badges. It had soon proved popular, with forty thousand volunteers enrolled and willing to serve by 1916, including a number of women from Jersey. Faced with a growing shortage of men, the military authorities had come to recognise the potential of this group, and the value of women serving in the armed forces. The situation was formalised in 1917 with the creation of the Women's Auxiliary Army Corps (WAAC) and the Women's Royal Naval Service (WRNS), and in 1918, the Women's Royal Air Force (WRAF). The members of these organisations would be formally recognised as military personnel for the first time. The WAAC soon recruited many of the former WL members, and took over their roles in the army's administrative, catering and support services. WAAC members would serve as clerks, cooks, mess waitresses, cleaners, storekeepers, drivers and mechanics, at home and on overseas service.

In search of volunteers, the WAAC had turned its attention to Jersey towards the end of 1917. The audience of a packed meeting at the Town Hall on 14 November that year heard an appeal from a Miss A. Deane, member of the WAAC and the Senior Organising Officer from the Ministry of Labour. The Ministry was reportedly responding to numerous requests from Island women for an opportunity to join the armed forces. Helping with the meeting's organisation and chairing was the Dean, Samuel Falle, who had now turned his ubiquitous attention and energy to this cause as well. Having first been warmly introduced, Miss Deane took the time to explain how the wartime roles of women had emerged during the previous three years and to underline the contribution that women had made to the war effort thus far. 'There is nothing too good to say about these women,' she declared, 'or the services rendered by those thousands of women and girls who have "stuck it" in the munitions factories on the mainland.'[4] Turning to the WAAC and its terms of service, she explained that women aged eighteen and over could join for service in Britain, and that to serve overseas meant being at least twenty-years-old. There were some restrictions on married women, who could enlist but not serve in the same location as their husband if he was in the armed forces also. Additionally, she explained that anyone in the Island who was then working in the agricultural industry could not apply. The rates of pay depended upon the work undertaken, but ranged from twenty shillings per week for unskilled work such as messengers and storekeepers up to thirty-nine shillings and sixpence per week for skilled workers such as shorthand typists. Furthermore, all WAAC members received two week's paid leave per year, with travel allowances for those who wanted to return home during this time. The organisation welcomed all women, Miss Deane announced, adding that it was, 'free from the nonsense of class distinction. Just like the men in the army stood shoulder to shoulder as brothers, so they served loyally as sisters.'[5]

At the end of the meeting, around fifty women came forward to express an interest in joining the WAAC. Yet although Miss Deane was able to offer advice to them, she could not enrol any of the women for service. For while the Island authorities had allowed her to make an appeal on behalf of the WAAC, they also wanted to retain firm control as to which and how many Islanders could join the organisation. There had previously been official alarm expressed over an earlier attempt to encourage Islanders to take up administrative posts in

Britain. A request by the Department of Agriculture and Fisheries seeking to establish a recruiting panel in the Island was rebuffed in May 1917, due to 'the very great shortage of labour in the Island, especially as regards agriculture.'[6] Preventing the Island's women joining the WAAC was less straightforward, especially given the clear interest that existed and because ultimately, candidates could travel to Britain independently if they so wished and apply to join the WAAC there. A compromise was agreed. Jersey would allow a limited number of women from the Island to join, after they had been approved to do so by local authorities. Medical examinations would take place in the Island, with those who passed being given free transport to Britain where they could enrol in the WAAC or in one of the other women's military corps.

Just how many women went through this particular route to enlist in the WAAC or other women's armed forces, or had joined before or subsequently of their own volition, is unknown. But from the few surviving records, it is clear that the majority who did chose to joined the WAAC, which received Royal recognition to become the Queen Mary's Army Auxiliary Corps (QMAAC) in April 1918. Prior to joining, most had been working in clerical or domestic duties in the Island, although some had already left Jersey for Britain to work in the munitions industry. They were of various ages, but the majority were in their twenties and most were unmarried.

Twenty-four-year-old Aileen Lillicrap from St Helier, for example, joined the WAAC in February 1918. She had worked at the General Hospital as a clerk before leaving the Island in 1917 to become a munitions worker in Woolwich, London. On 22 February 1918, she was accepted into the WAAC as a clerk and posted to France in May that year, serving first in Rouen and then at Paris Plage near Etaples on the Channel coast, which was the site of a large British base. Lillicrap had a good knowledge of the French language, something she may have acquired from her mother who was of French descent and which would have made her and other bi-lingual Island women excellent candidates for such a role. After completing her first year, she agreed to extend her service and she remained in the QMAAC until 1920. By contrast, Florence Le Riche was thirty-five, married and with a thirteen-year-old son when she joined the QMAAC in October 1918 to work as a storekeeper and packer in Bristol. Le Riche only remained in the corps for six months, being discharged in April 1919. Lillian Cole had been an office worker before joining the QMAAC in May 1918 aged twenty-four. She too served in France after a transfer to the WRNS. Violet Barnes, on the other hand, remained in Britain as a storekeeper after joining aged twenty-six in August 1917 and with a strong personal endorsement from the Reverend Samuel Falle. She remained in service for nearly two years, before returning home like the others.

Not all of Jersey's overseas servicewomen, volunteers and workers returned home safely however. Nellie Rault was just nineteen-years-old when she joined the WAAC in 1917. It was not her first experience of wartime service, as she had already volunteered for the WL two years earlier. Prior to this Nellie had worked as a tea packer in Jersey, at a factory not far from the St Helier home of her mother, Anne Rault and step-father, John Bewhay. In 1917, members of the WL had transferred to the WAAC and Nellie was posted to the Royal Engineers' Signals Depot at Haynes Park in Bedfordshire where she worked as a cook in the officers' mess there. She was described as a cheerful girl, bright and good looking with a happy outlook who kept in touch with her family regularly, returning to the Island when granted leave. Nellie enjoyed her work, agreeing to sign-on for an additional year once her original twelve month term had expired.

Nellie's decision to remain in the QMAAC rather than to return home to Jersey proved to be a fateful one. On 10 May 1919, her friends missed her at morning roll call. None of them had seen anything of Nellie since the afternoon of the previous day. Search parties were organised on the following morning when she had again failed to appear. One of the parties discovered Nellie's body on 12 May in woodland near the camp, having been roughly hidden in the undergrowth. She had been stabbed several times. Suspicion soon fell upon a Sergeant Major Montague Hepburn who had been at a dance with Nellie on the evening that she went missing. Hepburn, who served with the Royal Engineers at the camp, had also been out with her on previous occasions. Charged with murdering Nellie, the long-serving and decorated soldier was put on trial, protesting his innocence. Despite having his alibis discredited, the case against Hepburn collapsed due to conflicting and confusing evidence provided by the key prosecution witnesses. After the Director of Public Prosecutions had decided that 'the best interests of justice would not be served by immediately proceeding further with this enquiry.'[7] Hepburn was discharged by the court, and despite further investigations into a number of other suspects, no one was ever convicted of Nellie Rault's murder.

Her colleagues in QMAAC had buried her in the churchyard at Haynes with full military honours, although sadly her mother received the news too late for her to make the journey from Jersey. News of her daughter's death reached Queen Mary, who sent a consolation telegram to Mrs Bewhay:

> The Queen has heard from the headquarters of the Queen Mary's Army Auxiliary Corps of your daughter's fine record of good behaviour and splendid work since her enrolment, and Her Majesty cannot help hoping that the knowledge that your

> daughter in her short life was able to render such honourable service to the Corps may be some consolation to you in your bereavement.[8]

Nellie Rault's grave is still found in Bedfordshire near to where she was brutally murdered and a long way from her home in Jersey. Her name is also recorded on the Commonwealth War Grave Commission's Roll of Honour, one of only eight hundred women from the First World War to be accorded that sad honour.

While there may have been official recognition of Nellie's tragic wartime sacrifice, the reward for the majority of other Jersey women who took on new roles and challenges during the First World War was far less obvious. At the end of the conflict, most would be forced to give up their wartime positions and jobs, as communities returned to peacetime arrangements. Yet through their actions between 1914 and 1918, they undoubtedly advanced the cause of women's rights and their status in society, although it is unlikely that this was the motivation for most when volunteering or applying for a position or post. In common with their male counterparts who volunteered for military service, one woman's reason for coming forward would have been different from the next person. Collectively, however, their commitment contributed to Britain's victory and helped pave the way for realising the pre-war ambitions of the Suffragette movement through the post-war granting of equal voting rights and equal equality laws. In Jersey, those rights and equalities would take longer to come about, but through their commitment and sacrifice, Jersey's women had started an irreversible progression towards today's modern world.

12 MONEY, FOOD AND MEN

The challenges and demands faced by Jersey in a fourth year of war

During the Second World War that followed, it had become obvious by the winter of 1944/45 to even those with the narrowest of views that the Allies were going to win. Yet twenty-seven years earlier, during the final winter of the First World War, it is reasonable to say that the outcome was far less certain. In fact, given the prevailing situation at that time, it would have appeared more likely that Germany was on course for victory.

On the Eastern Front, an exhausted Russia and its army were leaving the war following defeat on the battlefield and after revolutionary turmoil at home had swept the Tsar and his Romanov dynasty from power in the spring of 1917. One outcome of this situation was that large numbers of German troops who had been fighting in the east were steadily moving across Europe for deployment in France and Belgium. There, the Allies could only nervously wait for a widely expected German offensive. The leaders of France and Britain knew that in due course, the departure of Russia would be offset by the arrival of the United States, which had entered the war on the Allied side in April 1917. Yet the reality was that it was going to take considerable time to equip and train an American Army that was capable of making a decisive contribution to the war, something not expected to occur before the summer of 1918. In the meantime, France remained weakened by a series of mutinies that had swept through its army during the summer of 1917 and was running out of men to replace the enormous losses sustained in three years of fighting. Britain too was feeling the effects of yet another year of mostly unsuccessful and very costly offensives, with its army short of the men needed to replace the losses incurred. During 1917, Britain had also been under siege at home as Germany sent its U-boat fleet on a campaign planned to starve the country into submission. The resulting struggle not only threatened Britain but also had potentially very serious consequences for Jersey.

Given the nature of their home, Islanders had a long and complex relationship with the sea. For centuries, generations of fishermen, mariners and ship-builders had been an integral part of Jersey's population. While the shipbuilding and fishing industries may have declined in the nineteenth century, at the start of the First World War men from Jersey still served throughout the world on all manner of vessels. A considerable number of them were in the

Royal Navy. In 1914, there were 650 men from Jersey serving on His Majesty's ships and among Royal Navy shore establishments, both as full-time sailors and as reservists recalled for service on the outbreak of war. More Islanders had subsequently joined them in the years that followed, as volunteering and conscription had taken men into the Britain's armed forces. The Island's first naval death had come within weeks of the war starting when, on 22 September 1914, Able Seaman Francis Hoffman lost his life along with 526 comrades when his ship, the cruiser HMS *Aboukir*, was sunk by a German submarine in the North Sea. Six weeks later, far away off the coast of Chile, fifteen more Jersey sailors would die in a single day's action when Britain lost HMS *Good Hope* and HMS *Monmouth* to the guns of Germany's East Asia Squadron at the Battle of Coronel. It was a salutary reminder that modern naval warfare could exact a sudden and heavy cost on those communities whose men served at sea. This was underlined by a 1916 naval battle that resulted in the greatest one-day loss of life suffered by the Island during the war. After almost two years of inconclusive sparring in the North Sea, the British Grand Fleet and the German High Seas Fleet finally clashed on 31 May 1916 in the Battle of Jutland. On that day and during the night that followed, 250 warships fought a series of encounters that resulted in the sinking of eleven German and fourteen British vessels. Just over six thousand Royal Navy sailors were killed, twenty-six of whom were from Jersey. Among them was eighteen-year-old Midshipman Philip Malet De Carteret, a member of one of Jersey most prestigious families who died along with 1,265 of his comrades when the battlecruiser HMS *Queen Mary* exploded and then sank within minutes.

Jersey seamen also served extensively on merchant vessels during the First World War. More than seven hundred Islanders could be found on board all classes of ship, from small ketches and schooners up to busy cross-channel steamers and grand ocean-going liners. While life on a merchant ship may have been thought less glamorous than that of their Royal Navy counterparts, the threats faced by merchant seamen were just as deadly. On 12 December 1914, Deckhand William Gallichan had been the first merchant seaman from Jersey to lose his life when the steam trawler *Cygnus* was sunk by a mine in the North Sea. Before the end of the war, the Island would lose at least sixty other merchant seamen.

Aside from the ever present challenges of heavy seas and poor weather, the greatest threat to British merchant seamen came from enemy submarines. Germany had entered the war with a small U-boat fleet that had initially confined its activity to the North Sea, attacking warships such as HMS *Aboukir* and laying mines to sink unwary vessels such as the *Cygnus*. Towards the end of that year, they had begun to venture into the English Channel, causing some anxiety but not having any significant effect. This situation would change in 1915 as the war at sea intensified. German submarines based in captured Belgian ports now began making their presence felt around the British Isles, sinking an increasing number of merchant ships in an attempt to blockade Britain. They were also a cause for concern in Jersey, which relied on its daily cross-Channel sailings to bring passengers and provisions to and from the Island. The first brush with a U-boat came in March 1915 when the master of the London and South Western Railways ship SS *Lydia* reported that a submarine had attempted to torpedo his ship not far north of the Channel Islands. As noted in an earlier chapter, there had also been concerns expressed by French naval commanders that U-boats may have been using the Channel Islands as supply bases. Although these suspicions were unfounded, in 1915 a small flotilla of French Navy torpedo boats took up residence in St Helier Harbour to provide protection for shipping in the Bay of St Malo. Later in the war, a French seaplane base in Guernsey and a Royal Naval Air Service (RNAS) squadron based in Cherbourg would strengthen local anti-submarine defences, with their aircraft engaged in hunting down enemy submarines and in spotting minefields. Among the British pilots based in France was Jerseyman Lieutenant Charles Mossop, who would win the Distinguished Service Cross (DSC) on 18 August 1917 for sinking the German mine-laying submarine UB-32 in waters north of the Channel Islands. Sadly, the young airman was killed a few months later when his aircraft crashed off the coast of France.

In due course, Germany would scale back its initial submarine operations after U-20 had sunk the liner RMS *Lusitania* in May 1915. The deaths of more than one thousand passengers, among which were women and children, caused international outrage, including in the then neutral United States that lost more than one hundred of its citizens in the sinking. Thereafter, U-boats began to operate under more restrictive practices that included surfacing to warn ships they were about to be attacked and to allow the crews to abandon ship. The loss of ships went on nevertheless, and this would include a number of Jersey-connected vessels that were sunk near the Channel Islands, among them the SS *Maud*, a 120-ton sailing vessel destroyed by submarine gunfire on 2 May 1916. On 3 December that year, U-boats had also attacked three more vessels in nearby waters, the sailing boats *Seeker* and *Mizpah* and the Danish-owned steamer *Yrsa*. In all of these cases, the vessels were stopped and their crews permitted to abandon ship before it was sunk. But all such notions of civilised behaviour would again disappear in February 1917 when the Germans resumed unrestricted submarine warfare once more.

Germany's military leaders had persuaded the Kaiser that only by adopting the severest of measures could they guarantee a successful outcome to the war.

This included launching a concentrated submarine campaign against Britain's vulnerable supply lines, while accepting the risk that an outraged United States would enter the war on the Allied side. Their argument was that Britain would have to sue for peace before the small American Army could be expanded to any significant size. At the start of 1917, the Kaiser agreed to recommence a campaign of unrestricted submarine warfare that would dispense with the need to warn merchant ships before they were attacked and which considered any vessel entering a designated war zone as a legitimate target. As a result, in February 1917, U-boats sunk over four hundred thousand tons of shipping around the coast of Britain, in March five hundred thousand tons and in April the figure climbed to over six hundred thousand tons. As the losses continued into the summer of that year, the outlook for Britain became increasingly bleak, with vital stocks of food and other essentials dwindling. It was total warfare, and it now affected all of the British Isles including Jersey.

It had not just been the direct threat of U-boats sinking ships bound to and from Jersey that had worried the States in the summer and autumn of 1917. While the danger posed to those ships crossing the Channel was undoubtedly very real, of more concern were the consequences arising from the dire losses then being inflicted upon Britain's merchant fleet. There was simply an increasing shortage of ships available to carry provisions to Jersey. Moreover, as Britain's own stockpiles of food and fuel had dwindled, it had become more difficult – and certainly more expensive – to procure what the Island needed to import. As the war entered its fourth year, Jersey faced a worrying winter of uncertainty over the availability of vital supplies.

Things could have been far worse however. That they were not was due to some far-sighted measures that had been taken earlier in the war and then by subsequent action of the Island's civilian and military authorities as concerns over the availability of supplies increased. The steps by the Lieutenant Governor and the States in August 1914 to control the distribution of food and the prices charged had been the start of this process. While this act may have appeared somewhat drastic at that time, it had served to underline the Island's vulnerability when it came to essential supplies. Despite its prosperous agricultural industry, Jersey still had to import a considerable amount of the food consumed by Islanders and the majority of the fuel that was needed for its lighting, heating and cooking. As would be the same for any community faced with this situation, it was not just the threat arising from a complete loss of supplies that concerned the authorities, but also the consequences of shortages and the resulting price rises that invariably affected the poorest in the population first. It had not taken long for these concerns to manifest themselves as public anxiety. As early as January 1915, the Island's newspapers were reporting disquiet over the price of bread, followed a month later by concerns regarding the increasing cost of coal. There were also worries over the price of butter, a commodity that Islanders were used to obtaining at a reasonable price given the quality and size of the local dairy industry. This situation would lead to a curious and prolonged debate both among the public and also in the States over the question of whether margarine should be introduced as a substitute for butter, and if so whether or not it should be coloured.

The option of using margarine as a substitute for butter had been a contentious issue in the years before the First World War. Seeking protection for their industry, farmers across the world had lobbied governments for legislation to prevent the sale of what was in effect a cheap substitute for butter, or at least to only permit its sale in an 'uncoloured' state so that margarine did not look like butter. In Jersey, the laws that had existed forbidding the sale of margarine had been lifted soon after the start of the war in order to protect the poor against rising butter prices. Yet margarine had only been allowed in a form that was not coloured yellow so that there was no mistaking exactly what it was. Then in December 1915, the Constable of St Helier tabled an amendment to allow the sale of coloured margarine, for the benefit of those who could no longer afford butter. Would members be happy to see uncoloured and insipid-looking white margarine on their tables, John Pinel asked States Members. 'The only possible reply was a negative. It was absolutely unnecessary to force poor people to eat it.'[1] Predictably, there was considerable resistance against the move from Members with a farming background who expressed their worries about the impact that low price margarine would have on the local dairy industry. There were also concerns expressed that such a move would allow unscrupulous merchants to mix margarine with butter to create some form of unwholesome product and then to sell it fraudulently. Despite the arguments against, the States recognised that the needs of the people came first and on 20 January 1916 Members finally passed the 'Margarine Bill' that allowed the sale of coloured margarine in the Island.

Early concerns over rising food prices and the contentious use of products such as margarine had clearly helped to focus the States' attention on the subject of essential supplies. Important steps had soon been taken to ensure their availability and distribution, and to control the prices that merchants could charge. Among the measures that were implemented was the creation of a new States' Food Production Committee that would work closely with the Island's farmers on maximising the amount of land under cultivation and ensuring that the best balance of crops were grown. The States' Defence Committee also turned its attention onto the Island's supply arrangements, working with merchants and retailers to manage imports, distribution and the pricing of essential goods such as bread, meat and potatoes. That the work undertaken was effective is evidenced by the fact that Jersey, unlike Britain, did not have to resort to widespread food rationing during the First World War. Aside from petrol, which had been restricted from soon after the start of the war, the only restriction faced by Islanders was a sugar ration imposed from October 1917. That is not to say that there were no efforts made to reduce consumption. From early 1917, the States had openly begun to encourage Islanders to reduce the amount of food that they were eating. In February that year the Defence Committee published dietary guidelines, 'in order to ensure a just and economical distribution of the principal important foodstuffs for all classes of the population…'[2] Among its recommendations were that people's weekly diet should include no more than four pounds of bread, two and a half pounds of meat and six ounces of sugar.

The adequate provision of bread had remained high on the list of the States' priorities throughout the war, but was something that was among the most challenging to achieve. Flour was one of the Island's most essential imports, with eighty tons needed each week in order to ensure that Islanders received their daily requirement of bread. Local production using the Island's antiquated watermills could only produce one quarter of this amount, with the flour that was made in this way being typically coarse and unsuited for bread. The balance had to be imported from Britain, which even by the start of 1915 was struggling to find the necessary rail and shipping capacity needed to carry flour to Jersey. Mindful of the possible implications of the supply of bread either becoming scarce or even running out, the States had intervened. While asking the Lieutenant Governor to lobby the British Government for the means to get flour to Jersey, the Defence Committee had established a storage depot at St Helier's West Park Pavilion. There, under armed guard, a minimum of one month's supply of flour was held, a reserve to be used should privately imported stocks have run out or the prices risen too high. It was a wise decision. After February 1917, the problem of local flour shortages became increasingly acute as the U-boats resumed their unrestricted campaign against merchant shipping around the British Isles. By November that year, the total stocks of flour in the Island had fallen to just 230 tons, which represented less than one-month's supply. It would lead to an urgent appeal to the British Government for assistance in obtaining the necessary flour stocks and for the shipping required to transport it to Jersey. Fortunately, determined persistence on this occasion paid off and Britain responded at the eleventh hour to prevent bread shortages on the Island.

Alongside the availability of flour, the other major concern for the States was over the supplies of fuel. The Island relied heavily on coal, for both domestic and business use. It was also the source of the local gas supply, which was provided by the Jersey Gas Light Company through a coal gasification process that took place at the company's works in St Helier. To satisfy normal consumption requirements, the Island needed to import forty thousand tons of coal annually. Concerns over its availability had led to rising prices in 1915, and further increases in 1916, which in turn caused considerable public agitation, particularly among the poorer members of the community. As a result of this, children and adults regularly followed the heavily laden coal carts leaving the harbour and collected any lumps that fell off as the carts bumped over the cobbles. Whatever the motive or circumstances of the collectors, coal merchants appealed for the Constable of St Helier to protect their supplies, particularly after it was found that some people were bringing along sticks to 'help' the coal fall off the carts.

The threat of rising fuel prices had already been recognised as a serious issue in Britain, and legislation was introduced there to impose price controls that protected the poorest in the community. As the winter of 1917/18 approached, there had been calls in Jersey for the States to introduce similar measures. One concerned St Helier businessman, a Mr Huelin of the Esplanade, went as far as to petition the British Government with an appeal to extend its 'Price of Coal Limitation Act' to the Island. It was unreasonable to expect the wife of a serving soldier who lived on twelve shillings a week separation allowance, he complained, to have to pay five shilling per week for her weekly coal supply. The British Government was sympathetic, but explained that it was a matter for the Island's authorities to address. The States were in the process of doing so at that time. By the autumn of 1917, it was becoming obvious that there was a need for further measures to ensure adequate coal supplies for the coming winter. Coal merchants had been raising concerns over the availability of supplies from August that year, leading to the States sending a special deputation to London for talks with the British Government. The British Government had responded in October by insisting that before coal could be provided, the Island's authorities had to do more to control the price of coal and to improve distribution. The States had quickly agreed, and appointed Deputy Francis Bois to the role of 'Coal Controller'. Despite these measures, coal was still not forthcoming, which led to rapidly dwindling local stocks and an exchange of increasingly urgent telegrams and letters with the British Government. The States' appeal finally succeeded, and the arrival of the SS *Alice Taylor* and her load of coal late in January 1918 meant that a potential crisis had been averted. Coal stocks would remain a concern until the end of the war, but Jersey had come through the worst.

Through measures such as these, the States and the Lieutenant Governor had been able to spare Islanders from any excessive hardships when it came to food and fuel, even during the most challenging winter of 1917/18. While similar actions in Britain had not prevented rationing there, they had helped overcome the crisis posed by Germany's unrestricted submarine campaign. By the start of 1918, Britain also appeared to have mastered the U-boat threat. After reaching a peak in the late spring of 1917, shipping losses had slowly declined and then levelled off at a costly yet bearable level. While the danger had not passed, enough supplies were reaching the country to avoid the threat of starvation. It meant that Britain could remain in the war during 1918.

Despite success against U-boats and an improving supply situation, the outlook for Britain and its allies had remained extremely grave at the start of 1918. If Britain was going to continue fighting the war and have any hope of emerging victorious, it was going to have to draw deeply upon its remaining resources and make more demands on those possessed by its Empire. With this in mind, a letter from the British Home Secretary, Sir George Cave, had arrived on the desk of Jersey's Lieutenant Governor on 13 April 1918. Although couched in polite prose, the letter's message was a simple one: Britain needed Jersey to make an even greater contribution to the nation's war effort. 'His Majesty's Government think it necessary, in the present national crisis,' the Home Secretary had announced, 'to bring before the Island of Jersey the urgent importance of their assisting, to the utmost extent of their resources, in the prosecution of the war.'[3]

It was not just Jersey that was being singled out, and the letter had gratefully acknowledged the contribution already made by Islanders up until that time. But more was needed. The demands were straightforward: the Island had to contribute more money, more food and more men. When it came to how this was to be achieved, Britain could offer advice and assistance, but it was for the Lieutenant Governor and the States to decide what was the most practical measures to take. Given the wartime situation, however, there was a need for firm action to be taken as soon as practically possible. 'The Government invite the Island of Jersey to take its full share now in the defence of the freedom and safety of the Empire with which their own safety and freedom are inseparably connected…,' the letter had concluded with a flourish. 'They feel sure that the people of Jersey do not fail to realise the greatness of the need and will respond to the utmost of their power.'[4]

Wilson must have thought long and hard about the letter before passing it on to the Bailiff for consideration two days later. He would have been very aware of the seriousness of the demands being made and that it was his duty to encourage the Island to do all that it could to meet them. Yet the previous eighteen months of fractious wrangling with the States over the Military Service

Act and the subsequent challenges over the implementation of conscription would have also warned him that there was likely to be further stress placed on the relationship between the British Government and the States. Earlier arguments may have also hardened Wilson's attitude towards the States. His actions during the months that followed do indicate that there was not the most harmonious relationship between the Island and its Lieutenant Governor, a situation that was not an ideal one given the magnitude of what was being asked for by the British Government.

The Bailiff's response to the letter was conciliatory and supportive however. 'I wish to place on record my sense of the importance and urgency of the message which Sir George Cave's letter of the 11th instant conveys to this Island,' Vernon had swiftly replied, 'and the assurance that every effort will, I trust, be made in order to effect its objects as far as local circumstances and resources may permit.'[5] A hastily convened conference of the Island's leaders had followed, at which there was a decision to place the request before the States. On 25 April 1918, the States had met in session to consider the letter and its implications for Jersey. The situation, Vernon informed them, was starkly clear. Jersey had lived and wished to remain under the Crown of England and was therefore tied to the fate of the mother country. Moreover, he informed a muted assembly, Islanders had further reasons to answer requests for help now that the enemy was in the ascendency. 'If Germany was to win and dictate terms of peace she would demand indemnities,' Vernon had dramatically asserted. 'One of the first things she would say in that case would be: "We take the Channel Islands." That was an absolute certainty.'[6] If Jersey was to avoid such a fate, he announced, the Island had to find the means of providing what the British Government had asked for. Whatever the validity of the Bailiff's ominous prediction, all three demands were given immediate attention. Perhaps the most straightforward demand to be addressed was the one asking for more money. Indeed the question of Jersey's financial contribution towards the cost of the war had been already under discussion, even before the arrival of the Home Secretary's letter. And it stemmed from the time when the Island's Militia had been disbanded and the new Military Service Act had come into force.

Up until February 1917, Jersey had been responsible for meeting the cost of the Militia's mobilisation. As noted in an earlier chapter, this unexpected expenditure had almost bankrupted the Island at the very start of the war, with the situation saved only by a loan funded by the issue of a £50,000 States' war bond. At that time, it was hoped that mobilisation was just a temporary measure, which had turned out to be somewhat optimistic. Between August 1914 and February 1917, expenditure on the Militia had amounted to £120,000, and this required the issuing of a second war bond for £100,000 in 1915 to cover the ongoing outlay. Yet from February 1917, the expenditure had stopped as responsibility for Jersey's defence passed to Britain under the terms of the Island's Military Service Act. The War Office had seen matters differently, however, and in June 1917 raised its disapproval of British taxpayers having to meet the cost of Jersey's defence. In a letter to the Home Office, the War Office made it clear that, 'the Army Council feel that such an arrangement is clearly inequitable and that it calls for amendment.'[7] Consequently, the Home Office had written to the Lieutenant Governor asking for Jersey to make a financial contribution towards the cost of the Island's continuing defence.

The initial response from the States to the request had been a vague suggestion that such matters were best left until after the war for settlement. But the Home Office was not in a mood to let the issue be forgotten, and wrote again in September 1917 asking to be advised as to what was being planned. Unable to put the question to one side as had been hoped for, after due deliberation in December that year the States agreed to offer a contribution of £25,000 towards the cost of its defence. The logic was that this amount represented the approximate annual expense of keeping the Militia mobilised. Yet while the British Government had gratefully accepted the offer, the Lieutenant Governor was less than satisfied with the amount proposed. In a forthright letter to the Home Office a few days after the States had agreed to pay, he made it clear that in his opinion the sum offered, 'is insufficient, and an inadequate return for the benefits that this Island has received…I consider that the Island could for the past year well afford to give more than double the amount that is now offered, and further, there should be an annual contribution dating from the 23rd February 1917, the date on which the Island's Militia was suspended.'[8] Home Secretary George Cave was persuaded, prompting him to include the demand for more money in his April letter.

The reaction of the States was commendably supportive of the request. There had already been an assurance given to the British Government that the £25,000 could be considered as an initial payment if necessary and that more money would be sent if needed. After further debate, and correspondence between the two governments, another payment of £50,000 was agreed, to be paid in October 1918 after a further loan for the same amount had been secured through the issuing of a third States war bond. Another £25,000 would follow immediately after the war ended to bring the total amount given by Jersey to £100,000. As a token of its appreciation, a grateful Home Office arranged to place special notes to record the donations in the Treasury minutes for presentation to both houses of the British Parliament.[*]

[*] The matter of Jersey's financial contribution to Britain's war effort was not completely settled at this time. After the war, the British Government requested an annual contribution of £275,000 from the Island towards the cost of defence and other Imperial services. The States had countered by offering a single payment of £300,000, which was finally accepted in 1927.

The Home Secretary's second request had been for the Island to provide more food for Britain. In effect, this had meant more potatoes. As with the request for defence funding, the question of potatoes was already under discussion when the letter arrived. The British Government had been taking an interest in Jersey's potato production since 1916. Towards the end of that year, representatives from the British Board of Agriculture and Fisheries and the Army Forage Corps approached the newly created Food Production Committee with a proposal. To feed its army, Britain wanted to requisition twenty-three thousand tons of Jersey Royals, which was approximately one third of the Island's annual crop. In return, farmers would receive a fixed price per ton, while Britain would supply all of the necessary freight and shipping facilities. The potatoes were not required until after June 1917, meaning that farmers would still enjoy good income from the sale of the choice early crop on the British market. Although no farmer was obliged to accept the offer, in truth the States had already committed the Island's growers to the arrangement. Britain was at war, it had been explained, and therefore Jersey had to conform to national expectations. To do so, the Island would have to increase the land under cultivation, wherever possible, and to give up growing non-staple crops including most of its tomatoes. For some growers the whole arrangement trampled upon Jersey's longstanding rights and privileges and on the principles of free trade. 'If England adopts a policy of colonial legislation towards us and violates our constitutional safeguards it is useless for our population to continue the struggle…'[9] wrote one indignant farmer. 'I have the honour to inform you that after much mature and careful consideration of the requisition order…I find myself reluctantly unable to comply…'[10] was the response in another letter.

Nonetheless, the requisition went ahead, and Jersey farmers duly delivered, although there was some wry amusement expressed when the promised ships failed to arrive and collect the potatoes at one point. By the end of the 1917 season, 52,200 tons had been shipped, with the British Army receiving its share as planned. This was an increase in supply of approximately 9,000 tons over the previous year's export crop. What's more, in value the exports achieved a record high of £807,495, a sum that was nearly £300,000 more than the amount that was earned in 1916. Despite the initial reservations over the principles of requisition and fixed prices, the scheme had worked very favourably and profitably for the benefit of the Island's farmers. This was an outcome that the Lieutenant Governor was determined would not be repeated in 1918. Taking the view that the farmers were manipulating the market to boost profits, and receiving overly generous terms, Wilson had set about revising the arrangements for 1918. The question that he faced was how to increase exports beyond those already shipped, particularly given the general shortage of agricultural labour, while also ensuring that local food stocks were provided for. Wilson believed that he had the answer, but he also knew that it was unlikely to be popular with the Island's farmers.

Wilson had turned his attention to the subject of Jersey's traditional early crop of potatoes. These 'earlies', as they were known, were highly sought after in Britain for their seasonal availability and their taste, allowing them to command the best prices – typically up to £100 a ton at times. Writing to the Home Secretary in February 1918, he demanded that the export price of potatoes be fixed again that year, but the question of 'earlies' addressed so that Britain received the greatest benefit. 'At present the Jersey farmer favoured by the milder climate of the Island has almost a free run of the early English market at what may be termed fancy prices,' Wilson explained. 'Consequently every effort is made to market potatoes before the English crop is fit to touch, the result being that large quantities of immature potatoes are exported (many about a third of the maximum size) with the resultant loss of some thousands of tons of foodstuff.'[11]

The suspicion that local farmers were putting profit before patriotism was one that had vexed his predecessor, General Rochfort. Wilson was determined to address the matter of possible profiteering, even if this meant further stormy arguments. The best way to do this, he had reasoned, was to impose a strict control over the harvest by preventing any farmer from exporting their potatoes before the start of June. This would eliminate the need for lifting the 'earlies' and thus increase the weight of the harvest available from June onwards. It would also limit the opportunity for speculation and excessive profit taking. That his letter on the matter was sent in confidence, without consultation with the Island's civilian authorities, indicates that he recognised there would be strong resistance to the proposals. In follow-up correspondence on behalf of the Lieutenant Governor, William Whitaker-Maitland, the Government Secretary, elaborated on the reasons for confidentiality and why it was considered important for Britain to intervene. 'You see the farming element prevails in the States, and the large profit realised by an early sale of [an] immature crop at fancy prices has great weight with them. It is useless to expect anything to be done on this side,' Whitaker-Maitland explained, 'but the regulation of prices in England would solve the problem without further difficulty.'[12]

There was a swift and indignant reaction from both the States and the Island's farmers when Wilson's proposals to control harvesting and prices became known in March 1918. In a detailed response, the Defence Committee firmly pointed out Wilson's lack of understanding over how Jersey's potato industry actually worked. Admittedly, the early potatoes commanded high prices on the British market, but they represented just a small fraction of the crop – no more than a few hundred tons. Leaving them in the ground for a longer period would not mean that they grew bigger since the type of soil in which these potatoes grew limited their size. Later harvesting would simply lead to them rotting in the ground, and it was the same for the main crop of potatoes that followed. They had to be lifted when the growing conditions dictated that they should, not when the Lieutenant Governor decided that it was appropriate. To delay harvesting would be of no benefit for Britain and it was likely to be ruinous for Jersey because it would mean they would come onto the market at the same time as British potatoes, rendering them almost valueless. The Defence Committee stressed that the whole point of Jersey Royals was that they were first to market. Take that advantage away and Jersey farmers simply could not compete given the additional costs incurred in shipping and transport. Furthermore, the Defence Committee had explained, local farmers needed to have the potato crop harvested as early as possible in order to replant the land with other staple crops for local use, and, most importantly, with the root crops used as animal feed during winter. Without these, it would not be possible to sustain Jersey's precious herd of cows, which provided the Island's milk and other vital dairy products. Finally, there was resentment stated as to any suggestion that Jersey was trying to manipulate the situation for reasons of profit. 'The Committee submit that they have never taken an insular view in connection with the matter of food production,' their report on the subject concluded indignantly. 'They have achieved a two-fold object which they set out to accomplish, of increasing supplies to the United Kingdom and at the same time making the Island of Jersey more self-supporting in the matter of foodstuffs.'[13]

Wilson was not entirely convinced. Submitting the Defence Committee's report to the Home Office, he accepted some of the points made, but still pressed for greater control from Britain. The result was a compromise agreement. No potatoes could be lifted before 15 May that year, two weeks earlier than the date that had been originally proposed, and the export of five hundred tons of 'earlies' between that date and the end of May would be permitted to help the farmers recoup their costs. From the start of June, price controls would be in force, starting at £25 per ton, and then progressively reducing to £14 per ton by the fourth week of June. Thereafter, farmers would be free to obtain whatever price they could. Yet as the Lieutenant Governor and the States argued over the matter, it soon became apparent that Mother Nature was going to intervene. A fine start to the year meant that the potato crop was growing faster than was expected. As a result, following a hurried exchange of telegrams, agreement was reached to double the quantity of 'earlies' that were allowed to be lifted. Yet it soon became obvious that even this was not enough as the crop quickly ripened in the fine weather. Eventually, after further appeals from the Defence Committee, Wilson agreed to lift all harvesting restrictions. He followed this by also admitting defeat on price fixing as well. Wholesale price controls were removed, although retail pricing for Jersey potatoes had to conform to the restrictions set by Britain's Food Controller. And inspectors were still required to monitor exports to ensure that, on no account, were unnecessary amounts of immature potatoes allowed to leave Jersey.

It had been a bruising tussle, but in the end all sides obtained what they had wanted. Britain received 61,885 tons of vital potatoes from Jersey – an increase of ten thousand tons over the previous year - while there was enough remaining to ensure Islanders did not go hungry in 1918. And the Island's farmers profited from a reduced, but still substantial export value of £537,295 that year, which was higher than the equivalent amount for 1914, the last harvest in peacetime.

With the provision of more food and money in hand, there had remained the third demand from the Home Secretary to be dealt with. While producing more food may have challenged the Island's farmers and finding the money to pay for Jersey's defence may have taxed the States financiers, neither had the human impact of the third demand on Jersey. Britain wanted more men from the Island and this would inevitably result in more of the Island's families facing hardship, uncertainty and for some, the ultimate sacrifice. The Island had little choice however. It was facing pressure from both Sir George Cave's letter and a further important development when it came to the subject of conscription. Britain had revised its Military Service Act in April 1918, and as was the case in 1916, Jersey was now expected to follow and do the same.

To replace the heavy losses still being incurred through 1917, Britain was having to find more men from its already overstretched reserves of manpower. One measure taken was to revoke all of the exemptions from military service that had been previously granted, and make every exempted man reapply to the Military Service Tribunals. Secondly, there was a revision of Britain's Military Service Act in April 1918 that raised the upper age for conscription from forty-one to fifty-one-years-old. At the same time, the minimum age at which a man could serve at the front was lowered from nineteen to eighteen years and six months. As with the adoption of the original Military Service Act, Jersey was expected to revise its own legislation accordingly. On 12 June 1918, the States had assembled to review the proposals to do exactly that.

In common with the previous debates on the subject of compulsory military service, and given what was at stake, the debate that day had led to acrimonious clashes between Members. On one side, there were those who believed that Jersey could and should give more to the war effort, on the other side were those who strongly felt the Island was already doing all that it could. The debate again centred on the subject of farming, and the question of sending married men to war while young, single men were being kept at home to work in agricultural jobs. Wilson was resolute on his position: he would have no hand in taking men above forty-one until it was impossible to find men under that age. In his view, there remained twelve or thirteen hundred suitable candidates in the Island. It was incumbent upon the States and the District Tribunals to ensure fairness in the selection of who should go and who should stay. That was all well and good, countered Jurat Thomas Payn, on behalf of the Defence Committee, but it would not help the Island meet the three demands made by the Home Secretary. 'Success in food production is dependent on the retention of a number of men sufficient to do that portion of the work which cannot be done by women and children,' he had announced, adding that, 'the financial well-being of the community is dependent entirely on the prosperity of the agricultural industry; and financial help can only be forthcoming if the community is in a position to pay such taxes as it may be found necessary to impose.'[14]

Although the question of who went and who stayed was not resolved on that day, within weeks, the States would pass the amendments to the Island's Military Service Act in line with those that had already been made by Britain. There was little choice. As the Bailiff had earlier pointed out, the fate of Jersey was now inextricably bound to that of Britain and its Empire. If Britain was defeated, who could say what would be the outcome for Islanders. One thing, at least, had become abundantly clear in the three and half years of war up until that time: Jersey was no longer a community that could pick and choose how it became involved in the affairs of the outside world and its wars. Britain needed more men – whatever age or fitness - and some at least would have to come from Jersey. They could not come soon enough. For the first six months of 1918, the armies of Britain, France and their allies had been fighting with their 'backs to the wall', as Field Marshal Haig, the Commander-in-Chief of the British Expeditionary Force had proclaimed, and suffering enormous numbers of casualties while desperately opposing a series of massive enemy offensives. By June 1918, the threat of a German victory was still a very real prospect. After three and half years of fighting, the outcome of the war remained in the balance. It meant that Jersey's soldiers still had a lot of fighting and further heavy casualties to endure before the war would come to an end.

JERSEY'S GREAT WAR

Volunteer now or face conscription: the Bailiff appeals to Militiamen in October 1915 to join the British Army or attest a willingness to do so under Britain's 'Derby Scheme'

More men: the first Jersey conscripts leave the Island to join the British Army in March 1917

More food: Jersey Royals on their way to Britain having been purchased by the Army Forage Corps

Pour Le Patrie: the Island's French Consul, *Monsieur* Auguste Jouve, in a ceremony to decorate a wounded member of Jersey's French community

Corporal John Veler who won a Military Medal on 1 July 1916 while serving with a Trench Mortar Battery and who would be killed later in the war

George Le Gresley, who served with the Royal Engineers in Macedonia where he won a Military Medal in September 1918 for a display of courage that inspired all

JERSEY'S GREAT WAR

Nineteen-year-old Bienaime Tirel of the *41e régiment d'infanterie coloniale* won a *médaille militaire* and the *croix de guerre* in April 1917 on the *Chemin Des Dames* where he was severely wounded

John Pinel, the Constable of St Helier, who was honoured for his efforts during the Spanish Flu epidemic in October and November 1918

Crowds gather outside the offices of the *Evening Post* newspaper in St Helier's Charles Street for news at the end of the war

JERSEY'S GREAT WAR

Members of the Island's newly formed trades union take part in a victory march

Société Jersiaise

The temporary cenotaph erected by the Constable of St Helier John Pinel in the Parade that stood until replaced by the permanent monument in 1923, which remains to the present time

13 TOMMIES AND POILUS

Jerseymen in the service of Britain and France

While the States of Jersey engaged in acrimonious debate over amending its Military Service Act in April 1918, the last remnants of the Jersey Company found themselves defending a small section of the front line near the French town of Hazebrouck. By then, few remained of the gallant band so earnestly sent off to war by those same politicians back in March 1915. In the three years since they had departed Jersey, the 320 original volunteers had been reduced to less than one hundred strong through losses caused by enemy action, illness and accidents. Yet despite the sacrifices that had already been made by April 1918, they and all of the other Jersey soldiers serving in the armies of Britain and France still had seven more long months of bitter and costly fighting to endure.

There were no real trenches to provide shelter for the Jersey Company members in that waterlogged area of farmland near to the Belgian border. After three years of stalemate, the fighting in France and Belgium had been driven into the open once more following a major German offensive. Employing new tactics and reinforced by thousands of soldiers released from the Eastern Front, the Germany Army had first swept through the British lines around the city of St Quentin on 21 March 1918 and then come very close to capturing Amiens, a strategically important Allied communications centre. The Jersey Company survivors were fortunate to be defending the line further north in Belgium when the German's first offensive, codenamed Operation *Michael*, had commenced and so avoided being engaged in the heavy fighting. The same fortune did not extent to April and a second German offensive, codenamed Operation *Georgette*, launched against the Allied line immediately south of the French-Belgian border. The British front line defences there had again crumbled and the British Army driven back towards the important communication centres of Bailleul and Hazebrouck and the vital Channel ports that lay beyond. Only through desperate defending and the arrival of reinforcements, among which were the men of the Jersey Company, had a complete German breakthrough been prevented, and a defensive front line been established once more. The cost of achieving this was a high one, however, with yet thousands more men killed, wounded or missing. Among them was Private Harry Richards of the Jersey Company, who had died on 10 April while defending the town of Ballieul.

Private Richards was one of the original volunteers to leave with the Jersey

Company in March 1915, departing from St Helier Harbour to spend nine months training, first in Ireland and then at Aldershot, before crossing the Channel with his comrades to enter the trenches at the start of 1916. The Jersey Company's first eight months at the front had been spent near the mining town of Loos, holding a front line that weaved around and through the winding towers and slagheaps to be found in that part of France. There, the volunteers had first encountered the reality of war, enduring a bitterly cold winter and a costly spring and summer in terms of casualties. While serving at Loos, illness, disease, sniping and shelling had bitten deeply into their ranks before there had even been a real chance to come to grips with the enemy. With no system in place to send reinforcements from Jersey to replace those lost, the strength of the small unit had declined. By September 1916, when the Jersey Company moved south to take part in the Battle of the Somme, its numbers were down by approximately a third to just two hundred men. Of these, only a handful would walk away from four days of intense fighting around the villages of Guillemont and Ginchy. Most of the others were either killed, wounded or reported as missing.

The Jersey Company had moved with its parent unit, the 7th Battalion of the Royal Irish Rifles, to Belgium after the fighting on the Somme, to recover following its costly ordeal. Strengthened by men returning after their recovery from wounds or illnesses, the Jersey Company had taken part in the successful storming of Messines Ridge on 7 June 1917. The ridge, which was known to be one of the most strongly defended positions on the Western Front, fell in just a single day's fighting, with the attackers aided by nineteen massive mine explosions that had destroyed or disrupted much of the German defences. Yet if Messines had been a triumph, the next battle for the Jersey Company would prove a disaster. On 16 August 1917, during the Third Battle of Ypres, or the Battle of Passchendaele as it has become more commonly known, they suffered heavy casualties once more, including nine men killed during an unsuccessful attack from the Frezenberg Ridge near the village of Zonnebeke.

One outcome of the fighting at Ypres was that 7th Royal Irish Rifles now came under suspicion of being unreliable. The accusations stemmed from the failed Easter Rising in April 1916 when Irish republicans had attempted to seize control of Dublin and to end British rule in Ireland. As a consequence, some senior British Army officers began to view certain Irish units with suspicion, believing that their soldiers held republican sympathies. Following a decision in September 1917 to disband 7th Royal Irish Rifles as a result of these suspicions, and to transfer the majority of its men to the 2nd Battalion of the Royal Irish Rifles, the surviving Jersey Company members decided to protest against the situation in which they now found themselves. Feeling let down through no reinforcements from home, under suspicion by association with their Irish comrades and threatened with dispersal, they had petitioned the Bailiff for permission to return to the Island. Given the wartime situation, Vernon was unable to grant the request, but with the assistance of the Lieutenant Governor, he was able to help arrange a transfer of the surviving members to a new regiment, one with stronger links to Jersey. The 2nd Battalion of the Hampshire Regiment already contained a number of Islanders who had joined either as volunteers or conscripts. It was with this unit that the last remnants of the Jersey Company – down in its strength to approximately seventy men at the start of 1918 – had helped repel a German attack on the town of Ballieul in April 1918. And it was as a member of the Hampshire Regiment that Harry Richards had lost his life in that fighting, becoming the sixty-sixth Jersey Company member to die since the unit's departure from Jersey.

By the time that the States were debating Jersey's revised Military Service Act in June 1918, the number of Jersey Company deaths had risen to sixty-eight as Private Louis Le Claire and Second Lieutenant Frank Lunn* had both lost their lives in May 1918. By the end of the war, the total would increase by ten more to seventy-eight. With two more men dying not long afterwards – victims of illness and an accident – the final count climbed to eighty. It meant that one in four of the Jersey Company members had died as a result of their military service, a figure that was three times higher than Britain's national average.

If losses such as these demonstrate the remarkable commitment of the Jersey Company between 1915 and 1918, the number of medals for bravery won by its members also shows their remarkable level of courage. By the end of the war, they had gained no fewer than twenty-two decorations including two Military Crosses (MC) and two Distinguished Conduct Medals (DCM), with the latter considered to be second only to the Victoria Cross. The two MCs went to Captain Cyril Ogier, who won his during the fighting at Bailleul in April 1918, and to Second Lieutenant Roy Binet†, who gained his for 'conspicuous gallantry and devotion to duty' in the October of that year. Sergeant Charles Laugeard, a former member of the States of Jersey Police Force, won the Jersey Company's first DCM for single-handedly destroying a German strongpoint during the fight for the village of Ginchy in September 1916. The other DCM went to Regimental Sergeant Major (RSM) Jack Le Breton, who was widely known as the 'father of the Jersey Company' for the devotion he had shown towards his men. Le Breton won his decoration during the Battle of Messines

---

* Lunn had left the Royal Irish Rifles in 1917 and been commissioned in the King's Liverpool Regiment at the time of his death.

† Binet had left the Royal Irish Rifles in 1917 and been commissioned into the King's Royal Rifle Corps at the time he won his MC.

Ridge in June 1917 for climbing down alone into a German dugout and single-handedly capturing a number of enemy soldiers who were sheltering there. While Ogier, Binet and Le Breton would return home after the war, Laugeard has the sad distinction of being one of the last members of the Jersey Company to be killed in action, dying of wounds near Ypres in October 1918.

While it is important to recall and single out the endeavours, losses and bravery of the Jersey Company, it is equally essential to remember that its members represented just a small fraction of the Jerseymen who left the Island between 1914 and 1918 to serve overseas. The majority of them joined the British Army or served with the Dominion contingents from Australia, Canada, New Zealand and South Africa. A small number of them also fought with the Indian Army, an all-volunteer force raised by Britain in the Subcontinent. Given that these Jersey 'Tommies', as British soldiers were nicknamed, served in so many different roles and in different regiments and corps, it is practically impossible to produce a fitting account or accurate record of their First World War service. Yet, in common with the men of the Jersey Company, many too faced moments of triumph and despair throughout the war, with some winning medals and others losing their lives. While all their individual stories may never been known, what it is possible to state with certainty is that Tommies from Jersey were present in every campaign fought by the British Army between 1914 and 1918, taking part in every major battle that took place and engaging in countless scraps, skirmishes and clashes in between.

The first Jersey soldiers to see action while serving in the British Army fought in the Battle of Mons in August 1914. Captain Ernest Briard was the first of them to lose his life, killed on the day following the battle while covering the British Expeditionary Force (BEF) as it retreated from Belgium. In the battles that followed to save Paris, and during the follow-up fighting along the Aisne River in September 1914, Jersey soldiers had their first real experience of the heavy casualties that would come to characterise First World War battles. Six Islanders would lose their lives in the attempt to dislodge the Germans from defensive positions on heights overlooking the Aisne River with little appreciable gain to show for their sacrifice. The Germans would still be on those same heights four years later. Yet the most costly fighting of that year took place in October and November, as both sides attempted to 'turn the flank' of their opponent during the so-called 'Race to the Sea'. In October, the BEF had moved from the Aisne to defend Ypres‡ in order to prevent the Germans breaking through to the Channel ports that lay some twenty-five miles west of the small Belgium city. The First Battle of Ypres that followed lasted from 19 October to 22 November, with intense fighting as the Germans

‡ Today the city is named Ieper.

had tried repeatedly to break through and capture the city. The majority of the BEF's units were involved at one point or another, and most suffered heavy casualties in the process. At least twenty-five men from Jersey died during the battle, with others killed in the weeks before and after the main fighting had died down.

It was shortly after the end of the First Battle of Ypres that Lieutenant William Bruce won the Victoria Cross (VC), Britain's highest award for bravery. Bruce, whose parents lived at Samarès in the parish of St Clement, had attended Victoria College between 1904 and 1908 after which time he had entered the Royal Military Academy at Sandhurst as a cadet. In 1914, he was a twenty-five-year-old officer serving in the 59th Scinde Rifles, a regiment of the Indian Army that had arrived in France in September that year. Bruce would win his VC on 19 December 1914 fighting near Givenchy-lès-la-Bassée, close to the French-Belgian border. His citation for the medal reads:

> For most conspicuous bravery and devotion to duty. On 19 December 1914, near Givenchy, during a night attack, Lieutenant Bruce was in command of a small party which captured one of the enemy trenches. In spite of being severely wounded in the neck, he walked up and down the trench encouraging his men to hold on against several counter-attacks for some hours until killed. The fire from rifles and bombs was very heavy all day, and it was due to the skilful disposition made and the example and encouragement shown by Lieutenant Bruce that his men were able to hold out until dusk, when the trench was finally captured by the enemy.[1]

The posthumous medal was not awarded until 1919 after soldiers who had fought with Bruce that night and been captured returned home to provide an account of the action.

In 1915, a renewed and expanded British Army had undertaken several offensives aimed at breaking through the German defences between Ypres and the French city of Lens. After attacking at Neuve Chapelle, Aubers Ridge and Festubert the largest offensive was the Battle of Loos, which began on 25 September and lasted until 14 October. In common with those preceding it that year, the offensive failed to achieve the planned breakthrough and resulted in very heavy casualties. Among those killed in the battle were at least fourteen Jerseymen including thirty-three-year-old Second Lieutenant Kenneth Dunlop, who was one those men who had volunteered for military service at the very start of the war. Tragically for his parents, Alice and Andrew Dunlop of St Helier, Kenneth was their third son to die since August 1914. Kenneth's older brother Julian had lost his life during the fighting at Ypres in October 1914 while serving as a captain in the South Staffordshire Regiment. A few weeks later, on 8 November, thirty-six-year-old Frederick Dunlop, who was a captain in the Manchester Regiment, had been killed near Armentières. The Dunlops had also lost two sons fifteen years earlier during the Boer War. They would not be the only Island parents to lose more than one son, with numerous examples of two or even three brothers killed or dying between 1914 and 1918. Yet given their losses from an earlier conflict, the Dunlop family's experience was a particularly tragic one. In addition to attacking the Germans in France, the British Army had been fighting in a number of more distant campaigns by 1915. The Ottoman Empire had joined the war on Germany's side in 1914, and Britain had hoped that easy victory against the Turks would both open the sea route to Russia and lead to Germany diverting forces from other fronts to assist their ally. In April 1915, following an unsuccessful naval attempt aimed at breaking through to the Ottoman capital, Constantinople, British, French, Australian and New Zealand forces landed on the Gallipoli Peninsular to try an overland offensive. The campaign soon turned into another costly stalemate, with the soldiers having to contend with heat, flies and disease as well as a skilful enemy. In January 1916, the Allied forces were withdrawn from the peninsular, having suffered quarter of a million casualties, among whom were at least twenty-seven Islanders. One of those who survived the campaign was RSM James Alexander who won the DCM in June while serving at Gallipoli with the Worcestershire Regiment. The medal citation for Alexander, who was badly wounded in the shoulder, chest and jaw, reveals that he won his award for showing the 'greatest coolness under hazardous conditions and critical periods.'

During 1915, Britain also fought in Mesopotamia§ against the Turks, after landing a force led by Jerseyman Brigadier General Walter Delamain on the Persian Gulf coast near the city of Basra in November 1914. It was a particularly challenging campaign for the hundreds of Jersey soldiers who served there. They not only found themselves up against Ottoman soldiers who proved to be tenacious adversaries for much of the time, but also a frequently hostile Arab population and a permanently hostile swarm of insects that were determined to make men's lives both miserable and unhealthy. The most challenging time had come between December 1915 and April 1916 when a British force was trapped and besieged in the town of Kut Al Amara. Among those who were surrounded there was Major Norman Rybot, a long-serving soldier from Jersey and later a renowned local historian. He was an officer in the 76th Punjabis, a regiment of the Indian Army that had provided many of the units for the Mesopotamian Campaign. Rybot went into Turkish captivity with his men

§ Modern day Iraq.

after a British relief force failed to break the siege. Yet while he and most other captured officers were subsequently treated reasonably and survived to be released at the end of the war, around three quarters of the other ranks who became prisoners would die of disease, starvation or neglect. Among them was Private Philip Whitley of the East Surrey Regiment, whose family lived in Gorey. Already sick through disease by the end of the siege, Whitley appears to have been one of those unfortunate enough to be force marched overland from Kut to Baghdad, where he died with hundreds of others in June 1916. After recovering from the setback at Kut, the British Army would go on to capture Baghdad in 1917 and continue advancing during 1918. The cost in lives for what was widely regarded as a 'sideshow' by many Western Front generals would be a heavy one, with men dying both in the fighting and due to disease. The final death toll of the Mesopotamian Campaign would include at least fifty men from Jersey, with many others being left permanently affected by malaria and the other tropical diseases contracted while serving there.

Jersey soldiers also fought elsewhere in the Middle East during the First World War, first defending the Suez Canal against an Ottoman invasion in 1915 and then taking part in the 1917 offensive into Palestine that culminated in the capture of Jerusalem in December that year. During the fighting in this region, which often proved as challenging as that taking place in Mesopotamia, a further twenty Islanders died. Across the eastern Mediterranean, another British force had landed at Salonica in Greece in 1915, partly to assist the Serbians who were then retreating before Austro-Hungarian, German and Bulgarian forces, and partly in an attempt to persuade Greece to join the war on the side of the Allies. They did not wholly succeed with either aim, with the Serbians soldiers driven from their country and Greeks hesitating to commit until 1917. Moreover, British soldiers soon found themselves facing a determined Bulgarian Army in the difficult Macedonian terrain north of Salonica. It was a costly campaign that by its conclusion in 1918 had taken the lives of fifteen Jerseymen who were there fighting with the British Army. It also saw many more individual acts of both resilience and bravery. Among those decorated during the campaign was Sergeant George Le Gresley, an army reservist living in Jersey at the beginning of the war and recalled to serve with the Royal Engineers, first in France and then later in Macedonia. On 1 September 1918, Sergeant Le Gresley spent a night consolidating a defensive position under heavy shellfire, displaying such courage that he inspired all those around him and for which he was awarded a Military Medal (MM).

As well as these campaigns in the Balkans, Mediterranean and Middle East, Jersey soldiers fought and died while serving with the British Army in East and South West Africa, in battles with German colonial forces there. They also fought in Italy after the Allies were forced to send troops there in 1917 to shore up a wavering Italian Army. The Italians, having originally been aligned with Germany and Austria-Hungary prior to the war, had entered the war on the Allied side on 1915 and soon found themselves in a trench-bound stalemate as well. British soldiers would even fight in Russia during its civil war, intervening against the Bolsheviks late in 1918 and into 1919. Rifleman Charles Chapman from Jersey was sent there with the King's Royal Rifle Corps in April 1919, having previously served on the Western Front where he had been wounded. In the fighting around the northern port city of Murmansk he won a MM for rescuing another Jersey soldier, William Machon, while under machine gun fire. Chapman survived and returned to Jersey, but a fellow islander, William Rendall, was not so fortunate. The twenty-one-year-old Royal Marine was killed in action in Northern Russia in August 1919.

Yet for all these distant and complex campaigns, the large majority of British soldiers, and thus most Jersey Tommies, spent their war serving on the Western Front in France and Belgium. In 1916, during the Battle of the Somme many had their real experience of attacking the enemy. The battle, which was part of a wider Allied strategy to engage their enemies on all fronts simultaneously, remains one of the most controversial of the war. Having failed in the original objective to break through the German defences, the British Commander-in-Chief, General Douglas Haig, had persisted with the fighting in the belief that it would eventually wear the enemy down. While such battles of attrition, as they are known, may result in a victory of sorts, it came at the cost of very heavy casualties. This is reflected in the number of Jerseymen who lost their lives in the four and a half months of fighting on the Somme. By its conclusion, the British Army had lost ninety-six thousand men killed in action, of which around 150 were from Jersey.

Throughout the Battle of the Somme, Islanders had served across the battlefield in various regiments and corps, and many won recognition for their actions there. Corporal John Veler, for example, who served in the Dorsetshire Regiment won the MM on 1 July 1916 for saving his mortar after the rest of its crew had been killed or wounded by enemy fire. Company Sergeant Major (CSM) Thomas Bennett of the Manchester Regiment also won a MM on the battle's opening day for bravery shown during the attack on the key German strongpoint of Thiepval while attached to a unit of the Royal Scots Regiment. After the officer commanding that unit was killed, Bennett, who had volunteered in August 1914, had taken charge of thirty-eight men and held on to an important position for fourteen hours during which time the original detachment was reduced to just six men. CSM Bennett survived the war; Corporal Veler, whose parents had come to Jersey from France, continued serving until October 1918 when he died after being severely wounded. Sadly for his parents, John Veler's younger brother Peter had been killed six months earlier near Loos.

Britain's Dominion contingents also fought in the Battle of the Somme, with Jersey-born soldiers present among the Australian, Canadian and New Zealand divisions that served there. Canadian divisions were engaged in September 1916 during an attack that featured the first ever use of tanks on the battlefield. Taking part was Sergeant Claude Reynolds who had left Jersey in 1911 to settle in Edmonton, Canada. After volunteering to serve in the Canadian contingent and returning to Europe, he won the DCM on 29 September 1916 for operating a machine gun while all around him were killed. Just over one week later, on 8 October, he won further acclaim for leading an attack through two lines of German trenches, advancing one thousand yards and capturing 270 enemy prisoners.

The Battle of the Somme also proved deadly for a high number of senior officers, including some from Jersey or with strong Island connections. They included Old Victorian Lieutenant Colonel Harry Allardice who was killed on 1 July leading the 13th Battalion, Northumberland Fusiliers, in an advance towards the village of Contalmaison. Lieutenant Colonel George Guyon, whose parents lived in St Martin, died on the same day leading the 16th Battalion, West Yorkshire Regiment, while attacking the village of Serre. Lieutenant Colonel Eric Benson, who had won the MC earlier in the war, was killed in September while commanding the 9th Battalion, King's Royal Rifle Corps, and Major Hugh Johnston DSO, who had been the Adjutant of the Militia's Royal Jersey Artillery, and presided over the trial of Edward Single in January 1915, died in October serving with the Royal Garrison Artillery. The most senior officer to die was Major General Edward Ingouville-Williams, whose mother was from Jersey. Generally known as 'Inky-Bill', he was killed by shrapnel on 22 July while reconnoitring the ground over which his 34th Division was due to attack.

While the Battle of the Somme may not have achieved the decisive results that had been hoped for, it did cause heavy German casualties. To minimise further such losses and reduce the length of front that had to be held, the German Army had withdrawn at the start of 1917 to a newly constructed defensive system known as the 'Hindenburg Line'. It would come to dominate much of the fighting that followed during 1917 as the British came up against the new concrete and steel fortifications. The first British troops to experience them did so during the Battle of Arras in April and May that year, an offensive designed to draw German attention away from a planned French attack on another part of the front. On the first day of the British offensive, the Canadian

Corps had stormed Vimy Ridge, a natural strongpoint upon which the Germans had constructed formidable defences. While the achievement was rightly hailed as a momentous victory, it still cost more than 3,500 Canadian lives, among whom were twelve men originally from Jersey. One was Sergeant Ernest Amourette who had enlisted in the 21st Battalion, Canadian Infantry (Eastern Ontario Regiment) in November 1914 and crossed to Europe in the summer of 1915. He had been in Jersey on leave to visit relatives only months before his death in the battle.

Jersey's losses, and accomplishments, had continued throughout 1917. The Battle of Arras, which lasted until 16 May, claimed the lives of approximately sixty Islanders. The battle had also marked a low point in Britain's air war on the Western Front, with its start being heralded as 'Bloody April' on account of the heavy losses in planes and airmen incurred. Both sides had started the war with only a limited number of aircraft each, whose role was mostly to undertake reconnaissance missions. It was not long before new purposes emerged, as planes designed as bombers and fighters took to the skies within a few months. Among the airmen of the recently formed Royal Flying Corps (RFC) was Jerseyman Thomas Bennett who won a DCM in September 1915 for shooting down a German plane at 11,000 feet. Flight Sergeant Thomas would survive the war, but twenty-two Jersey airmen and ground crew would lose their lives between 1914 and 1918, serving in the RFC and its successor from April 1918, the Royal Air Force.

Following the Battle of Arras, British attention moved north to Belgium where two Jerseymen would die in the storming of Messines Ridge on 7 June 1917. Having captured that important piece of high ground to the south of Ypres, the British had embarked upon a far larger offensive in front of the city that lasted from 31 July until mid-November that year when the village of Passchendaele was finally captured. It represented an advance of around five miles at a cost of perhaps four hundred thousand British casualties with the actual number being uncertain even to the present time. Among them there were at least seventy-five men from Jersey who lost their lives. One was Father Simon Knapp, a Roman Catholic padre with the Royal Army Chaplains' Department serving with the 2nd Battalion of the Irish Guards. Despite being a non-combatant, fifty-eight-year-old Knapp had already won an MC in 1916 and was awarded the Distinguished Service Order (DSO) just before his death, which came on the opening day of the Third Battle of Ypres while helping a wounded man. Later in the battle, Private Walter Coutanche won the MM for gallantry, but unlike Padre Knapp, he would survive the war. He had joined the 50th Battalion of the Canadian Army in December 1916, arriving in Europe just before the new offensive had begun. In September, while in charge of a

Lewis Gun, Coutanche showed 'conspicuous bravery and dash' in destroying an enemy machine gun position and thus allowing an advance to continue.

In the aftermath of Third Ypres, the British undertook one further major offensive in 1917, partly to deflect attention from the disappointing results of the fighting in Belgium, partly to try out newly developed tactics. The Battle of Cambrai would see a first use of massed tanks to spearhead an attack rather than just to support the infantry, and sophisticated artillery ranging techniques that replaced the lengthy opening bombardment that had preceded most British offensives up until that time. The tanks in particular proved to be a great success in the opening days of the battle, breaking through the Hindenburg Line and advancing towards Cambrai. Yet they failed to capture the city as breakdowns, a lack of reserves and the swift German response slowed down and then stopped the advance. During the battle, thirty-year-old Captain Allastair McReady-Diarmid, an Old Victorian whose mother was from Jersey, was awarded the VC. His citation reads:

> For most conspicuous bravery and brilliant leadership. When the enemy penetrated some distance into our position and the situation was extremely critical, Captain McReady-Diarmid at once led his company forward through a heavy barrage. He immediately engaged the enemy, with such success that he drove them back at least three hundred yards, causing numerous casualties and capturing twenty-seven prisoners. The following day the enemy again attacked and drove back another company which had lost all its officers. This gallant officer at once called for volunteers and attacked. He drove them back again for three hundred yards, with heavy casualties. Throughout this attack Captain McReady-Diarmid led the way himself, and it was absolutely and entirely due to his marvellous throwing of bombs that the ground was regained. His absolute disregard for danger, his cheerfulness and coolness at a most trying time, inspired all who saw him. This most gallant officer was eventually killed by a bomb when the enemy had been driven right back to their original starting point.[5]

In common with fellow Old Victorian and VC winner, William Bruce, McReady-Diarmid's bravery had cost him his life.

Despite its promising start, the Battle of Cambrai had ended in stalemate, like most First World War battles that had preceded it. Yet the initial British attack and a subsequent German counter-attack in which Captain McReady-

Diarmid died, had proved that both sides were close to developing the weapons and tactics that were needed to overcome the deadlock of the trenches. In the first half of 1918, the Germans would demonstrate this new capability with devastating effect. Their offensives launched against British line in March and April that year, and then against the French Army in May and June 1918, would push the Allies to the brink of defeat and result in more than half a million Allied casualties. Among those killed was Lance Corporal Vernon Andrews, who had been at the front with the Royal Army Medical Corps serving as part of a British cavalry unit since the start of the war. He had been recommended for the DCM in 1915, and subsequently won the MM and Bar as well as being twice officially 'Mentioned in Despatches' for his conduct. Caught up in the withdrawal following the German offensive on 21 March, he died of wounds on 24 March aged just twenty-one.

Despite their success in breaking through the Allied defences and causing enormous casualties, the German offensives in the spring and summer of 1918 had failed in their overall goal, which had been to win the war before the United States could intervene decisively. By July, heavy casualties had exhausted the German Army's reserves and left its front line units depleted while the Allies were gaining in strength as an expanding American Army took its place at the front. On 8 August, a British-led offensive outside the city of Amiens took the Germans by complete surprise and succeeded in driving them back for several miles and capturing thousands of prisoners in the process. The Battle of Amiens was a significant moment in the war. It had demonstrated that the Allies, and the British in particular, had finally created a successful combination of infantry, cavalry, artillery, tanks and aircraft that was capable of breaking through the enemy defences and advancing forward. It also indicated that the morale of German soldiers had declined since the failure of the German Army offensives earlier in the year. After four years of stoic fighting, many of them had chosen to surrender during the battle rather than resist to the end. This was an indication that the end of the war was in sight. Recognising this, its Commander-in-Chief, General Erich Ludendorff, had famously described the defeat in the Battle of Amiens as 'the black day of the German Army'.

In Jersey, people had devotedly followed the ebb and flow of distant battles with great interest since the start of the war. Daily accounts printed in the newspapers reported on the progress of the fighting while special features covered major battles and events. Given the controls on independent reporting that had been put in place by the British Government, the newspaper accounts tended to be upbeat versions of what was happening at the front, usually exaggerating Allied achievements and over emphasising enemy setbacks. But the reports could not hide the number of casualties. From the start of the war, the newspapers had reported the Island's military deaths under the heading 'Roll of Honour', and tried to include a small amount of personal information on each man's background, his family and on how he had died. There was barely a day in Jersey when one or more such reports were not included in the newspapers; during periods of heavy fighting they could take up whole columns. In most cases, the newspaper's Roll of Honour report had followed an official notification delivered by telegram to a man's family informing them that he had been killed. A letter would also usually arrive from the deceased man's commanding officer, or his senior non-commissioned officer, to offer condolences, say a few words about the man and to possibly explain how he had died. Almost invariably, the letter reported that death had been quick and painless – a sniper's bullet perhaps, or a sudden explosion. The reality may often have been far less straightforward, but it would have made little sense to provide a more honest version to grieving relatives. The War Office telegrams also notified whether a man had been wounded or reported missing. In the case of those who were reported as missing, there was hope that the man had been taken prisoner, in which case confirmation would be sent via the Red Cross in the weeks that followed. Sadly, it often meant that he had actually been killed but that his body had been subsequently lost or not identified. For many families, a 'missing' telegram would be followed up twelve months later with another one stating that the man was now considered to have died.

Given the scale of the losses being suffered by the Island, it was understandable that the authorities would seek to turn public attention away from the casualties wherever possible and onto the achievements of local soldiers. The newspapers carried stories of courageous acts by Islanders and published news of any bravery awards that had been won. They also interviewed men who returned to the Island from time to time, printing accounts that were invariably positive about the war, with only a few hints of the reality of life at the front. In 1916, the Constable of St Helier, John Pinel, had decided that it was necessary to do something more than simply print stories in a newspaper to recognise the individual bravery of Jersey servicemen. He instigated a public ceremony to honour those men who had won bravery medals, to be held when they subsequently returned to the Island on leave or when convalescing from wounds or illness. These became regular events at the Town Hall and usually took place in front of large audiences, with each man receiving warm recognition from the assembled dignitaries and the cheers of those who had gathered to watch. Each honoured man also received a gold watch and an illuminated scroll, with the costs of these gifts being met by public donations to a 'Heroes Fund', which had proved to be a popular cause.

None of the Island's French soldiers were honoured with Town Hall ceremonies and presentations. But some of those who did win bravery awards were given the thanks of the community in special events organised by the French Consul and held at either the Consulate offices in St Helier's Church Street or the nearby Royal Square. In one such ceremony held on 24 June 1917, three French soldiers were decorated for their bravery in front of a large crowd that included three hundred students from the French college of Notre Dame du Bon Secours, a military contingent from the Island's garrison and the Lieutenant Governor and Bailiff. *Adjutant* Louis de Gueser of the *1e régiment d'artillerie (RA)* was being decorated with the British MM, having already won the French m*édaille militaire* and c*roix de guerre* for bravery in 1914 during the Battle of Antwerp. *Caporal* Jerome Durand of the *94e régiment d'infanterie (RI)* was being awarded the *croix de guerre avec palme* to go with an earlier m*édaille militaire*. The third soldier was *Caporal* Pierre De Juvigny of the *306e RI* who had won the c*roix de guerre avec étoile en argent* for actions near Sapigneul during a recent French offensive.

The presence of these three French soldiers and others who attended similar ceremonies was a reminder that as well as those Jerseymen who served as British Tommies, there were thousands of Jersey '*Poilus*' who fought in the armies of France during the First World War. The nickname *Poilu* means 'hairy one' in French, both in recognition of the fact that many soldiers wore thick moustaches and beards during the war and also because it seemed to sum up the dogged determination of French soldiers to endure the bleak conditions of life at the front. Like the British Tommies they often fought alongside, the war took them to many locations between 1914 and 1918, including Africa, Gallipoli, Italy, the Middle East and Salonica. For the majority, however, the place they fought was on the Western Front in France and Belgium and therefore that was where most of Jersey's *Poilus* spent their war.

The conflict for the majority of Jersey's French soldiers had started in August 1914 when as reservists they had returned to their regiments in preparation for war. Many had gone to those that were stationed in the nearby *départements* of Brittany and Normandy, which jointly had formed the *10e corps d'armée (CA)*. In mid-August, its first action had come in the Battle of Charleroi on the French-Belgian border, two days before the BEF confronted the German advance in the Battle of Mons. Like their British allies, the French soldiers were unable to stop the Germans and they soon found themselves retreating south towards Paris as well. But on 29 August, the *47e RI* from St Malo was among a force that halted their retreat and made a brief stand during the Battle of Guise. It lost a number of men that day, including *Soldats* Leopold Decourtit and Guillaume Le Millin from Jersey, neither of whose bodies were ever found. In September, the *10e CA* fought in the Battle of the Marne, and then took part in the defence of the city of Reims, which had been partly surrounded by the Germans. At the end of that month, it moved to positions around the city of Arras to take part in the fighting there. *Adjutant* George Tremblay, who had worked as a clerk in Jersey before the war, was killed there on 1 November as a member of the *25e RI* from Cherbourg. He was just one of at least thirty-seven Jerseymen killed in 1914 while serving in the French Army.

The opening battles of the war had been extremely costly for France overall. The strategy and tactics that had been developed by its generals in the pre-war years had proved unsuccessful during the Battle of the Frontiers, although the traditional courage and determination of French soldiers had helped saved their country during the Battle of the Marne and the subsequent fighting in 1914. In the following year, France was determined to drive the Germans from its country. Germany was equally determined to hold onto its 1914 gains in the west while concentrating its military efforts on the Eastern Front against the Russians. To consolidate their hold on northern France and Belgium, the Germans built increasingly stronger and more complex trench systems. The first major test of these defences had come on 9 May in a French offensive launched around Arras. The Second Battle of Artois, which went on until 18 June, resulted in some early gains for the French but ultimately it failed to break through the German defences that included the strategically commanding Vimy Ridge. It would remain in German hands until April 1917 and the successful attack by the Canadian Corps. The *10e CA* had taken part in this offensive, fighting on the outskirts of Arras, around the villages of Saint-Laurent-Blangy, Écurie and Roclincourt. Among the Jersey dead in these battles was *Soldat* Joseph Renault who was killed on 11 May while serving there with the *71e RI* from Saint-Brieuc.

In the autumn of 1915, the French Army tried to breach the German defences around Arras once again, with another major offensive entitled the Third Battle of Artois that opened on 25 September. Fighting alongside, the British Army had begun the Battle of Loos on the same day in a joint attempt to overwhelm the German defences in that sector. Neither would succeed in achieving its objectives, with both Allied armies suffering heavy casualties in the fighting. At the same time as these battles were taking place, the largest French offensive of the war up until that time had begun on the rolling plains east of Reims. The Second Battle of Champagne resulted in six weeks of fighting that achieved only negligible gains in return for further heavy losses. Among the one hundred and forty-five thousand French casualties incurred during the battle were at least nine men from Jersey who were killed, including *Soldat* Yves-Marie Boustouller, who was serving in the *3e régiment d'artillerie à pied* (RAP), one of five brothers from Jersey who would serve in the war. His brother Emmanuel would die six months later in May 1916 while serving in the Argonne Forest with the *2e RI* from Granville.

The results of the 1915 battles did not deter the Allies from planning a further and even larger offensive for the following year. Their conviction was that with more men and heavier weapons it would be possible to break through the German defences and advance into the open country that lay beyond the lines of enemy trenches. Yet while they began preparations for the battle, which was planned to start in the summer of 1916, the German Army launched an offensive of their own. The Germans chose the eastern fortress city of Verdun as the objective and a plan designed to draw the French Army into the fighting there and progressively to destroy it in a battle of attrition. The Battle of Verdun would continue from February until December 1916, making it the longest battle of the war. It was also one of the most deadly, with each side suffering around one hundred and fifty thousand men killed, and more than three hundred thousand more wounded. Verdun would become a byword for suffering, in the minds of both the soldiers and their families as home. At Verdun men struggled not only against their enemy but also against the terrain, elements and conditions found on the cramped, undulating battlefield located either side of the River Meuse. At least thirteen Islanders would die there in the course of the ten months of fighting, among them *Soldat* Charles Boinville of the *49e Chasseurs à Pied* while defending the *Bois de Caures* woods during the first twenty-four hours of the battle.

Even with the heavy fighting still taking place at Verdun, the French Army had kept its commitment to the joint Allied offensive that had been planned for the summer of 1916. A smaller but more experienced French Army made better progress than its British 'New Army' counterpart did on the opening day of the Battle of the Somme, capturing most of its assigned objectives. Despite the success, there were still considerable casualties on 1 July, including Jersey's *Soldat* Adolphe Laulier who was killed while serving in the *84e RI*. The French effort would continue alongside that of the British until the end of the battle in November 1916, by which time eleven Jerseymen had died while fighting in the French Army there.

The fighting at Verdun and during the Battle of the Somme had resulted in further heavy losses for France to bear. Moreover, it had progressively weakened the morale and resolve of many French soldiers who had seen little success in the strategy and tactics of their leaders from the start of the war. Since 1914, they had also been forced to endure mostly poor living conditions while in the trenches and when resting in the camps behind the lines. Home leave was infrequent and usually badly organised, sometimes leaving soldiers stranded in railway stations for days. The army's medical services were often inadequate and could be easily overwhelmed by the number of casualties. Significantly, there was a strong feeling among the soldiers that French civilians did not have to suffer the same deprivations as they did, particular in cities such as Paris where life appeared to be continuing much the same as normal. As 1917 started, resentment against the war and French leadership was increasing among the troops. Their spirits were lifted – temporarily as it turned out – by a promise made by the new French Commander-in-Chief, *Général* Robert Nivelle, that he had developed the tactics that could defeat the Germans. Nivelle also promised that if they did not work then he would call an immediate halt to the next major offensive that was planned to start in April that year along a range of hills known as the *Chemin Des Dames*. Yet the battle, which commenced on 16 April, seven days after the British diversionary offensive at Arras had started, went wrong from the very beginning and then continued despite Nivelle's promise. Intact German defences caused unexpectedly heavy casualties among the attacking troops while the awful weather conditions encountered left the French troops soaked and frozen. One Jersey soldier, *Soldat* Pierre Euvrie, died on the first day of fighting serving with the *35e RI*. Another, nineteen-year-old *Soldat* Bienaime Tirel of the *41e Régiment d'Infanterie Coloniale (RIC)* won a *Médaille Militaire* and the *Croix de Guerre* at the start of the offensive, but would be severely wounded, with injuries to his head, hand, chest and leg. Before the battle ended on 9 May, at least seven Islanders were killed in the fighting there.

The failure on the *Chemin Des Dames* broke the spirit of many French regiments. From June 1917, some men began refusing to return to the trenches or to take part in any further attacks. A number of units went as far as threatening to march on Paris to demand that the French Government end the fighting. How far Jersey soldiers were involved in these mutinies is unknown as the affair went unreported at the time, and the official records of what happened remain closed to the present time. Yet for a time during the summer of 1917, it appeared that France may have to leave the war, such was the level of disquiet among its soldiers. It took a new Commander-in-Chief, *Général* Philippe Petain, who set about restoring discipline and morale through a combination of harsh repression against the leaders of the mutinies and, more importantly, through a series of reforms designed to improve the lives of French soldiers both at the front and while resting behind the lines. The measures worked, and by the start of 1918, the French Army was ready to play its part in the crucial battles of the war's final year.

French soldiers provided vital support to the British Army when it faced the German offensives in March and April. At the end of May, a third attack, codenamed Operation *Blücher-Yorck*, had struck the French defences along the

Chemin Des Dames, with German troops breaking through and threatening to advance on Paris. Among those killed on the opening day of that offensive was *Soldat* Louis Huby from Jersey, whose brother Emmanuel had also been killed in the previous month near Verdun. Now aided by significant numbers of American troops, the French Army succeeded in halting this German offensive. Determined to continue with their series of offensives, the German Army had begun the Battle of Reims in July, attacking the Allied defences to the east and west of that city. Once more, a decisive victory eluded the Germans, with staunch fighting by French, British, American and Italian troops halting the offensive. This success was a pivotal moment in the war. On 18 July 1918, a joint French and American force counter-attacked the overextended German Army in the Battle of Soissons and forced a major withdrawal. The scene was set for the victorious Battle of Amiens in August, and then a general Allied advance against the now exhausted Germans that pressed them gradually back in a series of coordinated offensives. France and its *Poilus* had survived their moment of crisis in 1917 and now had final victory in their sights.

Yet while hope was rising among the Allied leaders that the war could be brought to an end before the end of 1918, there was a new threat arising that would prove equally deadly for both soldiers and the civilians at home. While the First World War may have killed millions already, this new development would take the lives of millions more.

14 THE STORM AND THE CALM

Spanish Flu, the Armistice and the first challenges of peace

The global influenza pandemic of 1918, or Spanish Flu as it was widely known, remains one of the most deadly plagues of modern times. During the course of a few shocking months it killed more people than the four years of the First World War put together. Only a few communities were spared from its terrible affects. Jersey was not one of them.

The origins of Spanish Flu – so named because Spain was the first country to give it any widespread publicity - have never been satisfactorily explained. Competing theories exist to this day claiming that it had started in China or America, or possibly even in France among the many British Army camps that were located along the Channel Coast. Yet regardless of where it began or how it spread so quickly, it would prove devastating to both the military and civilians alike. In contrast to the expected seasonal influenza outbreaks that typically proved to be the greatest threat to the very old and young, Spanish Flu was lethal to all ages including healthy young adults, killing between 10 and 20 percent of all those who were infected. While its initial symptoms were similar to those found in milder forms of flu, including tiredness, headaches and fever, in the case of Spanish Flu, the victims swiftly deteriorated. Their skin would darken, turning shades of blue as the illness took hold. Coughing and wheezing would bring blood streaming from the noses and mouths of victims and even from their ears in some cases. Vomiting, diarrhoea and incontinence added to the misery of those suffering and those trying to treat the patients who were often delirious and writhing in agony. Death or recovery usually happened quickly. Most of those who died did so within three days of falling ill; most of those who survived quickly improved after three days of intense sickness.

The pandemic had swept the world in two stages, with the first outbreak being less serious than the one that followed in October and November 1918. Reports of the first phase of Spanish Flu had begun circulating in Jersey in late July 1918, although with no real sense of concern. Entrepreneurial Island pharmacists even seized upon the opportunity to market 'preventive medicines' and 'cures' for the disease. F.G. Picot offered any worried customers a potion that was made from essence of quinine mixed with cinnamon in bottled or tablet form that would help keep Spanish Flu at bay. Not to be outdone, his rival, A.A. Le Rossignol, announced the availability of 'Saltonica', made from unstated ingredients but which was claimed to provide an effective defence against the illness for only one shilling a bottle. One writer even offered some home grown advice in a letter to the *Evening Post*. 'Go straight to bed and keep warm for at least one day,' they recommended, 'take continual small doses of eucalyptus on sugar, two or three drops are sufficient, at intervals of about two hours during the day. At the same time keeping up the strength with very small doses of alcohol in almost any form such as brandy, champagne, etc., every few hours.'[1]

Offers and views such as these may have helped calm any anxieties that Islanders had felt, although there were soon indications that the epidemic was flaring up once more. In early October, the news from Britain began to make clear the seriousness of the situation. There were reports of a growing number of deaths and details of some of the measures being taken to isolate the disease such as closing schools and cancelling public meetings. It was becoming increasingly obvious that this was no seasonal flu.

Nevertheless, Jersey's authorities were resolutely determined that life should go on as normally as possible, even as the first reports of influenza cases had appeared in the Island. On 17 October, a meeting of the States' Primary Instruction Committee decided that schools should remain open, as to close them at that point would, 'not improve matters, but could only result in numbers of children being practically thrown on the street.'[2] Parents were encouraged keep sick children at home instead, with the recommended course of action being to put them to bed and keep them warm. Yet within days of this guidance, a number of deaths soon highlighted just how grave the situation was becoming, and signalled a need for more drastic measures. On 19 October, there was dismay at the deaths of husband and wife Richard and Edith Jeune of Halkett Street, St Helier, both of whom were in their early thirties and the parents of three young, and by then very sick, children. On that same day, seven-year-old Bert Holley died, while on 20 October, fifteen-year-old Marjorie Lawrence and six-year-old Florence Rondel were also among the victims. On 21 October, the thirty-seven-year-old editor of the local French language newspaper *Les Chroniques de Jersey*, Edward Luce, also died, much to the shock and dismay of his fellow editors and journalist colleagues. Clearly, the situation was not going to be simply resolved just by time in bed and by keeping warm. The epidemic was out of control and spreading across the Island. Town was the first part of Jersey to be seriously affected. By 22 October, there were several hundred cases of influenza reported in St Helier with more and more people falling ill with the disease. There were reports that in some streets there was hardly a household unaffected. Somewhat belatedly, the authorities now stepped up their efforts to control the disease and to help those it had already infected. The States' Sanitary Committee published instructions on how best to avoid catching influenza including the need to keep air circulating in the home, not to overcrowd rooms, to clean thoroughly and to avoid alcohol. There was also a strong warning against spitting, which was said to be especially dangerous, and a plea for anyone with symptoms of the disease not to go out in public. With this advice clearly in mind, it was announced that all schools would immediately close along with the Island's picture houses and theatres. People were also advised against attending any public gatherings. Yet even this was evidently insufficient, and after a few more days, closure orders were extended to include all places of entertainment and any planned public concerts or events. On 25 October, even the Island's church services were suspended, which must have been a blow to anyone seeking spiritual comfort in the middle of so much alarm and suffering. At the same time, the Island's newspapers were full of notices from local businesses announcing that they too were having to close or reduce their services as the epidemic took its toll upon staff.

Despite these counter-measures, the number of infections continued to rise. As they did, St Helier's General Hospital filled with sick and dying patients, crowding its wards and overstretching the staff who worked on them. With admissions climbing to 240 people, the hospital put out an appeal for any trained nurses in the Island to come forward and to help relieve the strain. A number of women did respond, even though such a well-meaning act would put them at a considerable personal risk of infection. One nurse, twenty-eight-year-old Harriet Laurens, did contract influenza while on duty at the hospital and sadly died at the beginning of November. Out in the community, exhausted general practitioners were also said be increasingly overwhelmed by the volume of cases that they were treating, with more appearing all the time. It prompted some people to question why the Island's VAD nurses were not doing more to help, an accusation that was strongly refuted by the Jersey Branch of the British Red Cross Society (BRCS). Although there were 162 VAD members on duty in Britain and elsewhere overseas at that time, there were still sixteen local volunteers who were working at the General Hospital, a representative of the organisation responded indignantly, and nine more serving at the Brighton Road Military Hospital. This was despite many of them also having members of their own family who were extremely sick at that time.

In addition to those who were assisting in the Island's hospitals, a further group of VAD members had joined other volunteers in a team that was working directly with households in St Helier. In charge of them was Matron Walton, a qualified nurse who had previously worked for the Hoxton Medical Mission in London's East End. Being in the Island at the time of the influenza outbreak, she had offered her services, particularly for work concentrating on the poorer parts of St Helier. Using the Town Hall as a base, Matron Walton and her team sallied out daily to deliver medicines, dispense advice and generally offer help wherever it was needed. Their efforts helped bring about a welcome decrease in new influenza cases occurring in St Helier as the month ended, with eleven recorded on 26 October, seven on 29 October and only one on the last day of that month.

While the epidemic had showed signs of abating in St Helier as October ended, the same was sadly not the case in the country parishes where the number of new infections continued to rise. There was some relief as recovering townspeople had left hospital, thereby freeing a bed for patients from the countryside. But for those who stayed at home, one of the biggest challenges was to get medicines to them, with the medical services short of vehicles and petrol. Help was at hand however. Having worked to establish Matron Walton and her team in town, the Constable of St Helier now turned his attention to those living in the countryside. On 30 October, John Pinel placed a newspaper notice appealing for anyone with a motorcycle, and ideally with a sidecar, to come forward if they were willing to help their fellow Islanders. The volunteers' job would be to collect medicines from the Town Hall twice daily and then deliver them to the local dispensary centres established by the Sanitary Committee across the Island. These were in parish halls, schools and other buildings that offered a convenient location from which people could collect prescriptions. Once again, these proactive steps were effective. After the start of November, the rate of new infections and deaths now declined in the country parishes also. The situation was improving everywhere.

With this positive news, thoughts could now turn to praising those who had gone out of their way to make a difference during the crisis. While thanks were given to all who had worked hard during the epidemic, there was a special recognition for the efforts of John Pinel. 'Before the epidemic the Constable was one of the busiest men in the Island,' declared the *Evening Post*, 'yet during the sad and trying weeks which have just elapsed he has voluntarily added to his activities by undertaking the direction of the relief work, which had its headquarters at the Town Hall. For what he had so well performed the public, and especially the poorer classes, owe Mr Pinel a debt of deep gratitude.'[3] On 18 November 1918, a deputation of worthy citizens called upon the Constable of St Helier to offer him their thanks on behalf of a grateful Island.

By 18 November, when Pinel was receiving his richly deserved plaudits, the epidemic was over. In common with the majority of other places, Spanish Flu had disappeared from Jersey as suddenly as it had arrived. Official records show that the outbreak lasted from 16 October until 15 November 1918, a period of thirty days. Reports suggested that it had first started spreading following the transfer of five infected members of a family from a house in St Helier's Waterloo Lane to the General Hospital. Thereafter, new cases of infection had climbed to a peak on 24 October and had remained high for the next ten or eleven days. Then, in early November, the outbreak had gradually declined until there were no reported new cases by 15 November. During those thirty days, Spanish Flu had claimed the lives of 308 Islanders who came from a variety of backgrounds, all age groups and both sexes. They also came from all of the Island's parishes with the exception of St Clement, which appears to have been spared any loss of life. Not surprisingly, St Helier was the worst affected, with 169 deaths, just over half of the overall total. St Saviour suffered the next highest number of dead, with thirty-nine parishioners succumbing during the epidemic. Six parishes, Grouville, St Brelade, St Lawrence, St John, St Peter and St Ouen all suffered between ten and twenty deaths, while the lowest were Trinity with eight dead, St Martin with seven and St Mary where only three people died. For those who survived, whether they had been infected or not, it had been a distressing, painful and often frightening ordeal. Yet it was also a period during which a long hoped for event had occurred. On the eleventh hour of the eleventh day of the eleventh month of 1918, the First World War had ended.

Somewhat ironically, the conflict concluded in the same sudden and largely unheralded fashion as it had started. Although there had been clear indications that Germany and its allies were losing the war during the days that would lead up to the Armistice being signed on 11 November, it was not certain until the very last that the fighting was going to end. Newspapers contained contradictory statements, with reports of peace talks alongside those of continuing battles, and there was certainly no reduction in the number of men being killed and wounded. Yet events that had begun with Germany's defeat in August's Battle of Amiens were destined to bring the war to a conclusion.

Following the failure of its offensives between March and July 1918 and after the Battle of Amiens, Germany's military leaders had realised that they could no longer win the war. Strong Allied advances in September had moreover shown that the German Army was becoming increasingly incapable of defending the country from a possible invasion. With food shortages brought about by a British naval blockade also causing increasing public disquiet among its civilian population, Germany had entered into peace negotiations with President Wilson of the United States in an attempt to bypass the wrath of the British and French governments. While reports of the discussions had appeared in Jersey's newspapers, it was still unclear to Islanders whether these talks would end successfully. Perhaps few dared to hope for peace given the cataclysmic events of the past four years. Bulgaria's request for an armistice on 29 September had been seen as a cautious yet positive sign that recent Allied victories were finally achieving successful results. And an armistice with the Ottoman Empire a month later would appear to have confirmed this. These two armistices meant that fighting in the Balkans, the Middle East and Mesopotamia was over at least, which must have been an enormous relief for the many Island families who had relatives serving in those regions. Finally, after the news of an Austro-Hungarian collapse had come through at the beginning of the November, there was a report on 7 November that German delegates were discussing the terms of a ceasefire. At last, people could dare to hope that an end to the fighting was in sight.

By the evening of 10 November, some form of announcement was widely anticipated. As a result, a large crowd had assembled outside the offices of the *Evening Post* in St Helier's Charles Street knowing that any news that arrived via the Island's telegraph network would be displayed there first. There was widespread disappointment when nothing appeared, and so people went home to await any overnight developments. A smaller crowd was present on the following day when the notice announcing the Armistice did finally appear at exactly eleven o'clock that morning. The momentous news that the war was over had soon spread throughout the town and out into the countryside by horse, bike, train and motorcar. Despite continuing fears over the still ongoing influenza epidemic, people flocked into the centre of St Helier to join impromptu celebrations that had broken out there immediately following the announcement. To those who were observing events, it was as though someone had uncorked a bottle. 'Simultaneously the whole town seemed to awaken from a lethargy,' reported the *Evening Post*. 'In a few minutes shopkeepers and householders were hoisting bunting that had not seen the light of day for several years. Friends eagerly congratulated one another and themselves on the joyful fact that the Hun was now beaten, and all seemed to breathe easier at the news that peace would soon reign over a world that for over four years had been devastated by war.'[4]

Soon the whole centre of St Helier was awash with red, white and blue as flags, banners and patriotic emblems had appeared. They were carried by revellers marching through the streets, or waved from passing bicycles and from motorcars now driving slowly around the town sounding their horns. The never ending peel of church bells added to clamour, while from the harbour came the noisy blasts of ships' horns and wailing sirens. Shop workers had joined the celebrations, which were centred on Halkett Place and along King Street and Queen Street, after many shop owners had decided to close at one o'clock that afternoon. Above the crowds, soldiers stationed at Fort Regent lined up on the ramparts, cheering, sounding bugles and waving down to those celebrating below. While there was no 'mafeking', reported the newspapers, everyone was determined to celebrate the cessation of hostilities in a good-humoured way.

The newspapers also noted that the celebrations on that day were not as enthusiastic or excessive as might have been expected given the significance of the occasion. This reflected the situation in which Islanders now found themselves. While the influenza epidemic was clearly declining by then, no one could say with certainty that it would not flare up again. Schools, cinemas and other places of entertainment still remained closed, with no plans to reopen them until the following week at the earliest. It was also impossible to overlook the fact that victory had come at such a heavy price. Few things had underlined this more than the sight of four soldiers taking part in the celebrations, each of whom had lost a leg in the fighting. While they had draped themselves in flags and cheerily joined in the festivities, their presence was a stark reminder of the war's brutal impact on the Island. There was also a more subtle reminder that the price of war was still being paid as telegram delivery boys continued to press though the crowds to carry their unwelcome messages that yet another islander had been wounded, killed or had been reported as missing.

Even while negotiations for an armistice had been taking place, the fighting in France and Belgium had continued right up to eleven o'clock on the morning of 11 November. Men continued to be killed and wounded until the very end, and then would continue to die from their wounds or illness once the fighting had stopped. Tragically, in the final days of the war, men from Jersey were still losing their lives. On 9 November, Able Seaman Arthur Rickett was reported missing when HMS *Britannia* became the last British warship to be sunk in the war, while Private Jack Mourant died of dysentery in the Mesopotamian city of Basra. On that same day twenty-three-year-old *Soldat* Sylvère Le Nouvel, who was in the French Army's *1e régiment d'infanterie coloniale (RIC)*, had died of illness while serving in the Balkans. On 10 November, the day before the Armistice had come into effect, Corporal Arthur Warren of the Lancashire Fusiliers died in a hospital at Etaples on the Channel Coast. On that day also, Private John Malzard serving with the Canadian Corps was killed in some of the final fighting of the war which took place near the Belgian city of Mons, which ironically was the same place as where it had all started for the BEF just over four years earlier. The deaths continued after the Armistice. On 12 November, Captain Philip Mallett, who had won the MC in 1917 for 'conspicuous gallantry and devotion to duty' shown during the Battle of Passchendaele and a Bar to his award in October 1918 during the fight for the villages of Fresnoy and Gricourt, died of his wounds at a military hospital in

Rouen. The deaths and suffering would continue for the remainder of 1918 and into the following year.

Given this, it was appropriate that Jersey's jubilant celebrations of 11 November were replaced on the following day with a more sombre event. A service of thanksgiving was held in St Helier's Royal Square that would set the tone for future commemorations. It was an impromptu affair as the sudden end to hostilities had caught everyone by surprise. Notices were hastily posted up that morning inviting Islanders to gather for the service, which was scheduled to commence at 4.30pm. The Lieutenant Governor and the Bailiff were present, along with a host of politicians, army officers and members of the clergy led by the Dean of Jersey. The French Consul, *Monsieur* Jouve, was also among the dignitaries who had assembled on the balcony of the gentlemen's club overlooking the Royal Square, which was reportedly filled with such a large crowd that it spilled into the side streets as well. Over two thousand people were present, along with bands from the Salvation Army, the Jersey Musical Union and the RJGB that had brought its fife and drums to add a martial air. After the music had stopped, the service began with three hearty cheers for 'our beloved French *confrères*', a symbolic gesture that seems to have been appreciated by the French Consul. The Constable of St Helier then gave the opening address. 'They were met to celebrate the signing of the Armistice, after four years of strenuous fighting by the British troops and Allies to obtain universal peace,' John Pinel announced. 'This was the most eventful day any of them could remember, and they had met…not only to rejoice because of the Armistice which would bring about the long-desired peace, but also to remember their fallen heroes and those of their Allies.'[5]

Whether heroes or not, these wartime losses were going affect societies and communities for years to come. Wartime sacrifice was understandably the subject of the first States' debate following the Armistice. Thanking 'Providence for the colossal victory achieved', the Bailiff solemnly told the assembly on 26 November that, 'the sense of joy at the great victory was unfortunately in many cases marred by the sacrifices that had been made, but it must be a satisfaction to realise that those sacrifices had not been in vain. Jersey must now take its share in the work of reconstruction, and he felt quite certain that the population would do it in the same spirit which had characterised them during the war.'[6]

The foremost task for Jersey was to reintegrate the thousands of returning servicemen back into civilian life now that the war had ended. Most had joined under terms that had required them to serve for the duration of the war only, with an implicit understanding that they would be allowed to return home once the war had ended. Now that it was, the majority desired to do just that. In preparation, the British Government had already drawn up plans for a controlled and orderly 'demobilisation' of the wartime armed forces and to return the services to a peacetime establishment. Initially, the intention had been to release those men who were important to industry first. But there had been a reassessment following recognition that this plan would be unfair on those who had been serving the longest and who therefore would naturally expect to be among the first candidates for release. This revised approach was broadly adopted, with the criteria for demobilisation based on factors such as a man's length of service, his age and the number of wounds he may have received.

Yet even this concession seemed unfair to some men. Many soldiers serving in the Dominion contingents protested at what they saw was an unnecessary and enforced stay in Europe after they had completed what had been asked of them. The reality was that a lack of shipping now existed after German submarines had decimated Britain's merchant fleet, leaving the military authorities with little choice but to send men back home in batches. To occupy those who had to stay behind in Europe, there were training schemes developed to provide skills that might be useful after returning to civilian life. Agriculture was a popular choice, and Jersey was selected as the location for one group of Australian soldiers to undertake their studies. They were in the Island between late 1918 and 1919, spending time working directly with farmers and learning at the States Experimental Farm. Accommodation was found at military establishments such as Grève de Lecq Barracks or among the population where the men were boarders in private homes. It seems that these Australian soldiers were popular with Islanders, especially with some of the young women. When they did depart, a number took newly acquired wives and fiancées with them, much to the dismay of some of the girls' fathers.

Soldiers from the Dominions were not alone in feeling unhappy at the prospect of spending more time in uniform than they felt was strictly necessary. 'When we volunteered in the early days of the war, many things were promised us by the public at home,' wrote three former members of the Jersey Company who found themselves stationed at Portsmouth in December 1918. 'We ask the authorities who helped us greatly in getting us away on that memorable day in March 1915, to exert their influence and get us all back again, thereby showing recognition of the services the boys have rendered for democracy.'[7] But the decision was not a matter for the Jersey authorities; it rested with the British Army, who at the end of 1918, still needed many of its troops for post-war duties.

Britain's biggest commitment after the Armistice was to provide part of the Allied force required to occupy Germany's Rhineland. In accordance with the agreement that ended the fighting, the German Army had been required to evacuate France and Belgium immediately and withdraw behind the River Rhine. The Allies were permitted to follow up and take control of all German lands west of that river, including the former French provinces of Alsace and Lorraine which were made part of France once more, and to occupy a number of 'bridgeheads' across the river until a permanent peace treaty had been signed. The force that Britain sent to undertake this task was named the British Army of the Rhine, and it took up station around the city of Cologne from late 1918. Among its ranks were a number of Jersey soldiers, some of them wartime volunteers and conscripts who were reluctant to be there while there were others who were pre-war regular soldiers and accepted that it was part of their job.

In addition to this ongoing commitment on the Continent, Britain had also needed to continue protecting and garrisoning its Empire, which had expanded considerably following victory. New mandates were acquired to govern former Ottoman territories in the Middle East and in Mesopotamia and to assume control of some of the conquered German colonies in Africa. Sadly, in all those locations, men continued to die in service, mostly through disease or accidents, although fighting carried on in northern Russia, that claimed more British and Jersey lives as noted in a previous chapter.

There were further practical reasons for planning a gradual rather than a sudden military demobilisation after the Armistice. Civilian society had to cope with the reintegration of the millions of returning ex-servicemen whose former peacetime roles and jobs had either disappeared or been taken over by someone else while they were away. Planning and careful management would be needed if this were to be achieved with the minimum of disruption. But it would unfortunately prove to be not so straightforward. There had been a promise made that the men who had fought and won the war deserved the nation's thanks in the form of decent housing, living conditions and jobs when they returned home. In the words of David Lloyd-George, the British Prime Minister, they were going to come back to 'a land fit for heroes'. Yet delivering such a land would always be a challenge.

In Jersey, the States set about meeting the promise with every good intent. The first step in the process was to help men smoothly make the transition from military to civilian life. In December 1918, the first batch of returning soldiers had arrived in the Island. They were men newly released from German prisoner of war camps where a number of them had been incarcerated for more than four years. Logically, those who had been prisoners were given the priority when it came to going home first. They received a hero's welcome on their return to the Island complete with ceremonies and presentations. After this, men steadily returned home each month throughout 1919, either individually or in small groups. Most had already gone through a formal process of military demobilisation before they arrived in Jersey. This included a final medical examination that would determine whether a man was entitled to a military pension due to disabilities that they may have incurred as a result of his service in the armed forces. Each man also received a 'Protection Certificate' to confirm that he had been demobilised, an 'Out-of-Work Donation Policy' that provided financial support for up to twenty-six weeks if he could not find a job, an advance on pay and a civilian suit or a clothing allowance so that he could buy one when he reached home.

Managing the process of demobilisation were specially formed 'Army Dispersal Units', one of which was established in Jersey in early January 1919. It was under the command of Captain Léonce L'H Ogier, who had previously served with the Militia and the Royal Jersey Garrison Battalion (RJGB) and who had been one of the military representatives on the District Tribunals. The role of his latest command was to oversee the demobilisation of the soldiers, to collect their uniforms and equipment, and receiving any weapons that a man might still possess. The Jersey unit also handed out coupons that enabled each demobilised man to obtain a made-to-measure suit from a local tailor. While Ogier's unit did deal with a number of soldiers returning from overseas' service, one of its prime tasks was to manage the demobilisation of those soldiers stationed in Jersey, many of whom had to wait longer than their comrades who had served overseas. It was not until November 1919 that the RJGB was finally stood down, having completed nearly three years of service. In common with its humble beginning, the RJGB's end would be an informal affair with speeches and a dinner held at a public house. Its garrison artillery counterparts had been disbanded earlier in the year.

Many Islanders serving in the French armed forces endured a process of demobilisation that retained them even beyond November 1919. Delays would be especially difficult for those survivors of the 1912 and 1913 *Classes* who had now been away from home for six or seven years. With concerns over German intentions after the Armistice, and with the same commitment as Britain had to occupying and garrison duties, it meant that the French Army was reluctant to let its men leave too soon. It was eventually agreed that those men who had served longest would be demobilised first, starting in the summer of 1919 and continuing through until 1921. Like their British allies, departing French soldiers also went through a process of medical examination, an issue of demobilisation documents and the exchange of uniforms for a civilian suit, which was rather contemptuously nicknamed *'Le suit 52 francs'* or *'Costume Abrami'* after its designer. And so dressed, Jersey's French ex-servicemen had also arrived home to pick up their lives once more.

The process of finding work for these men was made somewhat easier by a general agreement that any women who had been employed to replace them would relinquish their job on the men's return from the war. It meant an end to the novelty of women postal workers, bus drivers and the Women's Land Army. The same principle applied in Britain, ending the need for munitionettes as the munitions industry contracted to peacetime production levels and men came back to reclaim those jobs that remained. As the Jersey volunteers returned home at the start of 1919, the Constable of St Helier received a letter from the Works Manager at Kynochs Limited where many of the women had been employed. 'You will, I am sure, be very glad to hear that individually, and as a whole, the Jersey girls created a most favourable impression in these works,' wrote Mr Finch. 'They were always good tempered, attentive and hardworking, and I do not remember having heard a single complaint against any of them.'[8] A number of the girls found Birmingham to their liking too, with some deciding to remain there after the war.

To assist ex-servicemen following their return to Jersey, the States established the Demobilisation Employment Exchange, whose role was to match men unable to return to their former peacetime jobs to employers looking for men to hire. It was not a straightforward matter, despite appeals for patriotic support from local companies. The widespread economic recession that had followed the end of the war led to global austerity, with Britain especially affected. The huge cost of four years fighting had left the country heavily indebted, and with many of its traditional export markets such as Germany now closed. While the situation was not so pronounced in Jersey, the effect of the general economic downturn was felt, particularly by those unable to find work. To assist further in finding men suitable employment, the States also created a number of work schemes aimed at improving public infrastructure and also placed special effort on finding work for disabled ex-servicemen. Despite this, at the end of 1919 there remained more than one hundred men on the Employment Exchange's register looking for employment, the majority of whom were reported to be labourers, storemen, clerks and other unskilled trades. With their original 'Out-of-Work Donation Policy' either having expired or about to run out, many were forced to seek handouts in order to survive. Some financial support was received from the Parish-based welfare system that was already in existence, while other support came from ex-servicemen's associations formed in the aftermath of the war. One of the first of these established in Jersey was a local 'post' of the Comrades of the Great War, which had begun in November 1918. Others soon followed including a Jersey branch of the Officer's Association. Within a few years, many of these ex-servicemen's organisations would come together to form the Royal British Legion, which exists to the present time. French ex-servicemen formed a branch of the *L'Union Nationale des Combattants* in March 1919 following a meeting of over five hundred veterans and the families of some of those who had been killed. Not all were linked to larger, overseas organisations however. One of the smallest and most fiercely proud of them was the Original Jersey Overseas Contingent Association, formed in 1920 by the surviving members of the Jersey Company. Its purpose was to exist for the 'good comradeship and mutual benefit' of its members – something that it would successfully manage to achieve for decades to come.

This sense of coming together for mutual benefit was not solely limited to those who had been in uniform during the war. Many civilians who had lived through the conflict and had endured its deprivations felt that they too deserved better recognition and reward for their sacrifices. Prior to the war, there had been a strong political stirring among the British working classes over the inequalities that existed in society. The trade union movement had fostered aspirations for change during wartime years, using the opportunity to press for better pay and for improved working conditions. With the end of the war, many in Britain believed that it was the time to bring about real and permanent political change. While Jersey may have been far removed from the class struggle waged in Britain's industrialised communities, there were Islanders who believed that a change was also needed in Jersey. Some has gone as far as to form the Island's first trade union in September 1918, a local branch of the Dock, Wharf, Riverside and General Workers Union. It had been a new development for the Island, where trade unions were technically illegal under a law dating back to 1771. Regardless of this, the new workers' body had soon made its presence felt by organising two strikes in November 1918 in protest against non-union labour being employed at St Helier Harbour. In both cases, they were successful in getting their demands agreed. Other grievances were fuelled by a growing resentment over wartime conditions and a desire to see change in the political establishment that had existed in the Island before the war and which was still very much in power at its end.

Much of the resentment had initially centred upon the cost of food and fuel, whose prices been steadily rising throughout the war. On 5 July 1918, a group calling itself the Jersey Political Association (JPA) held a meeting at St Helier's Town Hall to discuss the subject of living costs. The strength of feeling was evident from the outset. The crowd, which was reported to be the largest audience ever seen in the Assembly Room, and which included a 'large sprinkling of ladies', spilled out of the room and onto the street outside. It was chaired by the Constable of St Helier who called for all speakers to be given a fair hearing, and started with the reading of a special resolution. 'That this meeting of Jersey inhabitants protests against the increased charges made for gas consumption, and to the excessive prices demanded to food necessities… being of opinion that such are harsh and extortionate and constitute a heavy tax upon all classes, particularly the poorer classes…'[9] The first address came from Deputy Gray, a recently elected States Member for St Helier. To the applause and cheers of most of those in the room, Gray pointed out that local gas prices had gone up from three shilling and sixpence per unit in 1914 to seven and six by 1918. The directors of the local gas company were clearly thinking about their wives, children and shareholders, he told the audience, and not about the poor people of St Helier. The company, he stated, had followed a policy of 'heads I win, tails you lose,'[10] It was the same principle when it came to food prices, Gray continued, with the cost of butter, eggs and vegetables reaching prices that he claimed were scandalous. At a time of war, he solemnly announced, what we want is equality of sacrifice, something that was clearly not happening in Jersey. Speakers who followed trying to justify the price rises were shouted down.

Imbued with the success of that first meeting, the JPA held another meeting on 10 July 1918. Although the Association had links to those behind Jersey's emerging trade unions, it was more broadly based, having both workers and employers among its supporters and with intentions to pursue a wider agenda than just workers' rights. In this second meeting, there was an agreement that the JPA stood for the 'advancement of welfare generally in the Island'. The audience that night heard why this cause was so important. It was unfair that only those with money could send their children into secondary education at schools such as Victoria College, Deputy Gray told them, and then on to university. Such opportunities should also be open to the sons of labourers. Doctor Fergusson, a local physician known for his work among the Island's poor, spoke about concerns over the levels of poverty present in Jersey. He told the surprised audience that there were far more cases of tuberculosis in Jersey children than there should be, and it was increasing due to a lack of fruit and vegetables and as a result of the insanitary conditions that many lived in. A Mrs Trachy spoke strongly against food prices in Jersey, claiming that despite the assurances from Island politicians Islanders were paying more for essentials than most people in Britain.

The presence of Mrs Trachy on the platform, who seemed quite at ease addressing the audience noted an apparently surprised newspaper reporter, was an indication of another clear JPA policy. They demanded that women should be able to vote in the Island's elections. It was a subject that was already being discussed by the States. A special Committee has been established at the end of 1917 to consider this after the British Government had begun the process of extending the franchise to women. Yet with little progress apparently being made, Deputy Gray had attempted to hasten matters. On 8 October 1918 – which was the same day that a Women's Branch of the JPA was formed – he brought a proposition to the States that would allow all women in Jersey to vote. On that occasion, it was rejected by Members. It was no more than a rearguard action by the States however. With a new British law allowing women over the age of thirty to vote having already been passed in February 1918, even the most conservative of Jersey politicians must have realised that change was in the air. In February 1919, the States debated the principle of giving the vote to women aged over thirty and also extending it to all men aged twenty or over. The debate would rumble on until 22 May 1919, when the proposition was finally passed.

One debate that had quickly ended after the war was what should be done to commemorate those who had died while serving their country. There was a strong feeling that something tangible and public was needed. This was particularly important for the families of those who had died, most of whom were unable to bring home the remains of a son, husband, father or brother for burial in the Island. The British Government had decided early in the war that the fallen should not be repatriated, so as to ensure equality between those who could afford to make such arrangements and those who could not. While schemes were organised in the post-war years to allow families to visit war cemeteries and memorials in France, Belgium and elsewhere, there was a demand for a location in the Island as a place to mourn loved ones who had not come home. In April 1919, the States agreed to create a permanent memorial. The only question was in what form and where. One commentator felt strongly that they had the answer. 'Why not remove the inartistic effigy of German George from the pedestal in the square,' they wrote in a letter to the *Evening Post*, 'and erect instead a figure of a typical Jersey soldier, with the names on the Roll of Honour inscribed on the pediment.'[11] The gilded statue of King George II would remain, however, as the attention turned to an initiative by the Constable of St Helier instead.

Mindful of the British Government's plan to erect a cenotaph, which in Greek means 'empty tomb', in London, the Constable of St Helier proposed that the States consider a similar approach to be adopted by Jersey. The location suggested was at one end of the Royal Parade, a stretch of gardens in the west of the town that had originally been created as a parade ground for troops. A grand monument to General Don, who had originally laid it out, already stood there in great splendour. With agreement that the place and the principle was acceptable, it was decided to hold the first commemoration ceremony on 4 August 1919, to mark the fifth anniversary of the outbreak of war. Lacking the time to create a permanent memorial, Pinel had asked the Town Architect to design and build a temporary structure in the time available. The result was a wooden cenotaph, although as one commentator would remark, it looked like stone and was a splendid and beautiful thing.

One side of monument was inscribed 'Our Glorious Dead'. On the other were the words 'Their Name Liveth for Evermore'. Everyone agreed that it was a fitting tribute.

15 ONE HUNDRED YEARS SINCE

Assessing Jersey's Great War

The new monument had stood out sombre yet splendid in the middle of the assembled crowd. Crafted from specially chosen grey granite, it glimmered slightly as the watery afternoon sunlight picked out tiny quartz flecks on its austere sides and ornately carved crown. Around the base, soldiers stood at each of the four corners with heads bowed, their hands resting gently on the butts of reversed rifles. A little further off, outside the encircling low wall and railing, a guard of honour stood to attention while a line of nearby buglers nervously licked their lips, waiting for the signal to play 'Last Post' once the ceremony began. It was 11 November 1923, exactly five years since the First World War had ended. The people of Jersey were gathered to mark the occasion. The temporary structure symbolising an 'empty tomb' erected through the initiative of the Constable of St Helier in 1919 had soon become a place for thousands of Islanders, both privileged and humble, to remember loved ones who had not returned. As a result, the States had decided that the plot of ground on which it stood should become sacred for generations to come, and that a permanent monument should replace the temporary wooden one.

At three o'clock that afternoon, the crowd fell silent as the Island's latest Lieutenant Governor, Major General Sir William Douglas Smith KCB KCVO, stepped forward to unveil the newly constructed memorial. Among those who were watching him was an assembly of almost one thousand ex-servicemen, men who had served in the armed forces of Britain and France between 1914 and 1918. They had gathered earlier that day in the Triangle Park near to St Helier's seafront to renew old friendships and swap stories before marching into the Parade accompanied by serving soldiers from the British Army garrison and the Island's reformed Militia. Now, they all stood to attention, headwear removed, to observe the unfolding ceremony. Clustered on the opposite side of the monument were a host of dignitaries, politicians and churchmen, many of whom had led Jersey through some of the most challenging years in its recent history. Drawn up on either side were choirs and bands who had earlier lent their songs and music to the occasion, but who now stood in silence along with everyone else in the large crowd that surrounded the monument. Prominent among them was a younger generation of Islanders, who were waiting in a specially constructed stand. Two children from each of the Island's schools had been given this place of honour to watch events and, as the Bailiff, Sir William Vernon, had reminded them in a special speech before the ceremony, to remember the sons of Jersey who had fought and died on land and sea between 1914 and 1918.

After the buglers had finished their call and as the echoes of the gunfire salutes from Fort Regent had faded away, the Bailiff addressed the watching crowd. Rolls containing the names of those from Jersey who had given their service and lives during the war had been ceremoniously placed in a sealed sarcophagus on top of the memorial. This was the price paid by the Island, Vernon reminded them, for its part in the war. 'In its noble simplicity the granite monument which the States of Jersey had erected to the memory of fallen Jerseymen would endure...this day, this moment, it should not serve merely as an emblem of mourning, it should be remembered with pride as an emblem of victory.'[1] Above all, Vernon had concluded, the Cenotaph would show how Jersey had responded in the national hour of need and helped win victory from the enemy.

The Cenotaph would not be the only monument erected to show how Jersey had responded in the national hour of need. In the war's aftermath, Islanders had embarked upon a remarkable programme of memorial building. More than fifty monuments, tablets and panels were erected throughout the Island in the years following 1918, along with many private tributes to the dead. Aside from the Cenotaph, the most prominent were the parish memorials, carved from stone or wood and constructed in a variety of designs, shapes and forms. Surprisingly, there were only eleven. One parish chose not to inscribe the names of its wartime dead for posterity. Perhaps St Helier thought that the presence of a parish memorial would somehow diminish the importance of the Cenotaph as the Island's principal monument to its war dead. Or perhaps there were just too many names to fit onto a parish memorial that needed to be both modest and respectful; St Helier had lost more than five hundred men in the war after all. Whatever the reason, the sacrifice of men from the town was not commemorated in the same fashion as those of the other parishes. Given the widely held belief during the war that St Helier had made proportionately a greater sacrifice than the other parishes had, there does seem to be an unfortunate injustice in this decision.

In addition to the parishes, many of the Island's churches also chose to remember the sacrifice made by their parishioners by erecting memorials of their own. Their congregations had decided that it was important to keep the names of the dead in the sight of the living as well as in their hearts. The churches also became the home for private memorials commemorating the losses suffered by individual families, which in some cases commemorated more than one fallen son. For some of the Island's schools it was also important to record the names of past pupils who had lost their lives. Victoria College erected the most impressive memorial, unveiled in 1924 and topped by a striking effigy of Sir Galahad complete with a shield and reversed sword representing a crucifix. It now records the names of 130 former masters and pupils who died in the First World War, among whom are the two Victoria Cross winners, William Bruce and Allastair McReady-Diarmid, who both have college houses named after them.

Any attempt to evaluate how the First World War affected Jersey and its people, must start with these memorials. Or rather, it must start with the dead whose names they bear, along with those men who were denied immortalisation in stone, metal or wood due to the fortunes of commemoration after the war. There is simply no escaping the amount of names and the even greater number of dead. One of the first tasks following the war was to gather the names of all those who had lost their lives. In Jersey, this process had actually commenced before an end of the conflict had even been in sight, with the formation in April 1917 of a special States' War Roll Committee led by Jurat Reginald Malet De Carteret. Its purpose was to create a 'Roll of Honour' containing the names of all of Jersey's war dead. By the time that the Roll was published in 1919, the Committee had recorded the details of 862 men who had died while serving in Britain's armed forces and noted that a further 264 had died while fighting for France.*

How does Jersey's wartime loss compare to that of other countries and communities? The percentage of military deaths among Britain's population has been calculated as 2 percent, while the same figure for France is 3.5 percent. Taking just the number of deaths contained on the Island's 1919 Roll of Honour, the equivalent figure for Jersey is 2.2 percent. A comparable figure for the Isle of Man indicates that its population suffered a wartime loss of 2.1 percent. It is more difficult to draw a direct comparison with Guernsey because no similar effort was made in that Island immediately after the war to record the names of its wartime dead. Recent analysis suggests a figure that is similar to that of Jersey however.[2] Of course, it could be reasonably argued that the number of deaths suffered by a country or community is not strictly representative of their commitment or sacrifice. Moreover, it is clear that the statistics on populations and military deaths from the First World War are imprecise and vary from source to source. Accepting these inadequacies, however, this analysis does indicate that Jersey's sacrifice was comparable to

---

* Recent analysis has shown that the number of men from Jersey, or who had a strong connection to the Island, who died during the First World War is actually far higher than the 1919 figure. The variance comes from the data gathering techniques used when compiling the Roll of Honour, which relied on the public putting forward the names of those who had died. While the total number may never be known, it is almost certainly closer to 1,600 men and possibly even higher.

that of Britain and the other Crown Dependencies, a fact that runs counter to wartime suggestions by the military authorities and some States Members that the Island was holding back its men from military service. Further analysis also indicates that the losses were shared almost equally between the town and the country parishes, despite a strong sense in the Island that St Helier was shouldering a disproportionally high share of the recruitment burden. Around 58 percent of those who died came from St Helier, a figure that is just a little higher than the 54 percent of the Island's population who lived in that parish.[3]

What was the impact of this sacrifice on Jersey? The popular notion is that nations suffered from a 'lost generation' given the number of deaths during the First World War, and were somehow diminished in the years that followed as a result. It is impossible to say how much validity there is in such an idea, but perhaps among Jersey's dead there were men who would have made a significant difference had they lived. Perhaps the Island lost some who would have become great politicians, entrepreneurs, teachers, artists and so forth. No one will ever know. But it can be said with certainty that for every man's death, there was an impact on his family, relatives and friends, immediately and in the months and years that followed. Those who were left without a son, husband, father, relative or friend individually experienced the tragedy of Jersey's 'lost generation' for the rest of their lives. The high number of deaths and the intimate nature of the community from which the men came also left a collective sense of loss in the Island. It was experienced most strongly in the years immediately after the war, leading to the many monuments that appeared during that period. Ultimately, this collective impact of the First World War was channelled into Remembrance Day on 11 November each year, and the associated ceremonies that continue to the present time. By doing so, it placed respectful boundaries around the individual and collective grief, allowing the Island to move forward while still remembering the sacrifices of those who had died.

In his 1923 speech at the unveiling of the Island's Cenotaph, the Bailiff had also said that the monument should represent Jersey's contribution to winning victory over the enemy. Yet amid the great efforts being made to remember the wartime dead, it seems that little thought was given in the post-war years to celebrating the wartime achievements. Jersey's soldiers, sailors and airmen had been a part of the victorious armies of Britain and France after all. Partly in recognition of this, the States had created a Roll of Service in 1919 to sit alongside the Island's Roll of Honour, but it appears to have been something of an afterthought. This Roll recorded the names of men who had fought in and survived the war, although it omitted for unknown reasons those who had served in the French armed forces. Taken jointly, the 1919 Rolls of Honour and Service record that 7,154 Jerseymen had served outside the Island in Britain's armed forces and in the Merchant Navy during the war. How did this number compare with others? After adding in the 2,450 Islanders who had fought for France, it indicates that Jersey mobilised approximately 19 percent of its population for military service outside the island during the First World War. By comparison, the equivalent figure for Britain is 13 percent while that of France is 22 percent. Even taking into account the deficiencies in the data, this indicates that Jersey's commitment to the war was a remarkable one that was worthy of more recognition.[4]

In the years following 1918, Britain's Dominions would place a great emphasis on recognising the achievements and sacrifices of their servicemen during the First World War. At significant locations on the old Western Front, and elsewhere in the world where their men had fought, Australia, Canada, New Zealand and South Africa preserved important battlefield sites and constructed impressive monuments to their nation's achievements. Even Newfoundland, then a self-governing Dominion of two hundred and fifty thousand people, constructed five magnificent memorials in places where its regiment had fought and its men had died. Yet there has been no comparable effort made by Jersey (or Guernsey). In many ways, this is understandable. For Britain's Dominions, the First World War was a 'coming of age' moment, with their progress towards independent nationhood helped by the commitment and sacrifice of their troops. There was no such outlook or outcome for the Channel Islands as a result of taking part in the war, and thus no real motive for drawing attention to the efforts of Islanders as distinct from those of Britain. Furthermore, as most Jerseymen had enlisted as individuals and fought separately in many units throughout the world, it would have been practically impossible to highlight a single action or location as the place worthy of preservation or where a Jersey memorial should have been erected.

There is one important exception of course. For its endeavours, achievements and losses, the Jersey Company was deserving of a memorial more tangible than just a page in the foreword of the Island's Roll of Honour and Service or a belated thanks from the States. Nothing was erected in Guillemont and Ginchy, on Messines Ridge, at Frezenberg near Ypres or indeed elsewhere to recall this unique and very courageous band of Jersey soldiers, and that remains the situation at the time of writing. Perhaps it was inappropriate to single out this one small group from among so many Jerseymen who had served. With nothing done officially, it was sadly left to the men themselves to place a memorial of their own to the Jersey Company in the parish church of Grouville in 1961.

If no effort was made to mark the achievements and sacrifices of Jerseymen on the battlefield during the First World War, it should not be surprising to find that nothing was done to mark the endeavours of those who stayed at home to defend their Island. While Jersey may not have had a regiment to send overseas, it did have military units that loyally stood on home guard duties during the war. The commitment of the Jersey Militia and its successors, the Royal Jersey Garrison Battalion and the 110th Company, Royal Garrison Artillery, between 1914 and 1918 sits proudly as the culmination of at least seven centuries of tradition and service. Jointly, the Royal Jersey Light Infantry, the Royal Jersey Artillery, the Engineer Company and the Medical Company represented the strongest, best trained and most well equipped military force that the Island had ever mobilised. Their men had stoically stood on duty day after day and night after night guarding the Island's coast and key facilities. The fact that the war stayed away from Jersey's shores should not diminish from their commitment or the sacrifice of a number of Militiamen who contracted illnesses while serving during the winter months and who subsequently died. They did the job that they were ordered to do, as they had done in the years leading up to 1914. As such, it seems that the Jersey Militia was a force that the Island should be more aware and proud of in the present time.

Although the men who stood on guard between 1914 and 1918 would have been unaware of the fact, the Militia was also a force that was nearing the end of its time. After seven centuries, the prevailing belief following the First World War was that Jersey's strategic military value was finally at an end. With Germany humbled and France now an ally bonded in blood, another war seemed inconceivable, much to the relief of an overdrawn and overstretched Britain that was focused on reducing its defence commitments and expenditure. In 1921, the Militia was re-established, but as a single infantry battalion and an artillery company, in total 625 men. Then in 1927, it was reduced in size again to just 250 men formed into a rifle company and a machine gun detachment. At the same time, Militia service became voluntary, with Jerseymen no longer compelled to defend their Island by law. It was almost the end of an era.

There was also little recognition given in the post-war years to the men who had directed the Island's defences between 1914 and 1918. In contrast to their famous predecessor, General Don, who had also successfully defended the Island one hundred years earlier, there was no monument erected to acknowledge the efforts of either Major General Alexander Rochfort or Major General Alexander Wilson, his successor from October 1916. Of the two, it seems that Rochfort was more deserving of some form of recognition. While the circumstances he had faced between 1914 and 1916 were admittedly less threatening than those faced by Don, the situation may have been changed had the war's opening battles of movement gone differently and the Germans won the Battle of the Marne in September 1914. In that eventuality, there was every chance that the German Army would have arrived on the nearby French coast, in which case the threat to the Island would have become critical. Rochfort had worked steadily before 1914 and tirelessly during the early years of the war to ensure that Jersey had a strong and modern Militia capable of offering a robust defence against any hostile force trying to invade the Island. The effort put into this, and in working with the States to ensure the well-being and security of the civilian population, may well have cost the sixty-eight-year-old his health and ultimately his life. It is unfortunate that his contribution has been overlooked, since it is worthy of more than just a brief footnote in the Island's history.

The contribution of Jersey's civilian population between 1914 and 1918 is also worthy of greater recognition. The First World War was not just about the soldiers, sailors and airmen who had fought and died; it had been a 'total war' that demanded Britain's entire strength to wage and ultimately win victory. Those who served on the 'home front', as it was termed, between 1914 and 1918 would assume a new importance alongside those fighting on the battlefields. As a result, Jersey's civilian population, both women and men, were forced to accept change, suffer hardships and make personal sacrifices. They became part of Britain's home front, and therefore contributors to the nation's war effort. The Empire's needs had demanded that civilians accept change in their lives, whether they were directly involved in the war effort or not. Islanders had to adjust to the sudden departure of men for service overseas and to the disruption caused by the Militia's mobilisation. As a result, they had to take up new roles and new responsibilities to ensure that daily life could continue. They had to accept a loss of personal rights, freedoms and choice, from inconveniences such as the reduction in public house opening hours to the threat of a court martial for spreading false rumours. They had to cope with rising food and fuel prices and the threatened shortages in these essentials on occasions. They had to live with nearly two thousand German prisoners of war present in their Island and with dozens of Austro-Hungarian internee labourers within their community. They had helped to fund the nation's war effort, both directly by giving to good causes and indirectly through the States' donations towards Britain's cost of the war. While the war may have been harder on some Islanders, everyone would have felt its impact in one way or another. Like it or not, the people of Jersey had been all in this together.

Islanders had also contributed directly to Britain's home front by sending hundreds of workers to serve in the armament's industry, making munitions, weapons and other war materials. The majority of these were women, who had also taken on roles as nurses and VAD volunteers, as army, naval and air force auxiliaries and as Land Girls who would work on farms in Britain as well as in Jersey. Indirectly, women had also taken on jobs and roles in the Island, thus allowing Britain to draw more Jerseymen into the armed forces for service overseas. In common with most other places, the contribution made by Jersey's women during the war was largely overlooked after 1918 when there was a desire among many individuals (mainly men) to return to the pre-war world. But there would be no going back to the Victorian and Edwardian society and values of 1914. Too much had changed as a result of the war. After wearing practical short haircuts and trousers as munitionettes or land girls, there was reluctance among women to return to starched dresses and whalebone corsets. The progressive enablement of women's political rights had also continued after 1918, though it was slower in Jersey than was the case in Britain. British women were permitted to stand for Parliament from 1918, and would receive equal voting rights with men from 1928. In Jersey, women were permitted to stand for the States from 1924, although it would not be until 1948 when the first woman won her seat. And equal voting rights for Island's female population would have to wait until after the Second World War and the changes to Jersey's government following the Occupation.

Those who clamoured for political change at the end of the war in recognition of the commitment and sacrifice of Islanders would also have to wait until after 1945 for their efforts to bear fruit. The reality was that in 1918 there was no compelling reason for political change. The Island's politicians, government and institutions had successfully steered Jersey through its most challenging period in one hundred years; why consider changing something that appeared to have worked perfectly? During the war, the States had shown itself to be capable of managing the challenging wartime situation without the need for significant changes to its structure or constitution. The States' Committees had worked hard to mitigate the worst effects of war on Islanders wherever possible, while still patriotically supporting Britain and the Allied cause. As a group, its Members had remained outwardly calm and measured as they coped with the impositions of war, only fracturing at times of high pressure such as during the Military Service Law debates. There can be no doubt that on occasions, States Members had acted with self-interest, both individually and collectively. This was most evident whenever the demands of Britain and the war threatened to impact upon the Island's dominant agricultural industry. But then would any small nation have behaved differently in such a position? Even in the darkest times of war, countries needed to look towards a time of peace and to ensure that their communities were able to resume normal life and be able to prosper in the future. Jersey had certainly emerged from the war ready to build on its pre-war economic success, and would prosper during the interwar years as a result.

Sir William Vernon led the States and the Island into those interwar years, remaining Bailiff until 1931 when ill health would force him to retire. In common with the States and the Island, he had come through the wartime years with a great deal of credit. Vernon had faced considerable personal challenges between 1914 and 1918, with much of his constitutional position reduced by the greater wartime role of the Lieutenant Governor and the imposition of the Defence of the Realm (DORA) regulations. Nevertheless, Vernon had adopted a pragmatic approach from the start that had sought to balance the proper demands of Britain with the protection of the Island's long held independence, rights and privileges. There had been times when these were under significant threat, with the possibility of a German attack at the beginning of the war and through the British demands for manpower towards its end. Yet Vernon had helped ensure the Island was able to defend itself on these and other occasions. He had also ensured that Jersey continued to function as normally as possible at all other times, with little sense of public panic or tension, despite the uncertainties brought about by the war. At its end, he oversaw a swift and smooth transition into peacetime normality once again. Vernon would die in 1934 at the age of eighty-two, much to the sadness of Islanders who clearly felt that he had served them well. Unlike Sir Alexander Coutanche, who was Bailiff during the Second World War, there are no monuments to recall Vernon's wartime leadership in the Island. As is the case with his colleague, and on occasions his adversary, General Rochfort, this does appear to be a regretful oversight.

Despite the continued presence of Vernon and other wartime leaders, the interwar years were a time of change for Jersey. The Island's French community, which had numbered more than six thousand permanent residents before 1914, had gradually declined after the First World War. By 1921, the number of French-born people in the Island was down to little more than four thousand, while ten years later it had reduced again to just over three thousand and it would continue to decline. The war was partly responsible for this, drawing over two thousand men away to serve, with many never returning to the Island. It had also hastened the assimilation of Jersey's French community, which had been so distinctive before 1914. Many sons of French families had volunteered for or been conscripted into the British Army during the war, choosing to serve their new country rather than the old. Some had even 'anglicised' their names to make it easier for fellow soldiers to pronounce, thus Alexandre became Alexander, Bastard became Basford and Jean became John. The States' educational and immigration policies contributed to this process of assimilation designed as they were to counter the perceived threat of a strong French presence and influence in the Island. In the post-Second World War years, the full-time

French Consul would also disappear, along with his wartime Consulate offices in St Helier's Church Street. By that time, the French Jesuit and other religious communities had also largely left the Island, as their organisers returned home and demand for their services decreased.

The process of 'anglicisation' would not only affect the Island's French community in the interwar years. The unique language and traditions of Jersey's 'native' population had already been under considerable pressure from English-speaking immigrants prior to 1914, and the First World War would play a part in accelerating the loss of a distinct Jersey identity. While wartime challenges had brought the town versus country division sharply into focus, the war had also helped to unite the Island in a common purpose, that of supporting Britain. Islanders had faced a common enemy, had joined in with patriotic collections and fundraising and had been challenged by a call to arms and the subsequent loss of life that had affected all levels of Island society. Moreover, the war had caused an unprecedented number of Islanders to leave Jersey, the majority for the first time. The destination of these men and women in most cases had been Britain, where they had lived alongside, formed relationships with and married British people. The trend was irreversible, and would continue in the years leading up the Second World War and beyond.

It is probably just as well that Sir William Vernon did not live to see the Second World War. In May and June 1940, German forces had swept through the new Western Front to drive a reconstituted BEF from the Continent and compel France into signing an armistice in the same railway carriage at Compiègne in which Germany had accepted defeat in November 1918. It was with a heavy sense of despair that Islanders who had lived through the First World War now watched German troops arrive in Jersey on 1 July 1940. A few days before this, they had also watched as the small Jersey Militia had hurriedly left along with the handful of British Army soldiers who remained in the Island. The Militia never returned, as a formed unit at least.[†] It was all a very different outcome than that witnessed in 1914; Britain had neither the means nor the motivation in 1940 to hold onto the Channel Islands. For Islanders, it must have been a moment of great sadness, reflection and questioning as to what exactly all the sacrifices of the First World War had been for.

The first commandant of the occupying forces was *Hauptman* Erich Gussek, who ironically had been one of the German prisoners of war held in Jersey at Les Blanches Banques camp during the First World War. The triumph of returning to the Island as a conqueror would not have been lost on Gussek, nor would the symbolism of choosing St Brelade's Churchyard as the location for

---

† The Militia was disbanded in 1953, having not been reformed after 1945. In 1987, the Jersey Field Squadron (The Royal Militia Island of Jersey) was formed as a unit of the Territorial Army in response to a request from Britain for a defence contribution, assuming the lineage and emblems of the Jersey Militia.

the German forces' *Heldenfriedhof* or 'Heroes' Cemetery'. There the occupiers found the graves of seven men who had died while prisoners of war in Jersey along with Willy Riedl, an Austro-Hungarian internee labourer who had died of tuberculosis in September 1918 and who had been buried in the same plot. They had stayed in the Island despite negotiations between Jersey's authorities and the families of the deceased men over repatriating their remains in the interwar years. Nearby was the grave of one of the prisoners' former guards, Private George Hanlon. While the Germans and the Austro-Hungarian would remain in the cemetery during the Occupation, Private Hanlon was apparently found to be in the way of a planned pathway, and so was moved to a newly created Allied war cemetery in St Helier. At the present time only Private Hanlon rests in Jersey; all the former First World War prisoners of war and Willy Riedl, along with the remains of 214 German servicemen who had been buried during the Second World War, were exhumed in 1961 and placed in a large ossuary located near Mont Saint-Michel in France.

Jersey's Second World War concluded in the joyous scenes of liberation on 9 May 1945 as British troops arrived to end the German occupation. In the years that followed, Islanders celebrated Liberation Day by coming together in a festive mood to honour those who had lived through the Occupation and to celebrate victory over the enemy. By contrast, Jersey's First World War continued to be commemorated by Remembrance Day with its mournful ceremonies and a focus on those who had died. After 1945, Remembrance Day came to encompass the Second World War also. The Cenotaph and a number of the other Island memorials now became monuments to not only the dead of the First World War, but also to those who had lost their lives between 1939 and 1945, and to those who have died in the many conflicts since. The President of the United States in 1918, Woodrow Wilson, had proclaimed that the First World War would be 'the war to end all wars'. How wrong he has proved to be.

Perhaps different ways of recalling the two world wars has been one of the reasons for Islanders to gradually overlook the Island's experiences in the First World War. This occurrence was not something that was confined to just Jersey. In the decades that followed 1945, general interest in the First World War declined as a fascination in the Second World War developed, helped by Hollywood stars in blockbuster movies. At the same time, many people accepted the 'Lions Led by Donkeys' theory of the First World that a number of authors and poets had advanced. In their view, it was possible to sum up four years of history by a depiction in which heroic soldiers, represented by lions, were needlessly sent to die by incompetent generals, who were represented by donkeys. This view persisted through the years during which First World War veterans, both military and civilian, whose first-hand experiences may have told a different story, were sadly passing away. Perhaps this was the reason why no one had thought that it was important to preserve the memories of the Jersey men and women who had lived through the First World War, or to set down an account of their experiences while they still lived. It is regrettable that Jersey's First World War passed from living memory into history with barely a thought.

Looking back, one hundred years after the events of 1914 to 1918, what should we make of Jersey's Great War? The instinct of the immediate post-war years was a correct one; the sacrifice made by those Jerseymen who had died fighting in foreign fields, hostile seas or distant skies should never be forgotten. Whether a regular, a reservist, a volunteer or a conscript, they had left the security and charm of their island home and had never came back. We should never tire of recalling their names, seeing images of their faces and hearing about their stories. But we should also be prepared to honour the memory and understand the achievements of those who served in the war and survived to return home. This recognition should encompass those men whose role it was to defend of their Island throughout the war, be it as a private soldier or a major general. Theirs was a (mostly) cheerful sacrifice that is worthy of remembrance.

We must also remember that Jersey's Great War experience was not just that of the Tommies and the *Poilus*. Jersey people as a whole lived through one of the most challenging times in their history and emerged from it a stronger and more unified people, and despite their losses and experiences, they were not a diminished people. And they were not a people that deserved to be overlooked by future generations.

ENDNOTES

CHAPTER 1
[1] *Morning News*, 1 January 1914
[2] *Morning News*, 13 August 1914
[3] JAS, A/E/10/7, correspondence between the Lieutenant Governor and the Home Office, August 1917
[4] 1916 *Evening Post* Jersey Almanac
[5] JAS A/E/3, Analysis of the Island of Jersey and Guernsey Census of 1911, H. Le Vavasseur dit Durell
[6] 1906 States Report on immigration into Jersey
[7] Ibid

CHAPTER 2
[1] JAS, D/AP/R/13/37, letter from the Lieutenant Governor to the Lieutenant Bailiff, 30 July 1914
[2] *Evening Post*, 6 December 1916
[3] JAS, A/C2/41/42/1, statement by the Lieutenant Governor to the States, 21 August 1905
[4] *Evening Post*, 10 October 1905
[5] *Evening Post*, 31 July 1914
[6] Ibid

CHAPTER 3
[1] Porch, D., The March to the Marne, p10
[2] Boleat, M., French Workers and the Jersey Population
[3] *Evening Post*, 3 August 1914
[4] *Evening Post*, 4 August 1917
[5] Ibid
[6] *Morning News*, 3 August 1914.
[7] Figures quoted in a number of documents held by the JAS, including a report from the Greffier in A/E/7 and a report by the Attorney General in D/AP/R/13/41.
[8] Clayton, A., Paths of Glory: The French Army 1914-18, p 195

CHAPTER 4
[1] *Evening Post*, 10 August 1914
[2] *Evening Post*, 3 August 1914
[3] Ibid
[4] *Evening Post*, 5 August 1914
[5] Le Brocq, E., *Memoirs*, p291
[6] *Evening Post*, 9 September 1914
[7] JAS, D/AP/R/13/41, report on recruiting; and EP 30 November 1915, statement by the Attorney General
[8] *Evening Post*, 15 October 1914
[9] JAS, D/AP/13/37, report from the Militia's Senior Medical Officer, 14 August 1914
[10] Militia Reserve numbers taken from Jersey's Roll of Service and Honour
[11] *Morning News*, 22 September 1914

CHAPTER 5
[1] *Morning News*, 17 September 1914
[2] JAS, D/AP/R/13/37, letter from the Lieutenant Governor to the Secretary, War Office, 16 September 1914
[3] JAS, D/AP/R/13/37, letter from the War Office to the Lieutenant Governor, 25 September 1914
[4] Analysis of reports in the *Evening Post* and *Morning News*
[5] *Morning News*, 5 December 1914
[6] *Evening Post*, 7 December 1914
[7] *Morning News*, 14 December 1914
[8] *Evening Post*, 15 December 1914
[9] Ibid
[10] Ibid
[11] Ibid
[12] Ibid
[13] Analysis based on report printed in *Evening Post* on 2 March 1915
[14] Analysis based on Jersey Rolls of Honour and Service
[15] *Morning News*, 24 February 1915
[16] *Morning News*, 2 March 1915
[17] NAS, HO 45/100896/364571, report from the Lieutenant Governor to the Home Office, 18 December 1915
[18] *Morning News*, 13 August 1915
[19] NAS, WO 363, Army Service Record of Riflemen Arthur Mallet

CHAPTER 6

[1] JAS, D/Z/H2/5, letter from the Constable of St Helier to the Lieutenant Governor, 2 November 1914
[2] *Morning News*, 13 August 1914
[3] JAS, A/E/7, letter from Edward Troup to the Lieutenant Governor, 18 August 1914
[4] *Evening Post*, 8 September 1914
[5] Ibid
[6] *Morning News*, 1 January 1915
[7] JAS, D/Z/H2/7, memorandum from Boots to the Attorney General, 23 October 1916
[8] JAS, D/Z/H2/6, letter from Phyllis Good to the Attorney General, 6 November 1916
[9] JAS, D/AP/R/31/37, letter from the Bailiff to the Privy Council, 18 August, 1914
[10] Ibid

CHAPTER 7

[1] JAS, A/E/4, letter from the Chief Censor to the Government Secretary, 25 October 1914
[2] JAS, A/E/4, letter from the Chief Censor to the Government Secretary, 25 October 1914
[3] JAS, D/AP/R/13/37, letter from the Lieutenant Governor to the Bailiff, 9 September 1914
[4] JAS, D/AP/R/13/28, letter from the Aliens Officer to the Attorney General, 13 December 1915
[5] JAS, A/E/1, report by the Aliens Officer to Colonel Western, 22 December 1914
[6] JAS, A/E/1, undated letter from unnamed person to the Lieutenant Governor
[7] JAS, A/E/4, letter from Edward Troup to the Lieutenant Governor, 4 August 1914
[8] Ibid
[9] JAS, A/E/1, statement by Private G Howard, 30 June 1915
[10] JAS, A/E/1, letter from Colonel Western to the Officer Commanding 1st (West) Battalion, 2 July 1915, July 1915
[11] JAS, A/E/10, extract of letter from the *Préfet Martime* in Brest to the British War Office, 9 May 1915
[12] JAS, A/E/10, extract from report to the Lieutenant Governor to the War Office, 29 April 1915
[13] JAS, A/E/10, letter from the Lieutenant Governor to the Home Office, 15 June 1915
[14] JAS, A/E/1, report from Colonel Western to unnamed recipient, 11 June 1915
[15] JAS, A/E/4, report from the Censor to the General Staff Officer, October 1918
[16] JAS, A/E/4, letter from the Government Secretary to the Secretary of the Swiss Legation, 21 September 1918
[17] JAS, A/E/8/1, letter from the Guernsey Secretary to the Government to the Jersey Secretary to the Government, 1 January 1916
[18] NAS, T161/101, petition from Mrs Ramm to King George V, 7 February 1928

CHAPTER 8

[1] *Evening Post*, 20 March 1915
[2] *Evening Post*, 22 March 1915
[3] Ibid
[4] NAS, FO383/276, inspector's report covering conditions in British prisoner of war camps, 4 March 1919
[5] *Evening Post*, 23 March 1915
[6] Naish, T.E.
[7] The Treatment of Prisoners of War, HM Stationary Office, 1915
[8] JAS, A/E/5. letter from the War Office to the Lieutenant Governor, 30 November 1916
[9] JAS, A/E/5, notes from meeting between the Defence Committee president and the Lieutenant Governor, 3 November 1916
[10] JAS, A/E/5, letter from the War Office to the Lieutenant Governor, 30

November 1916
[11] JAS, A/E/5, letter from the Food Production Committee president to the Lieutenant Governor, 27 December 1916

CHAPTER 9
[1] JAS, D/Z/H2/5, Letter from the Home Office to the Lieutenant Governor, 2 July 1915
[2] JAS, D/A/P/R/13/38, Regulation on National Registration (1915), 6 August 1915
[3] *Morning News*, 19 August 1915
[4] JAS, A/D1/A1/2, report by the Defence Committee, 28 December 1915
[5] *Morning News*, 6 October 1915
[6] *Morning News*, 11 October 1915
[7] NAS, HO 45/100896/364571, newspaper cutting sent in a letter from the Attorney General to the Government Secretary, 20 December 1915
[8] Ibid
[9] Ibid
[10] NAS, HO 45/100896/364571, letter from the Lieutenant Governor to the Home Secretary, 18 December 1915
[11] JAS, A/E/3, comparative statement of recruitment figures between Jersey and the Isle of Man, undated
[12] *Morning News*, 3 May 1916
[13] *Evening Post*, 5 June 1916
[14] Ibid
[15] *Evening Post*, 24 July 1916
[16] Ibid
[17] Ibid
[18] Ibid
[19] Ibid
[20] Ibid
[21] Ibid
[22] NAS, HO 45/100896/364571, report from the Crown Officers to the Lieutenant Governor, 26 October 1916
[23] *Evening Post*, 21 November 1916
[24] *Evening Post*, 24 November 1916
[25] *Evening Post*, 23 November 1916

CHAPTER 10
[1] *Evening Post*, Official report by the Jersey District Office presented to the States on 15 February 1918
[2] Statistics drawn from several sources included 1911 national census results, JAS, A/E/3, for information on Isle of Man volunteering and NAS, HO45/12958, for information on Guernsey volunteering and UK Parliamentary Papers, 1921, for information on British volunteering.
[3] *Evening Post*, 12 March 1917
[4] *Morning News*, 15 March 1917
[5] JAS, A/E/3, translation of the 'Law on Military Service' approved by His Majesty in Council on 6 February 1917
[6] *Morning News*, 14 April 1917
[7] *Morning News*, 16 April 1917
[8] *Morning News*, 6 November 1917
[9] *Evening Post*, 10 October 1917
[10] JAS A/E/5, letter from the Lieutenant Governor to the Under Secretary of State at the Home Office, 11 June 1917
[11] *Evening Post*, 17 October 1917
[12] Ibid
[13] Ibid
[14] JAS, A/E/5, letter from the Lieutenant Governor to the Under Secretary of State at the Home Office, 13 June 1917
[15] JAS A/E/5, letter from the Constable of St Clement to the Attorney General, 26 October 1917
[16] JAS A/E/5, letter from the Attorney General to the Lieutenant Governor, 5 September 1917
[17] JAS A/E/5, letter from the Attorney General to the Lieutenant Governor, 1 September 1917
[18] JAS A/E/5, letter from Philip Le Feuvre to the Home Office, 16 March 1919

ENDNOTES

CHAPTER 11
[1] *Morning News*, 15 October 1917
[2] *Morning News*, 9 August 1913
[3] *Morning News*, 17 June 1918
[4] *Morning News*, 15 August 1917
[5] Ibid
[6] JAS, A/D/W6, letter from the Lieutenant Governor to the Director, Board of Agriculture and Fisheries, 5 May 1917
[7] *Evening Post*, May 1919
[8] *Evening Post*, May 1919

CHAPTER 12
[1] *Evening Post*, 15 December 1915
[2] *Morning News*, 27 February 1917
[3] JAS, A/E/3, letter from the Home Secretary to the Lieutenant Governor, 11 April 1918
[4] Ibid
[5] JAS, A/E/3, letter from the Bailiff to the Lieutenant Governor, 18 April 1918
[6] *Evening Post,* 25 April 1918
[7] JAS, A/E/3, letter from War Office to Home Office, 18 June 1917
[8] Ibid
[9] JAS, D/Z/H2/8, letter to the Secretary of the Board of Agriculture and Fisheries, 24 October 1917
[10] Ibid
[11] JAS, A/E/10/7, letter from the Lieutenant Governor to the Home Secretary, 4 February 1918
[12] JAS, A/E/10/7, letter from Government Secretary to Under Secretary of State, 5 February 1918
[13] JAS, D/Z/H2/8, report by the Special Committee on Food Production, undated
[14] *Evening Post*, 12 June 1918

CHAPTER 13
[1] London Gazette, 4 September 1919
[2] London Gazette, 12 March 1918

CHAPTER 14
[1] *Evening Post*, 23 October 1919
[2] *Evening Post*, 18 October 1918
[3] *Evening Post*, 16 November 1918
[4] *Evening Post*, 11 November 1918
[5] *Evening Post*, 12 November 1918
[6] *Evening Post*, 26 November 1918
[7] *Evening Post*, 19 December 1918
[8] *Evening Post*, 6 January 1919
[9] *Evening Post*, 6 July 1918
[10] Ibid
[11] *Evening Post*, 2 April 1919

CHAPTER 15
[1] *Evening Post,* 12 November 1923
[2] Figures drawn from several sources: for Britain see Commonwealth War Graves Commission Annual Report 2009–2010; for France see Clayton, A, *Paths of Glory: The French Army 1914-18*; for Isle of Man see website of Isle of Man Government, gov.im, Isle of Man's role in World War One; for Guernsey see the website of *Channel Islands' Great War Study Group*, greatwarci.net, Guernsey's Roll of Honour
[3] Analysis based upon Jersey's Roll of Honour published in 1919, which includes parish details
[4] Figures drawn from several sources: For British Army recruitment statistics see Beckett, I. *A Nation in Arms: A Social Study of the British Army in the First World War*; for France see Clayton, A, *Paths of Glory: The French Army 1914-18*

SOURCES & BIBLIOGRAPHY

1. Archival Sources

Jersey Archive

A	Records of the Lieutenant Governor of Jersey
B/D	Bailiff's Chambers Archive
C/A	States Assembly - includes minutes, correspondence, projets de loi and rapports
C/B	Minutes of States Standing and Major Committees
D/AP	Various States Greffe/States Committee correspondence files and other papers
D/Z	Law Officer's Department
J/A	Medical Officer of Health Annual Reports

National Archive

FO	Records of the Foreign Office
HO	Records of the Home Office
T	Records of the Treasury
WO	Records of the War Office

Société Jersiaise Library, Jersey

Various records on the Jersey Militia and the First World War held in box files

2. Published Works

Adie, K, *Fighting on the Home Front: The Legacy of Women in World War One*, Hodder & Stroughton, 2013

Balleine, G., *A Biographical Dictionary of Jersey*, Staples Press, 1948

Beckett, I., *A Nation in Arms: A Social Study of the British Army in the First World War*, Manchester University Press, 1985

Clayton, A., *Paths of Glory: The French Army 1914-1918*, Cassell, 2003

Cowman, K. and Jackson, A., *Women and Work Culture: Britain c.1850-1950 (Studies in Labour History)* Ashgate Publishing Limited, 2005

De La Bois, F., *A Constitutional History of Jersey*, States' Greffe, 1970

Everard J.A. & Holt J.C., *Jersey 1204: The Forging of an Island Community*, Thames & Hudson, 2004

Ginns, M., *Jersey Occupied: The German Armed Forces in Jersey 1940–1945*, Channel Island Publishing, 2009

Holmes R., *Tommy: The British Soldier on the Western Front 1914-1918*, Harper Perennial, 2004

Le Brocq, E., *Memoirs of Edward Le Brocq 1877-1964*, ELSP, 2000

Le Hérissier, R.G., *The Development of the Government of Jersey, 1771-1972*, The States of Jersey, 1972

Mark, G., *Prisoners of War in British Hands During WWI: A Study of Their History, the Camps and Their Mails*, The Postal History Society, 2007

Middlebrook, M, *The Kaiser's Battle: 21 March 1918: The First Day of the German Spring Offensive*, Penguin Books, 1978

Parks, E., *Diex Aix: God Help Us – The Guernseymen who Marched Away 1914-1918*, Guernsey Museums & Galleries, 1992

Porch, D., *The March to the Marne: The French Army 1871-1914*, Cambridge University Press, 1981

Rinaldi, R., *Order of Battle of the British Army 1914*, Tiger Lily Books, 2008

Ronayne, I., *Ours: The Jersey Pals in the First World War*, The History Press, 2009

Stevenson, D., *1914-1918: The History of the First World War*, Penguin Books, 2004

Storey, N. and Housego, M., *Women in the First World War*, Shire Publications, 2010

3. Unpublished Material

Boleat, M., *French Workers and the Jersey Population* (Société Jersiaise)

Boleat, M., *A Summary of Influences on Jersey's Population Levels* (Société Jersiaise)

Boleat, M., *The 1906 States Report on immigration into Jersey* (Société Jersiaise)

Boleat, M., *Jersey's Population – A History* (Société Jersiaise)

Cooper, E.C., *Victoria College Jersey, C.I. Activities 1852-1928* (Société Jersiaise)

De Gruchy, F, *The Militia and the Military Role of Jersey in History* (Société Jersiaise)

Ford, D., *Jersey in the First World War* (Jersey Heritage)

Marett, G., *A History of the Telegraph in Jersey 1858 – 1940*, 2009

4. Newspapers, periodicals and other materials

Evening Post newspaper (Jersey Library)

Morning News newspaper (Jersey Library)

Les Chroniques de Jersey newspaper (Jersey Library)

Jersey Times Almanacs (Jersey Library)

Evening Post Almanacs (Jersey Library)

National Archive: Military Unit War Diaries

Channel Islands' Great War Study Group Journals

Naish, T.E. Major, The German Prisoners of War Camp at Jersey, During the Great War, 1914-1918, in: *Société Jersiaise Bulletin*, Volume 16, Part 3, 269-280

Spence, N., *Language in Jersey*, (*Société Jersiaise Bulletin*, 2001 Annual Bulletin)

5. Websites

The website of the *Channel Islands' Great War Study Group*, greatwarci.net

INDEX

Agricultural industry, 8, 9-10, 24, 34, 148, 149, 150-151, 153, 164, 166, 168, 173, 184, 186, 193, 204, 254
Albert Pier, St Helier, 112, 117, 124
Alexander, RSM James, 218
Alfera, Ignatz, 170
Alhambra, 83
Alien internee labour in Jersey, 168-173, 184, 257
Aliens Officer, 98. *See also* Luxon, Arthur
Aliens Registration Office, 99
Aliens Restriction Act, 96, 97, 105, 106
Allardice, Lt Col Harry, 221
Allpress, Maj, 126
American Consular Agent, *see* Renouf, Edward
Amourette, Sgt Ernest, 222
Amy, Clarence, 165
Andrews, Lce Cpl Vernon, 224
Aquila Road, St Helier, 174-175
Arras, 227, 229
Archduke Franz Ferdinand, assassination of, 12
Armistice, the, 236-238
Army Forage Corps, 200
Arsenals, in Jersey, 16, 19-20, 24, 58, 80, 156, 158
Attorney General, 5-6. *See also* Le Vavasseur dit Durell, Henry
Aubin, Jurat Philip, 149
Aubin, Jurat Walter, 124, 148, 149
Australians, in Jersey, 239

Bailiff, of Jersey, 5-6, 51, 85. *See also* Vernon, Sir William; Coutanche, Baron Alexander

Barnbow munitions factory explosion, 183
Barnes, Violet, 187
Barracks, in Jersey, 21-22, 24, 79-80, 82, 123, 139, 156, 158
Battles and offensives
   Battle of Amiens, 224
   Battle of Arras, 221, 222
   Battle of Cambrai, 223
   Battle of Charleroi, 226
   Battle of Coronel, 191
   Battle of Jersey, 16
   Battle of Jutland, 191
   Battle of Mons, 54, 55, 79, 216, 226
   Battle of Messines Ridge, 214, 215, 222
   Battle of Passchendaele, 214, 222
   Battle of Reims, 230
   Battle of Soissons, 230
   Battle of the Frontiers, 54, 79
   Battle of the Marne, 60, 226
   Battle of the Somme, 135-136, 156, 220-221, 228
   Battle of Verdun, 228
   Battle of Vimy Ridge, 221-222, 227
   German Spring Offensive, 213, 224, 230
   Second Battle of Artois, 227
   Second Battle of Champagne, 227
   Third Battle of Artois, 227
Béghin, Sgt Louis, 65
Béghin, Pte Maurice, 65
Bennett, CSM Thomas, 220
Bennett, Flt Sgt Thomas, 222
Benson, Lt Col Eric, 221
Bewhay, John, 188
Binet, 2nd Lt Roy, 215
Bishop, Col Edward, 101, 106, 107

Bitot, Victorie, 165
Bitot, Albert, 165
Bitot, Alfred, 165
Bois, Deputy Francis, 124, 145-146, 148, 196
Bowles, Lt Col Ludlow, 158
Briard, Capt Ernest, 216
Brighton Road School (military hospital), 114, 161-162, 169, 170, 180, 233
British Army, 12, 17, 20, 22, 46, 52, 53, 55, 62, 74, 76-77, 80, 116, 119, 135, 136, 147, 178, 181, 213, 240. *See also* British Army Formations; Jersey Militia garrison in Jersey, 16, 17, 18, 21, 55, 56, 160, 256
  recruitment from Jersey, 53, 70, 140-141, 154-155, 251
  wartime campaigns, 216-224
British Army formations
  British Expeditionary Force, 53, 54, 55, 65, 114, 216-217, 256
  British Indian Army, 216
  British Army of the Rhine, 240
  Royal Army Medical Corps, 22, 53
  Royal Artillery, 53
  Royal Defence Corps, 117
  Royal Engineers, 22, 53, 115
  Sixteenth (Irish) Division, 73
  Devonshire Regiment, 21, 52, 55, 56
  Dorsetshire Regiment, 52, 75, 156
  East Surrey Regiment, 53, 73
  Hampshire Regiment, 74, 75, 116, 121, 156, 215
  King's Own Royal Lancaster Regiment, 21
  Leicester Regiment, 159
  London Regiment (Post Office Rifles), 73
  Northumberland Fusiliers, 159
  Royal Guernsey Light Infantry, 145, 157
  Royal Irish Fusiliers, 69
  Royal Irish Regiment, 69
  Royal Irish Rifles, 69, 73, 214
  Royal Jersey Garrison Battalion, 158-159, 168, 238, 241, 252
  South Staffordshire Regiment, 56-57, 71, 78, 82, 87, 89, 118, 159-160
  The Accrington Pals, 63, 156
  York and Lancaster Regiment, 159
  36th Fire Command, 159
  20th Company Royal Garrison Artillery, 22, 55
  110th Company Royal Garrison Artillery, 159, 252
British Board of Agriculture and Fisheries, 200
British Government, 4-5, 45, 49, 62, 83, 87, 96, 97, 98, 107, 136, 147, 148, 157, 176, 196, 198, 199, 200, 224, 238-239, 245. *See also* War Office
British Red Cross Society, Jersey Branch, 80, 177, 233
Bruce, Lt William, 217, 249
Brundig, Karl, 121
Buck, Alys, 180
Buckton, Agnes, 176
Burgera, Martinn, 170
Butel, Albert, 103
Canadian Army, 74, 221, 222, 227
Carace, Samuel, 170
Cave, Sir George, 197-198, 199
Cenotaph, 245-246, 247-248, 257

INDEX

Censorship, 46, 87, 100-102, 224
Ceselin, Henry, 173
Chapman, Rfn Charles, 220
Charles Street, St Helier, 236
Civilian campaigns in support of the war effort, 79-81
Cole, Lillian, 187
Committee for Imperial Defence, 84
Compulsory military service, *see* Conscription
Conscientious objection, 152, 163
Conscription, 136, 154, 155-156, 157, 203. *See also* Military Service Act; Military Service Tribunals
Cory, Deputy, 67
Court-martial of Edward Single, *see* Edward Single
Coutanche, Baron Alexander, 93
Coutanche, Pte Walter, 222-223

Davis, Pte Howard, 135
Davis, Thomas, 135
Deane, Miss A., 186
Dean of Jersey, *see* Falle, V Rev. Samuel
Declarations of war, 13, 36, 45
Decourtit, *Sdt* Leopold, 226
Defence of the Realm Act (DORA), 84-91
De Gruchy, Rev Francis, 152
De Gueser, *Adj* Louis, 226
De Juvigny, *Cap* Pierre, 226
Delamain, Brig Gen Walter, 218
Demobilisation Employment Exchange, 244
Demobilisation of the armed forces, 239-241
Department of Agriculture and Fisheries, 187
Derby Scheme, 139

Devonshire Regiment, *see* British Army formations
Dorsetshire Regiment, *see* British Army formations
Dunlop, Alice and Andrew, 217-218
Dunlop, Capt Frederick, 218
Dunlop, Capt Julian, 218
Dunlop, 2nd Lt Kenneth, 217
Du Prat, *Sdt* Jean, 79
Durand, *Cap* Jerome, 226
Education, in Jersey, 3, 224
Elizabeth Castle, 22, 56
Enemy Aliens, 96-98, 102-111
Entente Cordiale, 12, 27
Entertainment restrictions, 83
Ereaut, Ellen, 180
Espionage, concerns over, 47-48, 102-103
Euvrie, *Sdt* Pierre, 229
Evening Post newspaper, 32, 46, 236
Ex-servicemen's associations, 242-243

Falle, V Rev. Samuel, 66, 80, 181-182, 186, 187
Fergusson, Dr, 244
Fitzroy, Almeric, 93
Food restrictions and rationing, 194-195
Forbes, Leswick, 90
Forsyth, Lall, 176
Fort Regent, 19, 22, 56, 80, 154, 156, 158, 236
Franco-Prussian War, 11, 26, 29, 34
French Army, 26, 27-29, 30, 31, 32-34, 35-36, 53, 54, 180, 229-230, 241
  recruitment from Jersey, 34
  wartime campaigns, 225-230
French Army formations

10e corps d'armée, 30, 226, 227
2e régiment d'infanterie, 30, 228
25e régiment d'infanterie, 30, 227
41e régiment d'infanterie, 30
47e régiment d'infanterie, 30
48e régiment d'infanterie, 30
70e régiment d'infanterie, 30
71e régiment d'infanterie, 30
136e régiment d'infanterie, 30
202e régiment d'infanterie, 30
247e régiment d'infanterie, 30
1e régiment d'infanterie coloniale, 30
French community in Jersey, 8, 10-11, 255-256
French Consulate, 28, 29, 31, 32-33, 226, 256. *See also* Jouve, Auguste
French Jesuit institutions, 8, 34, 88, 101, 121, 226, 256
Food and fuel shortages and restrictions, 193-196
Frohmann, Ludovicus, 96
Fuchs, Ernest, 172
Gallichan, William, 191
Germany, plans for war, 25
Gibbons, L Cpl Frederick, 158
Gladstone, Florence, 180
Godfray, George, 165
Godfrey, Brig Gen John, 21, 69
Good, Phyllis, 91
Goupy, Alfred, 165
Government Secretary, *see* Whitaker-Maitland, William
Grand Hotel, 56, 82, 86
Granville, 10
Gray, Deputy, 244, 245
Guernsey, 66, 68, 69, 70, 249, 145, 152, 155, 157, 192, 249
Guiton, Walter, 87
Gussek, *Haupt* Erich, 256

Guyon, Lt Col George, 221

Hague Convention, on prisoners of war, 112, 123
Haig, FM Sir Douglas, 204, 220
Haines, Lt Col Gregory, 116
Hakin, Irvingston, 99
Hammond, Jean, 50
Hampshire Regiment, *see* British Army formations
Hanlon, Pte George, 121, 257
Hart, Gen Sir Reginald, 109, 145, 157
Hepburn, Sgt Maj Montague, 188
Hoffman, Francis, 191
Holley, Bert, 232
Home Office, British, *see* British Government
Home Secretary, British, 109, 140, 197. *See also* Cave, Sir George
Honorary Police force, 6, 32, 91
Horkey, Max, 172
Houillebecq, François, 184-185
Howard, Pte George, 102
Huby, *Sdt* Louis, 230
Ingouville-Williams, Maj Gen Edward, 221
Isle of Man, 98, 143, 155, 168, 249
Jèrriais (language), 6-7, 11
Jersey contingent, *see* Jersey Company
Jersey Company, 68, 69-70, 72, 73, 75, 76, 80, 125, 135, 136, 156, 213-216, 239, 243, 251
Jersey District army headquarters, 21, 73, 75, 78, 98, 143
Jersey Gas Light Company, 196, 244
Jersey, Island of
   constitutional rights, 4, 11, 85, 144, 150

INDEX

defence, 4, 8. *See also* British Army; Jersey Militia
economy, 8, 9, 254
government. *See* States of Jersey
history, 3-5
people, 6-8
wartime casualties, 249-250
Jersey Militia, 14-17, 18, 19, 20-21, 22-24, 57-58, 59, 92-93, 154, 252, 256
Jersey Political Association, 243, 244
Jersey Rifle Association, 20
Jersey Royal Potato, 9, 150, 200-203. *See also* agriculture industry
Jeune, Richard and Edith, 212
Johnston, Maj Hugh, 86, 221
Joint War Committee, 179
Jouve, Auguste, 32, 103, 143, 238

Kayser, Edwin and Minnie, 105-107, 110
King John of England, 4
Kitchener, FM Herbert, 62, 65
Knapp, Fra Simon, 22
Knockaloe Internment Camp, 98
Kroeggel, Charles, 109
Krudewig, Jacob, 109
Kynoch Ltd, 182, 242

Laugeard, Sgt Charles, 215, 216
Laulier, *Sdt* Adolphe, 228
Laurens, Harriet, 233
Lawrence, Marjorie, 232
Boustouller, *Sdt* Yves-Marie, 227
Boustouller, *Sdt* Emmanuel, 228
Le Boutillier, Auguste, 164
Le Boutillier, Jurat Edward, 167
Le Boutillier, Walter, 164
Le Breton, CSM Jack
Le Brocq, Alice, 180

Le Brocq, Samuel, 165-166
Le Brun, Clarence, 185
Le Claire, Pte Louis, 215
Le Cocq, George, 160
Le Feuvre, Philip, 173
Le Gresley, Sgt George, 219
Le Maistre Gruchy, Maj George, 70
Le Millin, *Sdt* Guillaume, 226
Le Nouvel, *Sdt* Sylvère, 237
Le Riche, Florence, 187
Le Riche, Jack, 179
Le Rossignol, Maj Herbert, 159
Le Vavasseur dit Durell, Henry, 58, 87, 106, 117, 140, 151, 172
Les Chroniques de Jersey newspaper, 46, 232
Licensing hours changes, 81-82
Lieutenant Governor, of Jersey, 4-5, 6, 14, 17, 21, 49, 51, 58, 84, 85, 93, 247. *See also* Rochfort, Maj Gen Alexander; Wilson, Maj Gen Alexander
Lighting restrictions, 90-91
Lillicrap, Aileen, 187
Linder, Franz, 97
Lindsell, Eileen, 180
Lojos, Josef, 170
London Channel Islanders' Society, 81
Luce, Edward, 232
Ludendorff, Gen Erich, 224
Lunn, 2nd Lt Frank, 215
Luxon, Arthur, 98-99, 100

Machon, Rfn William, 220
Madler, Arthur, 109
Maison St Louis, *see* French Jesuit institutions
Malet De Carteret, Charles, 147
Malet De Carteret, Mid Philip, 191

Malet De Carteret, Jurat Reginald, 249
Mallet, Rfn Arthur, 75
Mallet, Rfn Charles, 75
Mallett, Capt Philip, 237
Malzard, Pte John, 237
Margerine Bill, 194
Mauger, George, 47
McKenzie, Lt Col Gerald, 23
McQueen, Sarah, 183
McReady-Diarmid, Capt Allastair, 223, 249
Middleton, Deputy, 67
Military Service Act, 141-142, 143-153, 154, 155, 157, 161, 162,163, 203-204. *See also* conscription
Military Service Tribunals, 162-168
Militia Vingteniers, 19, 59,
Morning News newspaper, 46
Möschke, Charlotte, 100
Mossop, Lt Charles, 192
Mourant, Pte Jack, 237
Mourant, Walter, 165
Muller, Ruth, 99
Munitionettes, 182-183
Munitions Industry, 144, 181-182

Naish, Maj Theodore, 115, 116
National Registration, 137-138, 139, 142, 155, 161
National Service Bureau, 170
Newbegin, Agnes, 175
Newfoundland, 63, 156, 251
New Zealand, 74
Nivelle, *Gén* Robert, 229
Nordbruch, Gottlobb, 96
Notre Dame du Bon Secours, *see* French Jesuit institutions
Nugent, Capt John, 162
Nursing in the British Army,
    development of, 178
Ogier, Capt Cyril, 215, 216
Ogier, Capt Léonce L H, 162-163, 167, 241
Opera House, 83

Pals Battalions, 63, 65, 136
People's Park, St Helier, 23, 56
Petain, *Gén* Philippe, 229
Philip II of France, 4
Pinel, John, 67, 82, 182, 184, 185, 194, 225, 234, 238, 245
Prisoner of war camp, Les Blanches Banques
    arrival and departure of prisoners, 112, 117-118, 120, 124-125, 126
    camp guards, 116-117, 121-122
    design and construction, 114-116
    prisoner deaths, 121
    prisoner escapes, 122-123
Prisoners of war, return to Jersey, 240
Police forces in Jersey, 6

Queen Mary's Army Auxiliary Corps, *see* Women's Army Auxiliary Corps
Queen's Assembly Rooms, St Helier, 20

Ramm, Emma, 104-105, 110-111
Rault, Anne, 188
Rault, Nellie, 188-189
Redway, Major George, 140, 155
Renault, *Sdt* Joseph, 227
Rendall, Pte William, 220
Renouf, Edward, 97
Reynolds, Sgt Claude, 221
Richards, Pte Harry, 213, 215
Rickett, AB Arthur, 237
Riedl, Willy, 257

INDEX

Rifle ranges in Jersey, 20
Rochfort, Maj Gen Alexander, 13-14, 34, 48-49, 51, 64, 65, 68, 80, 82, 87, 90, 98, 103, 104, 108, 109, 123-124, 137, 139, 141, 146, 147, 157, 254-253
Roll of Honour and Service, Jersey, 250
Rondel, Florence, 232
Royal Court, 5, 85, 163, 167
Royal Guernsey Light Infantry, *see* British Army formations
Royal Irish Rifles, *see* British Army formations
Royal Jersey Garrison Battalion, *see* British Army formations
Royal Navy, 12, 22, 53, 70, 140, 155, 191, 192
Royal Square, St Helier, 1, 2, 23, 59, 69, 226, 238,
Rybot, Maj Norman, 218-129

Saint-Brieuc, 10
Saint-Malo, 68, 180
Schönbauer, Carl, 172
Scouts Defence Corps, 160-161
Ships and other vessels
  Alice Taylor, 196
  Cygnus, 191
  Ibex, 69-70
  Lusitania, 107, 192
  Lydia, 192
  Maud, 192
  Melillia, 126
  Mizpah, 192
  Scotian, 119
  Seeker, 192
  Villareal, 126
  Yrsa, 192
Single, Edward, 86-87

Smith, Lillian, 183
Société Française de Bienfaisance, 80-81
Solicitor General, 5. *See also* Charles Malet de Carteret
South Hill Battery, 22, 24, 159
South Staffordshire Regiment, *see* British Army formations
Spanish Flu epidemic, 231-235
Springfield Showground, 24, 56, 113-114
States of Jersey, x, 5-6, 9, 11, 18, 48-49, 66-67, 82-83, 85-86, 91-92, 137, 141, 143-147, 148-150, 151-152, 169, 194, 195, 196, 198, 199, 201, 203, 204, 238, 242, 245, 254. *See also* States of Jersey Committees.
States of Jersey Committees
  Defence Committee, 92, 124, 125, 145, 146, 147, 148, 149, 150, 151, 152, 169, 194, 195, 202, 204
  Finance Committee, 92, 93
  Food Production Committee, 124, 126, 194, 200
  Primary Instruction Committee, 232
  Sanitary Committee, 234
  War Roll Committee, 249
St Aubin, 7
St Helier, town of, 6, 7, 16, 23, 32, 51
St Mark's Church, 56
St Saviour's Parish Hall, 164
Stocker, Louisa, 117
Stocker, Lt Col Walter, 69, 125
Suffragettes, 176-177
Submarine threat, 102, 103, 191-193, 197

Tauber, Anton,

Telegraphy network, 46, 94-95, 236
Tennant, Cap Hugh, 162
Thielemann, Albert, 101
Tirel, *Sdt* Bienaime, 229
Tischmeyer, Mary, 108
Town Hall, St Helier, 32, 97, 99, 165, 174, 181, 182, 186, 225, 234, 243
Trachy, A., 224
Trade unions, in Jersey, 243
Tremblay, *Adjutant* George, 227
Triple Alliance, 12
Triple Entente, 12

Vallois, Pte Frank, 79
Variallon, *Sdt* Constant, 79
Veler, Cpl John, 220, 221
Veler, Pte Peter, 221
Vernon, Lady Julia, 177
Vernon, Sir William, 49-51, 67, 69, 85, 92-93, 105, 110, 117, 139, 142, 143-144, 152, 167, 198, 238, 248, 255. *See also* Bailiff, of Jersey
Victoria College OTC, 22, 59
Victoria Cross winners, *see* Bruce, Lt William; McReady-Diarmid, Capt Allastair
Voluntary Aid Detachments, 178-180, 233,
Volunteering for military service, 62, 63-64, 65, 66, 68, 70-72, 73, 74, 76, 140-141, 143, 154, 155. *See also* Jersey Company, the

Wagner, Wenzel, 172
Walters, Rev Carey, 66
Walton, Matron, 233-234
War memorials, 245, 248-249. *See also* Cenotaph
War Office, British, 17, 18, 21, 23, 55, 58, 64, 65, 68, 69, 83, 87, 114, 124, 147, 199, 225
War Relief Committees, 81
Warren, Cpl Arthur, 237
Western, Col J., 98
West Park Pavilion, 195
Wests, 83
Whitaker-Maitland, William, 107, 201
Whitley, Pte Philip, 219
Wilson, Maj Gen Alexander, 157, 160, 161, 166-167, 168-169, 171, 173, 197- 198, 200-201, 202, 204, 252
Women taking over men's jobs, 183-184
Women's Land Army, 184-185
Women's rights, the development of, 3, 176, 189, 244-245
Women's Auxiliary Army Corps, 185-187
Women's Royal Air Force, 185
Women's Royal Naval Service, 185
Worrall. Arthur, 59

Young Man's Christian Association, Jersey Branch, 79-80

Zeppelins, 47, 90
Zimmerman, August, 106, 107